John Stuart Mill

BY
KARL BRITTON

Second Edition

DOVER PUBLICATIONS, INC.
NEW YORK

Published in Canada by General Publishing Company, Ltd., 30 Lesmill Road, Don Mills, Toronto, Ontario.
Published in the United Kingdom by Constable and Company, Ltd., 10 Orange Street, London WC 2.

This Dover edition, first published in 1969, is an unabridged and corrected republication of the work originally published by Penguin Books, Ltd., in 1953.

Standard Book Number: 486-22251-9
Library of Congress Catalog Card Number: 70-78798

Manufactured in the United States of America
Dover Publications, Inc.
180 Varick Street
New York, N.Y. 10014

CONTENTS

EDITORIAL FOREWORD

Professor Karl Britton's book on the philosophy of John Stuart Mill is one of a series of philosophical works which are appearing in a similar form. The series consists mainly in original studies of the work of a number of outstanding philosophers, but besides these contributions to the history of philosophy it will also include books on more general topics, such as logic, the theory of knowledge, political philosophy, ethics, and the philosophy of science.

The series is not designed to reflect the standpoint or to advance the views of any one philosophical school. Since it is addressed to an audience of non-specialists as well as professional philosophers, the contributors to it have been asked to write in as untechnical a manner as their subjects allow, but they have not been expected to achieve simplicity at the cost of accuracy or completeness.

In the case of John Stuart Mill there is a very wide field to cover. He himself probably attached the greatest importance to his work on logic, and it is, indeed, for his investigation of the processes of inductive reasoning that contemporary philosophers chiefly value him. At the same time, his *Utilitarianism* remains one of the best introductions to the study of ethics, his book on *Liberty* is a classic of political philosophy, and, as Professor Britton shows, he made important contributions to the theory of knowledge. The most versatile and gifted of the philosophical radicals, he carries forward the tradition of the great British philosophers of the seventeenth and eighteenth centuries towards the empiricist movement of our own time.

A. J. AYER

CHAPTER ONE

The Life of John Stuart Mill

There are hints in Stuart Mill of an original nature, which
was sentimental and almost religious, and which was not
made for the purely intellectual and abstract system imposed
on it since childhood.   ÉLIE HALÉVY

*

I. INTRODUCTION: THE BENTHAMITES

JOHN STUART MILL was not one of England's greatest
philosophers: but he has had an influence on later philosophical thought both at home and abroad, hardly surpassed
by thinkers of the highest order. For Mill was born into a
powerful philosophical and political movement, deriving from
the previous century and dominated by the mighty Bentham.
Its teaching he understood as well as any of its members and
he made original contributions of great importance. But he
was also open to quite new influences: the historical, romantic,
religious influences which became dominant in the middle of
the nineteenth century. His own philosophy presents Benthamism in a form so modified and accommodated as to allow
it to be effective in the new age. Therefore the particular
character which empirical and naturalistic thought possessed
in the later Victorian era derives very largely from Mill: and
the vigorous survival of naturalism in an unfavourable climate
at home, and its propagation in America and on the Continent,
owes a great deal to his books, his journalistic writings, his
personal correspondence, and his personal influence.

Mill was also much more than a philosopher. He was a
radical reformer in political and social life; and it seems just
to say that his enquiries into logic and scientific method, his
theories of morals and of society, were all undertaken with

practical ends in view. In this, too, he was a typical disciple of the Philosophical Radicals. For Bentham, as for John Stuart Mill, Utilitarianism meant the perfect unity of theory and practice – of empirical theory with radical practice. This preoccupation with 'improvement' – or the application of knowledge to human welfare – distinguishes the Utilitarians from the earlier and greater empirical philosophers, above all from Hume, whose sceptical theories were suitably expressed in a mild and cautious Toryism. In fact the Benthamites are quite as much the successors of the English Agitators of 1794 as of Locke and Hume. For the earlier movement also had its theorists: Priestley, Godwin, Paine, and Horne Tooke, as well as its purely practical members, such as Hardy, who admitted to holding only one theory – that every citizen should possess arms and the knowledge of their use.[1]

The ferocity of a war-time government compelled the earlier radicals to walk in fear of their lives; the Philosophical Radicals of 1830 had their own Members of Parliament even before the Reform, their sympathizers in the government, and their own Lord Chancellor. Nevertheless, they were in their own way a kind of conspiracy, a clique, a cabal, plotting, wire-pulling, pamphleteering, against the peace of church and state, parliament, the courts of justice, and the ancient universities of Cambridge and Oxford. They aimed at nothing less than the new-modelling of all our institutions: and though they attempted this by legislation and denounced all violent methods, it happened that, in the great crisis of 1831, they found themselves allied with a movement more frankly revolutionary than anything that existed in 1794.

The Benthamites had plans and projects in a variety of different fields; and in each field they were as deeply concerned to work out first principles as to frame immediate programmes. 'The fact is,' wrote James Mill, ' that good practice can, in no case, have any solid foundation but in sound

1. The men of 1794 have been brought to life in H. N. Brailsford's study: *Shelley, Godwin and their Circle*. Francis Place, and others, took part in both the Radical movements.

theory. ... For, what is theory? The *whole* of the knowledge, which we possess upon any subject, put into that order and form in which it is most easy to draw from it good practical rules. ... To recommend the separation of practice from theory is, therefore, simply, to recommend bad practice.' [2]

John Stuart Mill grew up in the midst of this powerful movement: and in spite of many later changes he continued to profess many of the views and policies which he received from it. The dominant influences were his father, Bentham, and Ricardo; and Francis Place must also have taught him a good deal of the inner side of practical politics and of life in general. From John Austin, Mill received Bentham's ideas much modified; and from George Grote, Bentham's ideas unmodified. In his years of reaction against these first teachers, Mill wrote a famous *critique* of Bentham, which has so much in it that is convincing and illuminating that it is important to guard against what is distorted and exaggerated.

Bentham and his friends were at work along four main lines of action: (1) the foundations of jurisprudence, and the reform of the law; (2) a theory of representative government based upon Utility, and the radical reform of parliament; (3) the building of economics into a systematic body of knowledge, and the abolition of restraints upon trade and labour; (4) a utilitarian doctrine of morality, and the reform and secularization of education.

In all these undertakings, the rule to be applied was the principle of Utility, or the Greatest Happiness Principle. This was not, of course, Bentham's own invention. The notion that the rightness or wrongness of an action is to be judged entirely by the goodness or badness of its consequences, he took from Priestley; and the identification of good with pleasure, he found in Locke and Hume. In fact, hedonistic utilitarianism, often with a theological background, was a commonplace of eighteenth-century philosophers. What was new in Bentham was his analytical method, 'the method of

2. From the Introduction to his *Encyclopaedia Britannica* article on *Education*.

detail'; his detached and unprejudiced consideration of every aspect of every question; the recording and storing-up of his findings; and the unshakable assurance with which he finally produced his conclusion.

2. THE EARLY EDUCATION OF JOHN STUART MILL

In the year 1805, James Mill, being in a position (as he supposed) to scrape together some five or six hundred pounds a year, sought the hand of Harriet Burrow, whose mother kept an asylum for lunatics in Hoxton. The marriage was arranged. Miss Burrow was ten years younger than Mill and was no doubt enslaved by a clever, handsome, and self-confident Scotchman, pursuing the object of his desire. He saw her to be beautiful and believed that her innocence and ignorance could be improved by education. The happy couple (and for a time they were happy) went to live at No. 13, Rodney Street, Pentonville. Here the bride became the mother of a son, John Stuart, on 20 May, 1806; and as other children followed, found that her life was to be a hard one and that her husband's income and temper were both highly variable. James Mill had at this time no regular employment: his literary work had to be done at home. By the time John Stuart Mill was old enough to notice, his father had developed an irascible manner and was unable to conceal his contempt for his wife. In 1806 he began his *History of India*, which for twelve years occupied all the time he could spare from more remunerative work. In 1808 he made the acquaintance of Jeremy Bentham, then in his sixtieth year, but still without a sympathetic disciple of outstanding ability in his own country. The two became firm friends and after a short sojourn at Newington Green James Mill accepted from Bentham a house near his own: and at No. 1 Queen Square the Mills lived for sixteen years (1814–30). During four summers, 1815–18, the whole family (including five children) were transported to Bentham's country mansion, Ford Abbey in Devonshire. There they were visited by Francis Place, the Radical tailor of Charing Cross, who has left a picture of the strenuous intellectual life and the equally strenuous walks which made up the round of daily life at the Abbey. Place thought James Mill excessively severe with his children, but found Mrs Mill good-natured and peaceable. He also remarked that the children had 'a plentiful lack of manners, and as much impertinence, sometimes called impudence, as any children need have'; and that James Mill, Junior, was not prohibited from trundling his hoop round the great hall.[3]

John Mill also profited from 'the large and free character of the habitation': and the castle and its shaded and well-watered grounds inspired in him 'a sort of poetic cultivation'. Nor was Bentham's company the least attraction of the place. He was fond of the children, and especially of John, and there was (as Hazlitt says) 'a lackadaisical *bonhomie* about his whole aspect, none of the fierceness of pride or power'.

Unfortunately these summer migrations came to an end in 1818, when Bentham had to give up the lease on Ford Abbey, and James Mill was appointed Assistant Examiner at the East India Company. For the next ten years Mill was obliged to put in polite office hours for eleven months out of the twelve: but he now had a good salary and a position of great responsibility. This, however, was not allowed to interfere with his political and philosophical activities, nor to interrupt the education of his children which he conducted in his home, without any help from church or school.

The education of John Stuart Mill is one of the most celebrated in British annals, and has been the subject of much comment, both admiring and otherwise. His father began teaching him Greek at an age when most children are still learning to lisp their native tongue. At eight, Latin and arithmetic were begun; logic at twelve, and political economy at thirteen. The child was plunged at once into the greatest works of antiquity; poetry, history, and travel, in English, being added as a make-weight. The catalogue of works studied is given by Mill in a famous chapter in his *Autobiography*: it cannot fail to impress. But of all these works, the

3. Graham Wallas, *Life of Francis Place* (1898).

only ones whose influence can be clearly traced in his later thought are Plato's *Dialogues*, Hobbes's *Computation*, Aristotle's *Rhetoric*, and the writings of Ricardo. And, of course, all these works were re-studied later. Bain justly questions whether such extensive reading at such an age was of any great value. 'What his reading of Thucydides could be at eight, we may dimly imagine: it could be nothing but an exercise in the Greek language.' Mill, himself, remarks of the reading of the *Theaetetus* at the same age, that the dialogue 'would have been better omitted, as it was totally impossible I should understand it'.[4]

James Mill not only heard his son's recital of what he had been set to learn: he also required written summaries and comments, which were discussed between them at home or on the long walks which they took together. He always demanded more than his son was capable of giving, and his reproofs for premature opinions were immediate and crushing. Nevertheless, John somehow managed to survive this severity and to learn (as his father wished above all) to think for himself. The other children did not profit equally, though several showed great promise and the family was noted for vivacity and charm. As early as possible, the 'Lancasterian Method' was introduced into the family; and it was John's duty to pass on to his sisters and brothers as much as possible of the lessons he had learned from his father.

Until his fourteenth year John Mill was kept from all contact with the outside world, except for his father's own friends. At least three of these – Bentham, Ricardo, and Place – were of great value to all the children; and John's recollections of Ricardo (benevolent, kindly, modest, and gentle) are of the very warmest. But this isolation from other children is surely the feature of this famous education which one would wish to criticize most. No doubt there were (as James Mill believed) corrupting influences in the schools of his day: but for security from these, he sacrificed the free and equal society of boys and

4. See *Autobiography* (1873), p. 5, etc., and Alexander Bain: *J. S. Mill, A Criticism* (1882), p. 24.

girls outside the home. John Mill once remarked: 'I never was a boy; never played at cricket; it is better to let Nature have her way.' And in the *Autobiography* he tells us without the flicker of a smile, 'my amusements, which were mostly solitary, were in general, of a quiet, if not a bookish turn'.

3. YOUTHFUL PROPAGANDISM

Paternal despotisms have at least one redeeming feature: their time is not long. In 1820 John Mill was sent abroad for a year, and on his return, his father wisely dropped the role of schoolmaster for that of tutor. This early escape from England was a happy interlude: John was the guest of Sir Samuel Bentham and his wife and four children. The family took him on a long excursion through the Pyrenees, where Mill, duly prepared by an early reading of *The Lady of the Lake*, formed an attachment for mountain scenery which was to remain with him all his life, and which, in due course, made him an ardent Wordsworthian. He also learned to despise English manners in favour of French; and to realize for the first time that the utmost importance attaches to the sentiments expressed and assumed in ordinary intercourse; that the feelings, as well as the mind, are capable of education.

On his return, John was set to read certain books fundamental to Benthamism. The first of these, the *Analysis of the Influence of Natural Religion on the Temporal Happiness of Mankind*, was published under the pseudonym of 'Philip Beauchamp', and was actually written by Grote from Bentham's notebooks. The book tried to disprove the familiar thesis that some sort of religious sanctions are necessary if morality is to retain its hold on the generality of mankind. The argument made a profound impression on John Mill, and he returned to it again late in life. He had no faith to lose: for his father, having abandoned Christianity, was educating his son without church or creed.

Another book was Dumont's *Traité de Législation*, which set before him Bentham's philosophy as a whole and gave him a creed of his own, something to live for and to pass on to others. A third was the *Rationale of Judicial Evidence*, which he himself was asked to edit for publication in English – thus acting in the spirit of Hazlitt's remark on Bentham: 'His works have been translated into French – they ought to be translated into English.' It fell to John Mill to try to unroll the convolutions of the language, and to fill in gaps and to answer objections. This important part of his education was completed before the autumn of 1826.

In the meantime, there was the question of his career. For a time, he was set to read law with John Austin, and friendship with John Austin's younger brother Charles, who was an undergraduate, led to a visit to Cambridge in 1822. James Mill was urged to send his son to Trinity, where he might have the benefit of meeting his patrician contemporaries: but the bait failed to attract, and in 1823 James Mill entered his son as a clerk at the India House. There was an understanding that the way should be open to early promotion. John remained with the Company until its extinction in 1858.

The *Autobiography* shows how John Mill was now launched into the society of other young men, and how his home ceased to be the sole, or even the chief, means of his education. There were at least three important experimental groups to which John Mill became attached during the years of 'youthful propagandism'. The first of these was the Utilitarian Society, founded by John Mill himself in 1823, and meeting every fortnight at Bentham's house. The Society conducted its discussions on the lines of an undergraduate club:

It met in a low, half-furnished, desolate sort of room. ... The place was lighted by a few tallow candles. A desk was drawn across the end of the room, at which desk sat the chairman, and some half dozen young men sat in chairs round the room and formed the society.[5]

The Utilitarian Society seems to have come to an end about 1826. Between 1825 and 1830, another experiment was in progress. A dozen young men met each morning on their way

5. *Life and Letters of J. A. Roebuck*, London, 1897

to their offices, at the house of Grote, the banker, in Thread-needle Street. They began by reading and discussing James Mill's *Elements of Political Economy*, and Ricardo's *Principles*. From this, they went on in due course to deductive logic and to psychology – James Mill's greatest work, *The Analysis of the Human Mind*, was published in 1828. From these discussions Mill dates the beginnings of his own original and independent thinking.

At the same time, Mill became the leading figure in the London Debating Society, which held public debates on the model of the Cambridge Union Society. Membership was by no means confined to the Benthamites, but included a consortium of Liberals of many different shades: Macaulay, Edward Lytton Bulwer, Samuel Wilberforce, and Fonblanque. And some efforts were made to secure regular Tory speakers also. Mill spoke frequently at these meetings and made important acquaintances there. Gustave d'Eichthal came, and handed him an early political tract by Auguste Comte; John Sterling, and F. D. Maurice, the Coleridgeans, 'made their appearance in the Society as a second Liberal and even Radical party, on totally different grounds from Benthamism and vehemently opposed to it; bringing into these discussions the general doctrines and modes of thought of the European reaction against the philosophy of the eighteenth century'.[6]

Meanwhile, the older Philosophical Radicals had attained some solidarity and considerable influence. They appeared to stand, and to be the only party to stand, for a coherent policy of reform. The time had come for them to acquire a journal of their own in which to set forth their views at length before the educated public. Bentham, at his own expense, founded *The Westminster Review*. For the first number James Mill undertook to examine the history, composition, and pretensions of the Whig Party, and in particular of the *Edinburgh Review*,

6. *Autobiography*, p. 128. The World's Classics Edition of the *Autobiography* prints four of the speeches that Mill delivered at the London Debating Society, 1825–9.

the great Whig organ. With characteristic thoroughness he set his son to read through all the numbers of the *Edinburgh* since its foundation in 1802, and to prepare the ground for a thorough demolition of all its opinions. The remarkable article, which appeared in the first number of *The Westminster Review* in April 1824, surveyed the whole British scene, dissected the British constitution, exposed the dishonesty of the Whigs, and the vacillation of Jeffrey and his corps of reviewers. Never, said John Mill, had so great a blow been struck for Radicalism. The slaughter of Gifford, the *Quarterly*, and the Tory Party, was reserved for a later number. Indeed, Hazlitt remarked that the *Westminster Review* showed no tenderness towards any established institutions except the East India Company. John Mill himself wrote thirteen articles during the next five years, and many of the other Benthamites were regular or irregular contributors. The *Review* changed hands in 1828 and the Mills ceased to write for it. It was only after many vicissitudes that it came back into the hands of John Mill, under the title of *The London and Westminster Review* (1837).

In looking back at the period of his life between his return from France and the autumn of 1826, Mill saw that there was something excessively sectarian in the outlook of the younger Benthamites. The group were united in their adherence to Bentham's general point of view, to the economic views of Ricardo, to the Associationist psychology of Hartley, and to the population doctrine of Malthus. Their political views derived largely from James Mill's *Essay on Government*. They had disagreements among themselves, but these were less important than their thorough acceptance of James Mill's leadership and their contempt, not only for different points of view, but even for those whose interests lay in other directions. In a letter to Carlyle, of 1834, Mill says that he was himself at that time thought to be the narrowest of the Utilitarians:

That was not wonderful, because even in the narrowest of my then associates, they being older men, their ratiocinative and nicely concatenated dreams were at some point or other, and in some degree or other, corrected and limited by their experience of actual realities, while I, a schoolboy fresh from the logic school, had never conversed with a reality, never seen one, knew not what manner of thing it was, had only spun, first other people's and then my own deductions from assumed premises.[7]

How zealous he was at this time is well illustrated by an incident which led to John Mill's arrest and detention in a London jail in 1824. One of the principal tenets of the Benthamites was that the poor must learn to keep down their own numbers. Malthus himself had acknowledged, in the second edition of his *Essay on Population*, that war and famine are not the only means that limit the numbers of people. They could also be limited by 'moral restraints'; by which Malthus (conformably to his cloth) meant chiefly the deferment of marriage. But both James Mill and Francis Place had advocated the teaching of direct methods of birth control: and for his outspoken advocacy Place received the opprobrium which he fully expected.[8]

For if the Reverend Robert Malthus had already scandalized orthodox opinion by seeming to doubt whether the Lord would indeed provide for every soul born into the world, it needs no saying that Neo-Malthusianism, or the theory and practice of birth control, was regarded as tantamount to infanticide. John Mill, at all events, wished to make a distinction because he had become aware of a difference. On walking to his office through Kensington Gardens and Green Park he had witnessed the discovery of the dead bodies of unwanted infants. The wretched fate of these children gave him a glimpse of the real conditions of working life. He determined to act on his convictions: and he and a friend were arrested while trying to distribute birth control literature in the backyards of slum tenements. The pair were sentenced by the Lord Mayor to imprisonment for fourteen days, and actually served a part of their sentence. This example of

7. *Letters*, Edited by Hugh Elliot (1910), Vol. I, p. 88.
8. Francis Place himself had fifteen children, James Mill nine.

'Youthful Propagandism' was not included by Mill in the relevant chapter of his *Autobiography*.[9]

4. THE CRISIS OF 1826

In the autumn of 1826, John Stuart Mill was in his twenty-first year. For the past five years of his life he had had a definite object in view – the promotion of human happiness through the Benthamite programme of reforms. To this he had given himself without restraint and had found happiness in the society of his fellow-labourers. No doubt they had been years of strain, of gradual emancipation from his father, and of excessively hard and exacting work. He now found himself in a dull state of nerves, unsusceptible to enjoyment.

In this frame of mind it occurred to me to put the question directly to myself: 'Suppose that all your objects in life were realized; that all the changes in institutions and opinions which you are looking forward to, could be completely effected at this very instant: would this be a great joy and happiness to you?' And an irrepressible self-consciousness distinctly answered, 'No!' At this my heart sank within me: the whole foundation on which my life was constructed fell down.[10]

The depression which followed this shocking discovery did not leave him for many months; the stark and disillusioning fact could not be conjured away by company or books, and he had no one to whom to turn for advice. It seemed evident to

9. There are two sources for this story. It was told to Lord and Lady Amberley by John Robertson, who was a close colleague of Mill during his ownership of *The London and Westminster Review*. It is given in *The Amberley Papers*, edited by Bertrand and Patricia Russell (1937), II, p. 249. The other source is in a pamphlet by W. D. Christie, *J. S. Mill and Mr. Abraham Hayward, Q.C.*, H. S. King & Co. (1873). Christie wrote the pamphlet in defence of Mill's character against hints and rumours. The story is also referred to by G. J. Holyoake in *J. S. Mill as some of the Working-class knew him*, Trubner & Co. (1873). Holyoake believes that Mill may have been present, but taking no part, and that 'the police (as their custom is still) seized the only person who did not do it, who proved to be young Mr. Mill'.

10. *Autobiography*, p. 133.

him that his love for mankind and his love of excellence for its own sake had burnt themselves out. He seemed to have no deep feelings left. How long could he bear to go on living in these conditions? At most, he decided, for another year. Fortunately, before half that time had elapsed something happened. He was reading a pathetic French story and he was moved to tears. From this time forward his spirits began to revive: he realized that he still had hope, for he was not after all a stock or stone.

Mill represents this mental crisis as a sudden atrophy of all feeling. But his *recovery* was something much more important than a revival of the two ruling passions of his early life – the love of knowledge and the desire for political and social reforms. His recovery was marked by the awakening of new passions and interests which had hardly yet had a chance to show themselves.

James Mill was opposed to displays of feeling and his views of life were opposed to many of the most cherished feelings of his fellow men.

For passionate emotions of all sorts, and for everything which has been said or written in exaltation of them, he professed the greatest contempt. He regarded them as a form of madness. 'The intense' was with him a bye-word of scornful disapprobation. ... Feelings, as such, he considered to be no proper subjects of praise or blame. Right and wrong, good and bad, he regarded as qualities solely of conduct of acts and omissions.[11]

There, we may say, speaks the eighteenth century, protesting against the Romantic Movement. And from this undervaluing of feeling there naturally resulted 'an undervaluing of poetry and of Imagination generally, as an element in human nature'.

This antagonism conformed with James Mill's theory. He wished to assert a rational morality in opposition to a sentimental one: to discount conscience, affection, reverence, family feeling, impulsive generosity, as thoroughly as the Christian moralists had discounted pride, selfishness, malice, or sensuality.

11. *Autobiography*, p. 49.

But all this failed to satisfy John Stuart Mill. He found it necessary to ask again: From what state of character, from what feeling or motives, may an impulse to do the right action arise? What is the connexion of moral motives with other sentiments and feelings – with affection, gratitude, kindliness, reverence for the past, love of natural objects?

How all these questions came to be forced upon him is made clear in the *Autobiography*. He had been taught Hartley's doctrine of the association of ideas and feelings; he well understood how, by planned education, a youth may be made to find his greatest happiness in working for the general good. And he also understood the fortuitous and unnatural character of the associations thus contrived. But he was in a peculiar position: he had himself undergone the educational process, and at the hands of a master. For a time it seemed that *the education* had succeeded: but suddenly, in 1826, the associations broke down. The idea of the general good was still there, but the pleasurable feeling was altogether absent. Why was this? Because, in an emotional crisis of adolescence, it was all too easy for him to dissociate by intellectual analysis the feelings from their objects.

Analytic habits ... fearfully undermine all desires, and all pleasures, which are the effects of association, that is, according to the theory I held, all except the purely physical and organic.[12]

He therefore had to ask himself, was it possible for a person who understood psychology to achieve and retain a state of character, a balance of feelings, directed towards the good for man?

The *Autobiography* makes two suggestions: first, that a man should not make his own happiness an immediate aim; his aim should be some ideal object, such as the improvement of mankind or the pursuit of an art. Life's pleasures should be enjoyed as they come along: self-consciousness and scrutiny should be trained upon the character of the aim itself: pleasures themselves should always be accepted without scrutiny.

12. *Autobiography*, p. 138.

Second, the training of the individual for speculation and action is not the only thing of importance in life. Our susceptibilities, passive as well as active, need to be nourished and enriched as well as guided. The internal culture of the feelings is itself a necessity of life.

From these two suggestions, the *Autobiography* goes on to recount Mill's reading of Wordsworth's *Poems, 1815*, in the autumn of 1828. The poems, he tells us:

seemed to be the very culture of the feelings, which I was in quest of. In them I seemed to draw from a source of inward joy, of sympathetic and imaginative pleasure, which could be shared in by all human beings; which had no connexion with struggle or imperfection, but would be made richer by every improvement in the physical or social condition of mankind. From them I seemed to learn what would be the perennial sources of happiness, when all the greater evils of life shall have been removed.

We may perhaps object that this claims too much for Wordsworth; that men can find perennial sources of happiness in the city, or at court, or even in a university; that it is a somewhat narrow view to hold that we are all obliged to become Wordsworthians or to forfeit our millennium. But the nineteenth century was to justify Mill's verdict, at least as far as many of its noblest minds, and a considerable proportion of its reading public, were concerned. And Mill lost no time in nailing his new colours to the mast. The London Debating Society discussed for two evenings the comparative merits of Byron's poetry and Wordsworth's. The dubious Roebuck championed Byron's poetry as 'the poetry of human life, while Wordsworth's, according to him, was that of flowers and butterflies'. John Mill, for the first time, found himself on the opposite side from many of his friends and dated from that night his schism from the orthodox Utilitarians. He also began his friendship with Sterling, a man who like himself had begun life as a Benthamite, but who had fallen under the influence of Goethe and Coleridge. Sterling had hitherto regarded Mill as a 'manufactured man'; but a change took place in his feelings when, on the night of this debate, 'he found that Wordsworth, and all which that name implies, "belonged" to me as much as to him and his friends'.

Mill became more attached to Sterling than to any other man: and all his letters to Sterling are worth reading because they show a vitality and sensibility unequalled in his published writings. The correspondence ended only with the death of Sterling in 1844.

Meanwhile, many of his old associates either denounced him as a renegade or lived in fear of what he would say next. 'I think John Mill has made great progress in becoming a German metaphysical mystic', wrote Francis Place in 1838. And Sir John Bowring in 1840

spoke of Mill with evident contempt as a renegade from philosophy, i.e. a renouncer of Bentham's creed and an expounder of Coleridge's. ... Mill's newly-developed 'Imagination' puzzles him (Bowring) not a little; he was most emphatically a philosopher, but then he read Wordsworth, and that muddled him, and he has been in a strange confusion ever since, endeavouring to unite poetry and philosophy.[13]

This is no bad description of what Mill was trying to do during the years following 1826. His extreme reaction against his father's views began to be modified as early as the summer of 1833; after his father's death in 1836, and his own serious illness in the same year, he tried to draw up a programme for a new 'utilitarianism of the whole of human nature'. In this new Utilitarianism feeling was to be 'at least as valuable as thought, and Poetry not only on a par with, but the necessary condition of, any true and comprehensive Philosophy'.[14]

These conclusions, though expressed in such stilted and indefinite language, place Mill fairly and squarely outside the sectarian creed of rationalistic hedonism. From them we can trace the beginnings of his own moral and political theory; his personal emphasis on the intrinsic value of the individual character and individual differences.

13. *Caroline Fox, Journal and Letters*, edited by H. N. Pym (1883), p. 141.
14. *Letters*, I, p. 104 (to E. Lytton Bulwer).

In commenting upon the changes that took place in Mill's views at this time, Halévy says that it was impossible for Mill to interpret the Utilitarian morality as he did, 'without returning to that sentimentalism which the orthodox Benthamites had only defined in order to condemn'.

This seems to be a correct verdict. John Mill was attempting to insist upon the importance for morality of precisely those elements of feeling and of inwardness which Bentham and James Mill had rejected.[15]

5. HARRIET TAYLOR

The transformation in his opinions and character which took place after 1826 is described by John Mill himself as 'the only actual revolution which has ever taken place in my modes of thinking'. By 1830 that revolution was, he says, complete: but the new tendencies received an important modification through his friendship with Harriet, the wife of John Taylor a London merchant. Mrs Taylor was then twenty-two years old and known as a very pretty woman with a quick wit and vivid manner. Her husband, who was a good man, had neither the gifts nor the attainments to match those of a young woman who had read Berkeley's philosophy at the age of eleven and had studied logic at the age of fourteen. She seems to have been discontented before she met Mill, but had a small circle of congenial friends. To this circle Mill was admitted in 1830, and he early recognized in her the most admirable person he had ever known – as she was certainly the first young woman he had ever met outside his own family. In 1833 Harriet Taylor wrote of Mill as 'the type of the possible elevation of humanity' and avowed that 'to be with him wholly is my ideal of the noblest fate'.[16]

15. See Elie Halévy, *The Growth of Philosophic Radicalism* (translated by Mary Morris), London (1928), p. 469. Lord Morley told Mr Laski that Mill became a great reader of novels, Dickens being a particular favourite.

16. See *Letters*, I, *The Private Life of J. S. Mill*, by Mary Taylor, p. xli, and *J. S. Mill and Harriet Taylor*, correspondence edited by F. A. Hayek, Routledge (1951).

It was probably in this year that her husband vainly attempted to bring the friendship to an end: Mrs Taylor went to Paris, where Mill was also staying. On her return her husband seems to have accepted the situation, and the two afterwards lived apart a great deal. Mrs Taylor and her daughter Helen spent long periods at their country house and travelled abroad during the winters. But husband and wife continued to spend part of the year together in London, and after 1842 Mill dined there twice a week while Mrs Taylor was in residence, the husband conveniently dining out.

Naturally enough, there was also opposition to the friendship from Mill's family. James Mill, though believing that a greater freedom of relations between the sexes would some day be permitted, was not inclined to accept his son as a pioneer in this field. He 'openly taxed him with being in love with another man's wife'. Others of his friends were offended and estranged and the pair began to feel themselves isolated. At the end of 1835 John Mill suffered from a mysterious nervous complaint, and in the following summer his father wrote: 'John is still in a rather pining way; though as he does not tell the cause of his pining, he leaves other people to their conjectures.'[17]

In August 1836 Mill went abroad in an attempt to recover his health: Mrs Taylor accompanied him and Carlyle comments: 'They are innocent says Charity, they are guilty says Scandal: then why in the name of wonder are they dying broken hearted?'

From 1840 onwards, Mill virtually retired from London society. He indulged 'the inclination, natural to thinking persons when the age of boyish vanity is once passed, for limiting my own society to a very few persons'. These persons were Mrs Taylor, George Grote, Alexander Bain, and a very few others.

17. See *Letters*, I, pp. 66, 71, etc.; and Bain, *J. S. Mill, A Criticism*, p. 42, etc., and 163, etc., and *James Mill*, p. 406. Bain discusses the various illnesses from which Mill suffered. The family was, of course, consumptive.

Mill admits that his association with Mrs Taylor was liable to be 'falsely interpreted', but states categorically that their relation to each other 'was one of strong affection and confidential intimacy only'. They both disapproved of the marriage law and considered that no ordinances of society were binding in a matter so entirely personal. But they felt obliged to pursue a course which would in no degree bring discredit upon the husband, 'nor therefore on herself'. We may therefore conclude that Charity was right and Scandal mistaken.

Mill believed that Mrs Taylor had a great intellect and was a great imaginative thinker. He compares her very favourably indeed with Carlyle and with Shelley, and says that, had such a career been open to women, she would have become eminent among the rulers of mankind. And nobody else has ever been found who was able to confirm these views.

Mrs Taylor evidently possessed a remarkable gift of intuition: she could see at once the ultimate moral principles involved in a question; and there is no doubt that it was her way of making up her mind on such issues without argument and without reserve, that gave Mill the clue to Carlyle.

I conceive that most of the highest truths are, to persons endowed by nature in certain ways which I think I could state, intuitive; that is, they need neither explanation nor proof, but if not known before are assented to as soon as stated.[18]

Mill also pays tribute to her power of seeing what was the next immediately useful and practical step to be taken: and her power of applying their principles to human life with imagination. 'What was abstract and purely scientific was generally mine; the properly human element came from her.'[19]

This releasing of Mill's emotions and attaching of them both to herself and to their common aims, was no doubt of very great service indeed. Even if we suppose that Mrs

18. *Letters*, I, p. 54 (to Carlyle).
19. *Autobiography*, p. 247 (Mill is writing of the *Political Economy*).

Taylor's convictions were very largely an echo of Mill's own, it was surely of immense value to him to have an ally who could give them life and power. And there is no reason to doubt Mill's more sober statements of the directions in which she influenced his views. It was, he says, through her that he came to see the practical possibility of socialism and the vital importance of redressing the injustices suffered by the working classes. He says, also, that the *Liberty* was a joint work, and that it was she who helped to keep him a radical and democrat.

6. THE REFORM AGITATION

These changes of opinion and conduct naturally tended to divide John Mill from his father: but on both sides there was a sensible inclination to pass over the deeper disagreements in silence, and to co-operate upon those enterprises which still united them – especially upon the India Company's Charter and on Parliamentary Reform. John Mill shared in the family summer residence at Dorking and Mickleham, and removed with them from Queen Square to Vicarage Place, Kensington, in 1830. James Mill became head Examiner at India House in the same year: he was now fifty-seven years old, the father of nine children, a rich and powerful man, famous as a politician and philosopher. He was undoubtedly one of the men who guided the parliamentary leaders of the Reform Movement throughout the protracted and extremely painful struggles of 1830–2. He and Grote were in touch with Francis Place, and through him, with Parkes and the Birmingham Unions. While James Mill suggested to Lord Brougham the names of those who should speak for the Bill in Parliament, Francis Place helped to nominate the 'generals' who should meet the victor of Waterloo on the playing-fields of London.

Into the Reform Movement John Mill entered fully. He recognized its revolutionary character and assented to it. It seemed certain that the Church of England and the House of Lords were doomed and he had no regrets for either. But while he welcomed the work of destruction, John Mill was more keenly interested in the difficult question of reconstruction. This interest was quickened by his reading of Coleridge's *Church and State* and of Auguste Comte's *Système de Politique Positive*, and it was confirmed by his visit to Wordsworth and Southey in the autumn of 1831, and to the Saint-Simonists in Paris during July 1830. His public comments are given in five articles, entitled *The Spirit of the Age*, which appeared in *The Examiner*, and his private comments, in a long letter to John Sterling written in October 1831.[20]

John Mill's introduction to Saint-Simonism began in May 1828, when Gustave d'Eichthal attended a meeting of the London Debating Society. He handed on to Mill various writings of Saint-Simon and his followers and the early *Système* of Comte. These Mill read, and after some resistance he came to believe that some form of socialism might be the *ultimate* form of human society; but he refused to take it up as a practical issue and declined to become a member of the Saint-Simonist Society. In 1830 he hurried to Paris to observe the July Revolution and had long discussions with Enfantin and Bazard. But he seems not to have made any contact with Comte, from whose writings he immediately adopted certain leading principles which enabled him to understand better the deficiencies of the Radical theory of politics.

Mill's visit to Wordsworth and Southey also made a deep impression upon him. He felt their reverence for good government as something which men needed and of which men could not permanently be deprived. And he saw the shallowness of the Radicals, who would make every man his own guide and authority. The Radical view, he thought, showed a thorough ignorance of man's nature and of what is necessary for his true happiness. While he differed from Wordsworth

20. See *Letters*, I, p. 3, etc., and *The Spirit of the Age*, edited by Professor Hayek, Chicago University Press (1942). See also Professor Hayek's Introduction. Comte's essay was published in translation in Frederick Harrison's edition of the *Early Essays on Social Philosophy* (Routledge, London).

on all points of immediate policy, he felt that he now differed from the Radicals upon fundamental principles.[21]

Mill thus found himself asserting the value, for human happiness, of an *orthodoxy*, supported by institutions capable of supplying moral and intellectual leadership. But how could this desire for a settlement be reconciled with his rejection of the Church and his hopes of enormous improvements in society? The political writings of the Saint-Simonists and of Comte provided him with an answer to this question; a new view of Motion and Rest in politics. There are (he learned from them) natural stages in social development. At certain periods there are settled ideas and practices and a settled order of government; between such enviable times, there are Ages of Transition. In the Middle Ages there was a religious settlement: the theological view of the nature of man, and of morality, was taught and enforced by the Church, and no other leadership was possible or necessary. The Reformation shows the decay of the fundamental ideas of the Middle Ages: they became out-of-date and dangerous. Then came a new settlement, directed not by the Church but by the aristocracy, both lay and clerical. The height of this second period was reached in the days of Descartes, Newton, and Locke. The revolutions that marked the close of the eighteenth century also marked the beginning of a new Age of Transition. Mill was himself aware of the fact that he was living in such an age. But he could see (what was concealed from the Radicals) that transition is not natural, not *organic;* a new settlement would come in due course. And this new settlement will rest, not on theology, nor on *a priori* reasoning, but on positive notions – on principles verified by observation in the manner of the physical sciences.[22]

21. See *Letters, loc. cit.* This visit took place during the crisis of the Reform Bill: at this time Wordsworth was thoroughly horrified and incensed, and feared an immediate revolution. His son, William, Assistant Distributor of Stamps for Westmorland, was warned by the poet 'to stay at home and guard his stamps'. See the *Letters of William and Dorothy Wordsworth*, ed. De Selincourt, II, p. 584.

22. See *Autobiography*, pp. 164, etc., for the different ways in which the Saint-Simonists and Comte identified the stages in European history.

7. MILL AND CARLYLE

Mill tells us that *The Spirit of the Age* naturally failed to attract much attention in the height of the Reform crisis. But it was read with grim satisfaction by Thomas Carlyle, who was then finishing *Sartor Resartus* in the snowy isolation of Craigenputtock. Here, at last, he thought, is an Englishman who recognizes the deficiencies of the present age. Carlyle had come to the conclusion that man is a creature born *to believe*, to accept without question, and even without conscious recognition, the wisdom that shall rule his life in peace. He condemned alike the English Empiricists and the French Enlightenment and poured bitter scorn on the mechanical philosophy of the Benthamites. But he was himself sceptical of Christian orthodoxy and recognized that he lived in an Age of Unbelief. He proclaimed the coming of a new Idea, a new Faith – that men generally would acknowledge what the Poet, or Prophet, would discover. His reading of the German philosophers inclined him to believe that they would provide the new revelation of the godlike. Although the time of scepticism was not yet past, the joy had already gone out of it: 'the problem is not now to deny, but to ascertain and perform'.[23]

On reading Mill's essays, Carlyle exclaimed: 'Here is a new mystic'; a misjudgement which led to an intimate friendship and also considerable embarrassment for Mill. In 1831 Carlyle came to London, bringing with him the manuscript of *Sartor Resartus*. He was deeply impressed by Mill – his intelligence, good looks, graceful manners, and attentive homage. Mill had seen in Carlyle's earlier articles 'nothing but insane rhapsody'; he had now to read *Sartor Resartus* and little could he make of it. Nevertheless, Carlyle was there and was not a person to be ignored: a friendship had begun. When at last Carlyle returned to Craigenputtock in the following year, still carrying his manuscript in a paper parcel, Mill began an important corre-

23. Carlyle, *Characteristics*, Fraser's Magazine (1831) (written earlier). See also Emery Neff's *Carlyle and Mill*, New York (1926).

spondence in which their differences were for a time avoided, and the narrow grounds of their agreement fully exploited. Mill himself had a notion of a new orthodoxy: men must not always be expected to hold their fundamental beliefs as tentative: there are stages in the affairs of men – ages of transition and ages of settled opinion. Mill's own notion of a new orthodoxy was that it would be discovered by rational argument and experimental enquiry. But he was quite willing to believe that certain peculiarly gifted individuals might arrive at important truths by short cuts unknown to ordinary minds. More important still, the poet and the artist might be especially fitted to express the new truth in such a way as to move men to act on it. 'You I look upon as an artist,' he wrote to Carlyle, 'and perhaps the only genuine one now living in this country: the highest destiny of all lies in that direction; for it is the artist alone in whose hands Truth becomes impressive and a living principle of action.' His own task is the humbler one of removing intellectual objections to the new Truth.[24]

But though variations on the same theme recur in many later letters, by May 1833 Mill made up his mind that he had been deceiving both Carlyle and himself by pretending a wider agreement than he really felt. The occasion of this enlightenment was Carlyle's condemnation of Diderot. In a series of letters lasting over a year, Mill now says again and again that the differences he had represented so lightly, really amount to half a universe. He, like Diderot, believes that the existence of God can never be more than probable. To Carlyle, 'a probable God' may be worse than no God at all, but Mill can see no way of settling the question except by a consideration of the evidence. The bad news is wrapped in many professions of admiration for Carlyle's faith; but it gradually convinced Carlyle that he was not making a disciple. In the meantime *Sartor Resartus* had at last been published, and Mill, under the guidance of Mrs Taylor, began for the first time to understand it, and to feel strong agreement with many of its criticisms of

24. *Letters*, I, p. 35 (July 1832).

the Benthamites. But by this time his own position as an independent thinker was established. He would henceforth oppose the new Transcendentalism no less than the old narrow intellectualism of the Radicals.

8. MILL AND THE RADICALS, 1836–40

In 1832, at the height of the struggle for Parliamentary Reform, Jeremy Bentham had died at the age of eighty-four, and in June 1836, James Mill died.

John Mill no doubt hoped after his father's death to succeed to at least a part of his power and influence over the Radical group in the reformed Parliament. But it is doubtful whether he had at the time a sufficiently clear notion of his own aims to offer himself as a guide to others. From 1837–40 he was owner and director of the *London and Westminster Review:* but he did not succeed in pleasing the genuine Radicals, and failed to draw in the men of broader principles whom he wished to recruit. These failures were felt by Mill as personal defeats: he realized that his trimming and his 'many-sidedness' had defeated his chances of building a new Party. Sterling remarked at a later date:

He has made the sacrifice of being the undoubted leader of a powerful party for the higher glory of being a private in the army of Truth, ready to storm any of the strong places of Falsehood, even if defended by his late adherents.

But Mill knew better at the time:

I have long done what I could to prepare them for (office), but in vain: so I have given them up, and in fact they have given up me.[25]

The writings which, above all others, divided Mill from his former friends, were his 'Essay on Bentham' (1838) and his

25. *Journal of Caroline Fox*, p. 223 and p. 97. See also *Autobiography*, p. 216, on Mill's 'one success', in connexion with Lord Durham's Report on Canada. Mill's *Letters*, I, pp. 104, 108, 110, show his attempts to recruit Lytton Bulwer.

'Essay on Coleridge' (1840). In these great studies there is an attempt to view the rival philosophies in an *objective* manner. But there is something unsatisfactory in this exaggerated attempt to see both good and bad in both sides of a fundamental controversy. The writer seems committed to not committing himself. Moreover the character of Bentham, though not unsympathetically drawn, was shown up in all its narrowness. His philosophy is described as 'the empiricism of one who has had little experience'; of one whose life had been without inward conflict or suffering, whose character was really that of a prodigiously intellectual schoolboy; lacking imagination and self-analysis and unable to draw light from those who had it. In the Coleridge article, on the other hand, the poet is placed on an equal with Bentham. The English empiricists are now shown to lack an adequate notion of society, and to have adopted a false *apriorism* in their science of government. The Coleridgeans are the true successors of Bacon and Locke in this field: though their methodology may be wrong their methods are right. After reading this essay, Mill's friends experienced a painful misgiving as to his adhering to their principles or to any principles at all.

Meanwhile, however, Mill had discovered a new writer on politics, who seemed to him to follow a genuinely empirical and non-partisan method, without the encumbrance of transcendental principles. This was Alexis de Tocqueville, whose book on America both Mill and his father had read in 1835. In the *Edinburgh Review* (1840) Mill reviewed the book and dealt with one of its underlying themes: the dangers of majority rule. This article, which attracted little attention at the time, might have offered some assurance to his old associates. For Mill here showed himself capable of facing fundamental criticism of democracy and remaining unshaken by it.

In the spring of 1840, Mill suffered the loss of his favourite brother, Harry, who died of consumption at Falmouth. John and his sister Clara spent some weeks in Cornwall and were accompanied by John Sterling. This visit has been recorded by Caroline Fox, with whom they were acquainted: her

Journal gives us a picture of Mill in his thirty-fourth year as seen by a Quakeress of twenty:

He is a very uncommon-looking person – such acuteness and sensibility marked in his exquisitely chiselled countenance. . . . His voice is refinement itself and his mode of expressing himself tallies with voice and countenance.

Quite an ideal head so expanded with patient thought and a face of such exquisite refinement.

His manners greatly pleased her: his tenderness towards his brother, his amiability when with John Sterling. The friends had long conversations about poetry, beauty, and truth. Nor was sentimentalism entirely lacking: on leaving Pendennis Cavern, Mill suggested that they should leave the candles lighted as an offering to the gnomes.

But what most impressed Caroline Fox was Mill's devotion to his self-appointed task of educating his own age in the truth as he himself saw it. He realized the magnitude and loneliness of the task 'as is sufficiently attested by his careworn and anxious . . . countenance.' He had come to see that the utilitarian test of success was not the final criterion: that even if a man is certain to fail, it is yet of supreme importance that he should stick to the truth as he sees it, teach it without compromise, and live it without servile adaptation.

Find out your own individuality and live and act in the circle around it. . . . Everyone has a part to perform whilst stationed here, and he must strive with enthusiasm to perform it.

At a later meeting Mill 'alluded to the indescribable change and growth he experienced when he made the discovery that what was right for others might not be right for him.'

9. THE *LOGIC* AND THE *POLITICAL ECONOMY*

It was during the summer of the same year that Mill completed the first draft of his *Logic*. It had its first beginnings in the discussions in Threadneedle Street during the year 1826, and the first attempt to write down conclusions reached at these meetings was made in 1830: the topic was the meaning or 'import' of propositions.

Mill thus devoted the 'spare time' of the best years of his life to the completion of his greatest work; making use of the contemporary writings of Whewell, Herschel, and Auguste Comte. After the publication of the *Logic* he was a famous man. 'How the book came to have, for a work of the kind, so much success, and what sort of persons compose the bulk of those who have bought, I will not venture to say read, it, I have never thoroughly understood.'[26]

The *Logic* has continued to influence philosophers as well as to guide the reflections of undergraduates. Jevons and Venn, Johnson and Keynes, based their work avowedly upon his, and the writings of the later Idealist logicians reveal a debt even where their authors fail to acknowledge it. It was likewise from the basis of Mill's ideas that the philosophies of Frege and Meinong made their departure.[27]

The publication of the *Logic* marks the end of Mill's Coleridgean period. From this point on, he moved back towards many of the views with which he had been brough up, and which he had abandoned in the crisis of 1826. This reversion is noticeable along two main lines. First, he now rejects the doctrine that the mind has intuitive powers of discovering truths; or rather, he holds that any valid intuitive powers that the mind possesses can serve only to anticipate the senses and the analytic faculty. When he wrote the *Logic* he made some pretence of avoiding a dogmatic statement on this question. He was willing to learn from John Sterling more about the views of Kant, Hegel, and Schelling. But by the time he came to write his metaphysical treatise (*The Examination of Sir William Hamilton's Philosophy*), it was primarily with the idea of combatting the intuitionism of the Germans. This greater confidence did not come from a thorough study of Kant and Hegel: Kant was read (or at

26. See *Autobiography*, pp. 159, 180, 221, etc. See also Mill's letters of this period to Sterling, Lytton Bulwer and Bain.
27. See R. Jackson, *The Deductive Logic of J. S. Mill*, Preface.

least quoted) in translation: James Stirling's interpretation of Hegel sufficed to show Mill 'that conversancy with him tends to deprave one's intellect. ... For some time after I had finished the book all such words as *reflection, development, evolution,* etc., gave me a sort of sickening feeling which I have not entirely yet got rid of.'[28]

Secondly, in his *Political Economy* and *Claims of Labour,* Mill shows that he is now willing to accept the Radical view that man can find no *authority* competent to guide him in the discovery or verification of fundamental truths. Provided discussion is absolutely free (and endless), truth will make itself known. Paternalism, of the kind advocated by Coleridge and Carlyle, tends to degrade men and to delay their growth to full stature and self-dependence.

It seems likely that these revisions of opinion are due in part to the influence of Harriet Taylor, but in part to Mill's own further reflections and further experiences. It is important to notice, however, what remains with him of his earlier views; his conviction that it is the inner life of feeling that is of chief importance in morals. This is the basis of the ethical teaching of *Utilitarianism* and the *Essay on Liberty.* It embodies something not quite a mistrust of intellectualism. To every partisan conviction, there is opposed a contrary conviction, and on many questions an open mind is the only rational mind. And beyond all theory and all policy there is the life of the soul itself —

> the secret cup
> Of still and serious thought.

In 1844 Mill published the first of his works on economics: *Essays on Some Unsettled Questions in Political Economy,* which belong to the period 1830–4. In the following year appeared *The Claims of Labour (Edinburgh Review),* and in 1848 his comprehensive work, *The Principles of Political Economy.*

In this work Mill was certainly far more generous to the claims of the working-class than any of the previous political

28. *Letters,* II, p. 93 (1867).

economists: and the chapter on *The Probable Futurity of the Labouring Classes*, added in later drafts, paved the way to co-operation with the intellectual leaders of the workers. But this was a slow process; and the book was entirely incapable of arousing the noble and imaginative passion for reform which burned in Carlyle and his followers. Nevertheless, it would be true to say that from this time onwards, Mill's main concern in politics was to further the cause of working-class representation; and to guard against, or to mitigate, the difficulties and dangers of a transition to working-class domination.

10. LATER WORKS (1849–65)

In the year 1849 John Taylor died. On 6 March, 1851, Mill wrote out a solemn statement of his disapproval of the whole character of the marriage relation as constituted by law. Thereafter the two friends who had known each other and no one else for so many long years were at last united in marriage. This union, which lasted only seven years, was a source of the greatest happiness to them both. Unfortunately it was also the occasion of a division between John Mill and his mother and sisters. There exists a long correspondence on this subject. In his *Autobiography*, which was mostly written in 1861, Mill makes no mention of his mother's existence.[29]

The seven years of his married life were spent quietly enough, but the marriage did not immediately open the doors of all those who had looked askance at the long friendship. Nor did the house at Blackheath become the centre of political causes until many years later. Mill was occupied with a number of essays on fundamental questions: the restatement of his moral theories on Justice, Utility, Liberty, and on Religious Belief.

The *Essay on Liberty* was written jointly with his wife and

29. *Letters*, I, *The Private Life of J. S. Mill*, by Mary Taylor, granddaughter of Mill's wife: Professor Laski's *Introduction* to the World's Classics edition of the *Autobiography* : and Hayek, *J. S. Mill and Harriet Taylor*.

was regarded by Mill as likely to survive longer than any of his other works 'with the possible exception of the *Logic*.' In it Mill expresses his view of the value of individual character and individual differences, and the importance of protecting them against the power of society. In writing it, Mill had very much in mind that future state of industrial society in which the dominating positions would be in the hands of the working classes. The *Essay* expresses an inward, spiritual egotism – an egotism of the unworldly-minded, something of which is conveyed in Mill's light-hearted advice to Lady Amberley to 'establish a character for strangeness'. 'There is nothing like it,' he said, 'then one can do what one likes.'[30]

During the same years, Mill shaped his own views on *The Subjection of Women*. His belief in the equality of the sexes, as an intellectual conviction, dates from his earliest political reflections: but his association with Harriet Taylor transformed it into one of the major passions of his later life. From her he learned 'the vast practical bearings of women's disabilities' and their connexion with other evils of the age – over-population and the resulting evils to the working classes, servility, stupidity, superstition, and an over-emphasis on sexual interests which Mill thought to be characteristic of his age. From her he derived the extreme feminism which led him to see no essential differences between the best masculine characters and the best feminine characters. This is revealed as early as 1833 in a letter to Carlyle:

But the women, of all I have known, who possessed the highest measure of what are considered feminine qualities, have combined with them more of the highest *masculine* qualities than I have ever seen in any but one or two men, and those one or two men were also in many respects almost women. I suspect it is the second-rate people of the two sexes that are unlike ... but then, in this respect, my position has been and is, ... 'a peculiar one'.[31]

Mill held that a philosophy is to be judged by its conception of human nature: and it is somewhat disconcerting to find

30. *Amberley Papers*, I, p. 475 (1866).
31. *Letters*, I, p. 70.

that his own conception suffered from this eccentric limitation.

In 1856 Mill was made head of the Examiner's Department at India House and had to write the petition by which the Company tried to secure a renewal of their Charter. On the failure of the petition, Mill declined the offer of a seat on the new India Council and retired in 1858. In the same year his wife died at Avignon: the leisure which he had hoped to share with her he dedicated to the completion of those works in which she had had a part; and to the writing of his *Autobiography*. In this he was helped by his wife's daughter, Helen Taylor, who lived with him for the rest of his life. Part of each year was spent at Blackheath, and the remainder at a cottage at Avignon. During the years 1858–65, Mill described his retirement as that of 'a recluse who reads the newspapers'. But in fact he became a sociable man again: the friends of his later years were George Grote, W. T. Thornton, John Morley, and the omnicompetent Scotchman, Alexander Bain. In 1864 Mill made the acquaintance of Lord Amberley, who called on him first at Avignon. He and Miss Taylor recruited Lord and Lady Amberley for the feminist movement and many other good causes, and enjoyed their society for many years.

The essays on *Utilitarianism* appeared in *Fraser's Magazine* in 1861. In the same year Mill read the logical and metaphysical lectures of Sir William Hamilton, which had been published after his death by two of his pupils. Hamilton had been Professor of Logic and Metaphysics at Edinburgh for twenty years and had established himself as the leader of the British Kantians and as an authority on the history of philosophy. After reading his works, Mill determined to write an answer: but the answer turned out to be a thorough denunciation:

> It almost goes against me to write so complete a demolition of a brother-philosopher after he is dead, not having done it while he was alive, and the more when I consider what a furious retort I should infallibly have brought upon myself, if he had lived to make it.[32]

32. *Letters*, I, p. 311 (to Bain).

The *Examination* cannot be regarded as a philosophical work of the first rank: but certain chapters on mind and body and our knowledge of the physical world contain matter enough for a serious treatise on some of the most difficult questions of philosophy. They present phenomenalism, as transmitted through James Mill and Brown, in downright fashion, abandoning all Hume's subtle hesitations between the philosopher in his study and the philosopher in the world. Besides these, the later chapters of the *Examination* have in them the making of a treatise on the foundations of necessary truth and of formal logic and mathematics.

II. PARLIAMENT

In 1865 a group of citizens of Westminster asked Mill if he would stand as a working-men's candidate at the General Election. Mill agreed to stand, on condition that he should not be expected to contribute towards the expenses of the election in his own constituency, that he would not canvass, nor promise to give any of his time (if elected) to the local interests of Westminster, nor at any time give information on his religious views. His promoters accepted these conditions and Mill conducted a series of meetings and discussions which (to everyone's surprise) secured his return to Parliament.

This election had all the elements of poetic justice. No English philosopher since Locke had been so much devoted to the actual political questions of his day. Mill's real aim had been to secure a first share of power for the working-classes: but his programme was a stern one and often seemed to conflict directly with working-class aims. This election to the democratic constituency of Westminster, which had been captured by his father and Francis Place for Burdett in the early days of Reform, enabled Mill to cement that alliance between the intellectual left wing and the working classes which has been the foundation of British Socialism.

Mill's membership lasted until the General Election of

1868. During his time in Parliament he spoke in favour of extending the vote to the whole of the working class; and when Gladstone's Reform ministry was defeated and Disraeli came into office, Mill was much concerned in the working-class agitation against the Tory Government. This began in the provinces where Bright was master: but in the autumn of 1866 came London's turn. A monster demonstration was announced for Hyde Park. The meeting was forbidden and the Park picketed by the police. The leaders of the working men retired under protest: but a vast crowd assembled and with symbolic violence tore down the railings of the Park. In spite of the police ban, a second meeting was arranged, and it was expected that the Reformers would bring their weapons with them. At this point Mill and other Radical Members were called to a conference, and Mill relates in his *Autobiography* that it was by his own arguments that the meeting was convinced of the folly of inviting a clash with the military.

In the next session, Disraeli himself introduced a Bill for giving the vote to all municipal householders: and this was the occasion of a simple amendment, proposed by John Mill, for substituting the word 'person' for the word 'man'. The motion won the votes of seventy-three members, including John Bright.[33]

Two important questions of British rule overseas also led to Mill's active intervention. One was the Irish question; and Mill's speeches at the time of the Fenian outrages brought him considerable unpopularity. The other was the conduct of Governor Eyre in the mutiny in Jamaica. In his leadership of the Jamaica Committee Mill won a reputation for advocating ruthless and vindictive measures against a British proconsul, whose only offences had been committed against black people some thousands of miles across the water. He was opposed by a 'Governor Eyre Committee', which had been formed under the chairmanship of Carlyle. Behind Carlyle were ranged the Tories and the Whigs as a matter of course: but he also en-

33. See *Autobiography*, p. 279, etc.; also *Amberley Papers*, I, p. 468, etc., and II, p. 36, etc.; and G. J. Holyoake, *op. cit.*

listed Ruskin, Tennyson, Kingsley, and Charles Dickens. Mill, on the other hand, had the support of Darwin, Wallace, Huxley, Spencer, Frederick Harrison, Leslie Stephen, and John Morley, together with the working-class leaders and other Radicals. In the end Mill's party won a theoretical victory: the Lord Chief Justice, Sir Alexander Cockburn, delivered his charge at Old Bailey, making it clear that the Governor was indeed answerable for his offences, thus settling the question 'in favour of liberty', as far as the law went. But the jury threw out the bill and no trial ever took place.

On questions of foreign policy, Mill took the line that one would expect. He defended the Northern States against the opposition of Liberals and Tories, and at the same time tried to explain to his American friends the baffling ambiguities of Lord John Russell. He had been warmly in favour of the French Revolution of 1848, and continued to support the Socialists after the June Days. But after 1851, Mill became thoroughly disgusted with the French and was unable to see in the Franco-Prussian War anything more than the punishment of Napoleon's ambitions and treachery.[34]

12. AVIGNON

In the General Election of 1868 Mill was defeated by the Tory candidate. Every possible use was made by his opponents of the fact that Mill had contributed towards the election expenses of Charles Bradlaugh. Mill agreed with Bradlaugh in rejecting Christian beliefs: he had no sympathy with Bradlaugh's scornful manner and provocative language. But Bradlaugh was a working-men's candidate; willing to support Malthusianism, Proportional Representation, and Votes for Women.

After his defeat Mill and his step-daughter retired to Avignon: and during the last years of his life, the two spent only a short part of each year in London. Their home at Avignon

34. See *Frazer's Magazine*, January 1862, 'The Contest in America'; and *The Education of Henry Adams*. On French affairs, see *Letters*, II.

was a small white stone cottage a mile from the town, hidden behind a long garden. A vine-covered terrace on two sides of the house provided a Wordsworthian promenade for the rainy weather: and a herbarium was added to house Mill's collection of plants and botanical books. Beyond the garden was a prospect of meadows and mountains. The day's work began after an eight o'clock breakfast and continued until after midday. In the afternoon there were long country walks: and after supper the philosopher would read aloud 'some light book'. Few visitors were permitted: and Queen Victoria's daughter, the Princess Royal of Prussia, who wished to visit Mill at Avignon, was told that 'he was not in a condition to avail himself of the honour intended'. Besides the writing of *The Subjection of Women*, and the notes to his father's *Analysis of the Human Mind*, Mill wrote many long letters, and minor papers on the three subjects that interested him most deeply during his later life: scientific thought, socialism, and religion.

Scientific method was, of course, one of the principal themes of Mill's logic. His unflagging interest in this question is shown in the correspondence of the last fifteen years of his life. In 1860 he gives his views on a first reading of Darwin's *Origin of Species*:

It far surpasses my expectation. Though he cannot be said to have proved the truth of his doctrine, he does seem to have proved that it *may* be true, which I take to be as great a triumph as knowledge and ingenuity could possibly achieve on such a question. Certainly nothing can be at first sight more entirely unplausible than his theory, and yet after beginning by thinking it impossible, one arrives at something like an actual belief in it, and one certainly does not relapse into complete disbelief.[35]

Mill also read Tyndall's *Lectures on Heat*: his own reflections on the subject are full of perplexity, but well illustrate that mental habit of 'never accepting half-solutions of difficulties as complete; never abandoning a puzzle, but again and again returning to it until it was cleared up.'[36]

35. *Letters*, I, p. 236.
36. *Autobiography*, p. 123.

Mill was led to a re-examination of socialism by speculating as to what the working men of the towns would do with the help of the vote and by the use of strikes. Like other classical economists, Mill had always believed that strikes for higher wages would in the long run reduce the volume of industry, by cutting into that minimum profit which alone incited the employer to remain in business. But W. T. Thornton had convinced Mill that this 'wage-fund theory' was a mare's nest: and Mill at once saw the importance of this demonstration. If strikes were an economic possibility they would most certainly be used. Armed with the vote and the strike-weapon, the workers might achieve a large share of political power in a much shorter time than had seemed possible. What could be done to educate their leaders to use this power wisely and moderately? Mill had no particle of sentimentalism in his view of the working-class or of any other class, and saw with great clearness the dangers which a too-rapid advance of their power might bring. It seemed possible that Britain would face a long and bitter class struggle. But at the time there was still the chance that the leaders of both sides might be shown the wisdom of certain compromises.

These questions were raised by Mill in an article in John Morley's *Fortnightly Review*. He later undertook a thorough examination of socialism in a work which occupied him during the last three years of his life. Four completed chapters were published in the *Fortnightly* in 1879, and constitute one of the foundations of Fabian Socialism. The system of private property and private enterprise should be purged of its abuses, and at the same time experiments should be carried out in all eligible forms of socialistic or communistic ownership or control. The great means of preparing the workers were education (paid for, but not provided, by the State) and co-operation in local and national government, and in public enterprises of an unofficial character.

During the same last years, Mill also wrote a long essay on Theism. This was published after his death, together with two other essays on religion which had been written during

the period of his marriage. In her preface Helen Taylor anticipated the charge that Mill had kept these papers back because
he wished to avoid whatever odium might result from a full
expression of his opinions on religion. In fact the statement of
his disbeliefs could hardly have surprised Mill's readers: the
surprise came for Mill's more intimate friends. For in the last
essay there is a tentative attempt to put forward grounds for
believing in an after-life and in the existence of a finite Deity.
Bain says that he never received any hint of this from Mill's
letters or conversation.

It is highly characteristic of Mill that he loved to find points
upon which he could agree with thinking men in all parties,
including those in the Church; and that he was eager to
acknowledge the honesty, self-sacrifice, and love of our fellow
creatures, which he found in genuinely religious people. But
this did not abate his life-long opposition to the teaching and
influence of the Church and his distaste for its worship. He
once recommended Herbert Spencer on the grounds that he
was 'as anti-clergymenish as possible': this phrase remained
true of Mill himself.

In June 1871, Mill's oldest friend, George Grote, died and
was buried in Westminster Abbey with full ecclesiastical
honours. Mill was prevailed upon to act as a pall bearer; he
agreed with great reluctance. As he left the Abbey he remarked
to Bain: 'In no very long time, I shall be laid in the ground
with a very different ceremonial from that.' His health was
now very poor.

In 1872, his friends Lord and Lady Amberley asked him
to be god-father to their second son. This he agreed to be in
a purely secular sense, and the child, for whom the names of
Galahad and Hildebrand had been suggested by kindly rela-
tives, was duly named Bertrand Arthur William, in the
presence of the Russell family.

In May 1873, Mill died at Avignon, the victim of a local
fever. Three days before his death he had taken one of those
extremely long and arduous country walks which – like his
father – he so much enjoyed.

Ethics

*

I. INTRODUCTION

AT the age of fifteen John Stuart Mill gave his enthusiastic adherence to the Benthamite system of morals. The greatest happiness principle burst upon him with all the force of a novelty; he felt that all previous moralists had been superseded, and that here indeed was the commencement of a new era in thought. And, in fact, to the end of his days he professed the fundamental logic and psychology of Utilitarianism. But at the same time his attitude towards their distinctive moral teaching changed very greatly indeed; and it is true to say of him that he was no mere psychologist and grammarian of morals. He had his insights, his own individual moral premises: and while some of these fitted well enough into the basic psychology and logic of Benthamism, others were more remote and intractable. In later years he was inclined to judge the rightness or wrongness of an action very largely by its probable effects upon the characters of the individuals immediately concerned. Mill was a Wordsworthian. Inner character (not adventitious pleasures and pains) is the real focus of the teaching of the *Essay on Liberty*, of his address to the students of St Andrews University, and of his letters. This leads him to place the greatest importance upon sentiments of justice, honesty, purity, for their own sakes: and it accords ill with a purely hedonistic calculation of consequences – very ill indeed with any notions of quantitative assessment. On the other hand, it conforms with a deterministic doctrine of human conduct: it is possible for us to build our characters after the pattern of an ideal, precisely because habits determine conduct

45

and desires can establish or modify habits. And so, in various ways, the original grammar and psychology fits, or does not fit, the later moral and ethical insights. The result is that Mill's ethical writings are marked by serious strains and inconsistencies. I shall first try to show where the main tension lies, and how it appears in the 'proofs' contained in his essays on *Utilitarianism*, which commit some of the most advertised blunders in moral philosophy. I shall then try to give an analysis and criticism of his system of ethics, as this can be gathered from all his writings.

2. THE DESIRABLE AND THE DESIRED

Mill's earlier writings on ethics belong to his own Age of Transition – the years during which his first acceptance of Benthamism had been greatly modified by his mental crisis of 1826, and by his acquaintance with Wordsworth, Coleridge, Comte, and Carlyle. In the 1830's Mill was fully convinced that he was living in an Age of Transition, in which all the older authorities had become misleading and dangerous, and a temporary appeal to private judgement was inevitable. His view of private judgement, however, was very much the same as Mr T. S. Eliot's view of the 'inner light': 'the most untrustworthy and deceitful guide that ever offered itself to wandering humanity.'[1]

Mill believed that an objective standard of right and wrong could be found in the methods of the experimental sciences. The question: 'What is our duty?' need not be decided by an appeal to outmoded traditions or to individual caprice: 'An appeal lies, as on all other subjects, from a received opinion, however generally entertained, to the decisions of cultivated reason.'[2] By 'cultivated reason' Mill meant scientific method.

Utilitarianism is the only *scientific* morality. Hume and other empiricists had shown that the ground of morality is to

1. *After Strange Gods*, p. 59.
2. 'On Professor Sedgwick's Discourse on the Students of the University of Cambridge' (1835), *Dissertations and Discussions*, 1859, I, p. 158.

be found in the nature of man himself – in his appetites, sentiments, habits. But while Hume had shown that we judge things to be good if they please us or seem likely to bring us future pleasure, he had left the judgements of right and wrong to a ' sentiment of humanity' which is as a general rule guided by considerations of utility. It was Bentham who had employed the pleasure-principle, not simply to *explain* our judgements of the good, but as an objective test of right and wrong. 'He introduced into morals and politics those habits of thought and modes of investigation which are essential to the idea of science.'[3] Rightness depends upon pleasure-consequences; we ought therefore to be able to estimate rightness by observation, measurement, and induction.

This procedure rests upon certain presuppositions :
  (1) That if an object gives a man pleasure, he will know it and show it.
  (2) That men are moved to do what they believe will bring them pleasure immediately or remotely.
  (3) That if a certain kind of object has been found to please a man, then, other things being equal, it will always please him.
  (4) That the consequences of a proposed action can be foretold on the basis of past experience and generalization.
  (5) That degrees or amounts of pleasure can be measured.

What, in effect, Bentham supposed was that we can apply the methods of observation, analysis, and induction to questions of the kind: 'Would A or would B be the right thing to do in these circumstances?' It was during the 1830's that Mill was debating with himself the great question of *inference*, of induction and deduction, and of what is and what is not a genuine method of adding to knowledge. His conclusion was that only by *induction* can new general propositions be established. If, therefore, there are to be any valid general propositions in ethics, these must be established by induction also.

3. 'Essay on Bentham', *Dissertations and Discussions*, I, p. 339.

It follows that psychology must be deterministic: for induction presupposes the uniformity of nature, and morality is to be regarded as *natural*. Ethics must become a part of an empirical, inductive, 'science of human nature'. For such a system, hedonistic utilitarianism seemed to provide the only possible basis.

This hedonism, however, has to be brought face to face with the question: 'Upon *whose* pleasure does the rightness or wrongness of an action depend?' If we take an ethical view, and say: 'On anybody's pleasure, or the greatest possible pleasure of the greatest possible number', then the system seems to lose its cogency. For (1) it is no longer obvious that the idea of bringing pleasure 'to anybody or everybody' provides a *necessary* motive for me to perform a given action. The connexion is by no means the same as that between what pleases me and what I desire to do. And (2) we have to recall that, in connecting the judgement 'This is good' with 'This gives me pleasure', Hume and Locke certainly had the pleasure of the agent himself in mind. These considerations seem to drive us to a purely psychological view:

'This is good' = 'I desire this' = 'This gives me pleasure.'

But how is this equation ever to give rise to any notion of right and wrong? All that one would expect to derive from it is the altogether different notion of 'right-for-me' and 'wrong-for-me', which would be concerned only with my long-term happiness, and not at all with the general happiness. In fact, sympathy and self-love together do not seem capable of ensuring conduct that will lead to the general happiness, except by the entirely artificial expedient of a pre-established harmony. Mill, of course, always supposed that it would give me pleasure to please others: 'The idea of the pleasure of another is naturally pleasurable.' But this does not necessarily mean merely that the idea of the general pleasure would have a stronger appeal than the idea of the maximum possible pleasure for me and my friends. A pre-established harmony (if there were any evidence for it) could of course secure a long-term identity between the two: but this is a metaphysical doctrine deriving from Natural Law and Providence: it could be regarded by Mill only as a piece of sociological guess-work.

The means by which Mill tried to extricate himself from these difficulties will be examined later; it is now sufficient to see how he got into them. He got into them by his determination to adopt a naturalistic account of morality: for only a naturalistic account would allow for what Mill regarded as scientific methods of proof. The naturalistic key is the supposed connexion between the good and the pleasant and the object of desire. Mill argues as if a man does desire, and can desire, nothing but his own pleasure, and calls that pleasure ' good'. But in fact, of course, Mill assumes that a man can and does desire the pleasure of other people. Is this, then, to desire one's own pleasure? No doubt, if I want the pleasure of another, it will please me to get what I want. But this is a conditional statement: the consequential pleasure for me is not what I aim at, and would not be there at all *unless* I had something else (viz. the pleasure of another) as my aim, my desire. But if it appears that I can, after all, desire something quite other than my own pleasure, may it not be the case that I can also desire things other than pleasure, whether my own or somebody else's? Can I not also desire to see justice done, knowledge achieved, honour preserved, dignity and independence maintained?

It is well known that Mill tried to accommodate these aims by recognizing them as desires for peculiar sorts of pleasure, and arguing that pleasures differ in quality as well as in quantity. Such differences in quality, he said, ought not to be ignored in estimating the rightness or wrongness of an action. Since, in fact, the different 'weight' of the different kinds of pleasure cannot be measured in any scale, the only thing we can do is to accept the verdict of those persons of wisdom and experience who have themselves enjoyed all the different kinds. Like Plato, he held that 'the verdict of the wise is to be preferred'. This leads us to adopt a new equation:

'The good' = 'What the wise men desire' = 'What pleases
the wise.'

Mill wavers between these two definitions in his essays on
Utilitarianism.

3. UTILITARIANISM, HOW PROVED

Mill demurs about giving a proof of Utilitarianism: in the
strict sense of the word, it has no proof. That is to say, it
cannot be derived by evident steps from some more ultimate
and certain principles. But nevertheless, 'Considerations may
be presented capable of determining the intellect either to give
or withhold its assent to the doctrine; and this is equivalent to
proof' in a larger meaning of the word.[4] These considerations
are offered to the thoughtful – and charitable – reader in the
fourth essay. There are two separate principles to be proved:
(1) That happiness alone is intrinsically good, all other things
being good only because they contain, or are a means towards,
happiness; (2) That an action is right if it makes for the happiness of everyone – for the greatest happiness of the greatest
possible number, each one counting for one, and nobody for
more than one.

(1) *'That happiness is desirable, and the only thing desirable, as an
end'*

The use of 'desirable as an end' for 'intrinsically good'
allows Mill to proceed to an empirical proof. People do
actually desire happiness; both in theory and in practice, they
acknowledge it as an end of conduct. Hence it must be
desirable.

It is not enough to see that Mill confuses 'can be desired'
with 'ought to be desired'. There is at least a hundred years
of history behind this blunder. Mill confused the two because
he had been brought up in a tradition which never was quite
willing to distinguish them. He is speaking for Bentham,

4. *Utilitarianism*, Everyman Edition, p. 4.

Hume, and Locke, in this argument: he is moved by the conviction that the good must arouse desire, and that the only absolutely authentic natural desires are the simple organic desires for pleasure or relief from pain.

Happiness, then, is desirable: is it the only thing desirable as an end? Mill offers a simple enough 'proof' – one already implicit in his connexion between 'desirable' and 'desired'. We can see that

desiring a thing and finding it pleasant, aversion to it and thinking of it as painful, are phenomena entirely inseparable, or rather two parts of the same phenomenon; in strictness of language, two different modes of naming the same psychological fact: that to think of an object as desirable (unless for the sake of its consequences), and to think of it as pleasant, are one and the same thing; and that to desire anything, except in proportion as the idea of it is pleasant, is a physical and metaphysical impossibility.[5]

In other words, while busily collecting evidence that all men desire what they think will be pleasant, we suddenly realize that 'to be (anticipated as) pleasant' and 'to be desired' are terms which have the same meaning. So that, not only is our generalization immediately convertible, but the connexion is seen not to be a psychological one at all: it is a purely verbal one. To desire and not to regard as pleasant is, indeed, not a physical but a metaphysical impossibility. And 'what is the principle of utility, if it be not that "happiness" and "desirable" are synonymous terms?'[6]

But a discussion of virtue has already opened the door to a modification of this equation. Some men desire virtue *because it has become a part of their happiness*. They have become so strongly addicted to virtue that they would feel frustrated and ashamed if they could not achieve it to a degree. These, we say, are 'men of character', and their inclination to virtue is regarded by Mill as a matter of habit: he offers the addiction to money for its own sake as an analogy. Misers also are 'men of character'. Are there not then as many different kinds of

5. *Utilitarianism*, p. 36.
6. *Op. cit.*, p. 58, note. But for a defence of Mill see J. T. Wisdom, *Philosophy and Psycho-analyses* (1953), p. 107.

pleasure as there are different kinds of character? How are these different kinds of pleasure to be weighed in judging the probable consequences of an action?

In the second essay on *Utilitarianism*, Mill faces this problem:

It would be absurd that while, in estimating all other things, quality is considered as well as quantity, the estimation of pleasures should be supposed to depend on quantity alone.[7]

And on the *value* of the different kinds of pleasure (for that is the real question at issue) the *opinion of the wise* is to be preferred. The wise prefer those pleasures which are consonant with human dignity, pride, love of liberty, personal independence. The wise will not exchange such pleasures for *any* quantity of the fool's pleasures or the beast's.

And if the fool, or the pig, are of a different opinion, it is because they only know their own side of the question. The other party to the comparison knows both sides.[8]

Here again Mill makes a show of applying observational methods. We have already surveyed mankind to make sure that they all desire happiness: we are now to consult a special sub-group of mankind, 'those who are equally acquainted with, and equally capable of appreciating and enjoying, both', i.e., the higher and the lower pleasures. Mill has to admit that even those in whom the sense of human dignity is strong may make lower pleasures the object of a momentary desire; but not of a calm and informed choice. With such welcome unanimity we are able to proceed to an inductive inference. All (or almost all) of those who are competently acquainted with the different kinds of pleasures, agree in arranging them in a scale of value. And since measurement is impossible, the moralist is obliged to accept the results of this enquiry.

But in fact those who fundamentally disagree with this judgement will be said not to be competently acquainted with

7. *Utilitarianism*, p. 7.
8. *Op. cit.*, p. 9.

the different kinds of pleasures. The verdict of the wise is not found by scientific methods. There are many who agree on a scale: we agree with them and call them 'wise'. 'The good' is what a man will desire *if he is wise.*

(2) *'The happiness which forms the utilitarian standard of what is right in conduct, is not the agent's own happiness, but that of all concerned.'*

In his celebrated 'proof' of universalism, Mill argues:

(1) That the general happiness is desirable *because* each person desires his own happiness. And this might be a very sensible reason to advance, provided we can supply ourselves with some genuinely moral premise, such as that it is a good thing to give people what they want. But Mill wishes to avoid any such ethical premise. He proceeds:

(2) That the general happiness is in fact desired by the aggregate of all persons *since* each person desires his own happiness. And of course what is desired is also desirable. Unfortunately this is a fallacy of composition, and we have yet to discover whether anybody at all desires the happiness of everybody. It is at this point that we should consult the wise. They do indeed desire the general happiness for its own sake; for them, 'equal amounts of happiness are equally desirable, whether felt by the same or by different persons'. It is true of the wise that the desire for harmony with their fellow-creatures 'possesses all the character of a natural feeling'; and the only kind of society which they can tolerate is one in which 'the interests of all are to be regarded equally' – 'equally', as the wise estimate equality.[9]

The intricate convolutions of the argument may conceal from the writer the fact that a moral decision has to be made here. It is *possible* to make the general happiness an aim, or the supreme aim; it is possible not to do so. It is possible to regard it as the greatest of all good things, or even as the only thing intrinsically good. It is also possible to place other

9. Mill was challenged on the fallacy of this paragraph and made a most unsatisfactory reply: *Letters*, II, p. 116.

things alongside it and hence (sometimes) in competition with it. It seems to me quite clear that the choices here presented cannot be decided upon empirical evidence: certainly no considerations of what men in fact like or dislike can be decisive. Such considerations may indeed incline us to a decision: but they do not enable us to *infer* what the 'correct' decision is.

In my opinion, Mill's appeal to the wise is an expression of his own decision: for the wise are simply those he agrees with.

But to speak of a personal decision perhaps makes the matter seem too deliberate. For most of us there seems to be little freedom of choice in these matters. We have been brought up in a family and in a tradition which has trained us to regard the good of all as (at all events) one among the good things at which we ought to aim. To prefer our own good, then, is to fall below the standard which we have been led to acknowledge. We all sometimes do this. To proclaim defiance of this standard is to be known as a scamp. Indeed, so thoroughly have certain very general moral principles been incorporated into our ways of speech, that one might say: To ignore the happiness of mankind in general is *by definition* to be immoral. But these very important considerations only mean that the great moral decisions are usually taken by individuals under the guidance of societies and institutions.

It will be best to recognize this element of pure choice in Mill's ethical writings, and to discard altogether the view that he has offered us a proof of the pleasure principle, whether in its egotistical or its universalistic form. We should, rather, understand that in this essay Mill has expressed his adherence to the most general principles of Christian morality, with modifications deriving in part from Benthamism and in part from his own moral insight.

Utilitarianism – How proved? The answer to this question is that Utilitarianism cannot be proved. There is, however, a most important comment to be made about the sense in which Bentham and Mill understood the pleasure principle. 'The greatest happiness of the greatest possible number' introduces a distributive principle: each person is to count for one, and nobody for more than one. And questions of right and wrong turn upon the distribution, as well as on the amount, of the pleasure to be produced. A less amount for others might be preferable to a greater amount for me. A less amount, equally distributed, might be preferable to a greater amount unequally distributed. 'Equally' cannot possibly be taken to mean 'in equal measured amounts to each person'; it must obviously be related to the needs, desires, and opportunities, of the persons concerned. This principle of equality is not in any way based upon 'maximizing pleasure' or 'minimizing pain': it rests on precisely what we call 'a sense of justice'.

This, in practice, Mill understood: and he made a valiant attempt to formulate a doctrine of justice in purely utilitarian terms.[10] The argument is presumably based upon Hume's *Enquiry*. Justice is regarded by Hume as an artificial virtue which comes into existence as a consequence of certain social and political institutions whose *utility* depends upon a rigid uniformity of human conduct. Property, for example, which is necessary for the restraint of human greed, cannot survive as an institution unless it is almost always respected. If I give to a needy man what is not my property, I may, for the moment, increase the sum of human happiness: but in the long run this kind of action will undermine the laws by which property is defined, and so defeat its own intentions. For the needy would, in that event, have no title to what I gave them or to what they themselves have earned. Hume therefore argues that rules of justice are to be observed because they serve the good of mankind in the long run. Justice is thus shown as one of the greatest of all *utilities*.

Mill's chapter follows the same lines. The arguments against him have been put a very great many times and in a very great many ways. The following may serve as an illustration:

Surely I ought to repay a debt whether my not doing so would weaken the social structure *or not*. Moral philosophers have expended their ingenuity in constructing imaginary cases

10. *Utilitarianism*, ch. v.

where none of the further evil consequences to society could possibly occur. Should we, in such cases, feel free to violate rules of justice? I suppose that some might feel free, and if they did, I know of no argument that could demonstrate that they were mistaken. I should agree with Hume and Mill that many (at all events) of the situations in which I think it right to do an action that does not seem to conform to the maxim of general benevolence, arise out of the existence of institutions that, *as a general rule*, serve human happiness. Yet I still feel that my loyalty to such institutions does not rest *only* on considerations of their utility. And Mill's arguments are not, I think, very impressive if we remember how large an element of intuitive justice enters into his notion of the working of the happiness principle. Neither Bentham nor Mill ever attempts to show that rightness is to be determined simply by the *amount* of happiness produced. Since a tacit recognition of justice as an independent principle cannot be avoided by the Utilitarian, it seems idle to attempt to explain away those cases in which there appears to be a clash between the two principles. Justice is restrictive; benevolence expansive. The morality that Mill really adopted combined both elements.

4. THE GUESS-WORK OF CONSEQUENCES

In his *Essay on Bentham*, Mill says that rational persons of all schools hold the doctrine that the morality of actions depends upon their consequences; that the idea of an aim (whether human happiness or some other) is essential to 'moral philosophy; is, in fact, what renders argument or discussion on moral questions possible'.[11] It is notorious that Kant and other highly rational minds have argued that rightness and wrongness depend upon the motive of an action, and not at all upon its consequences. To this Mill replies that the nature of the motive has to do with the 'worth of the agent', not with the morality of the action.[12] The Benthamites had taken

11. *Dissertations and Discussions*, I, p. 385.
12. *Utilitarianism*, ch. ii.

this view from a wish to discourage a morality of mere good intentions and pure motives. They wished the word 'right' (with the imperative of duty attached to it) to be applied to conduct that would do *good in the world*, rather than to conduct which leaves the agent blameless. To Mill there seemed to be a most important moral judgement to be passed upon motives: but this judgement was separable and distinct from a judgement on the rightness or wrongness of particular actions.

This distinction is now widely adopted by moral philosophers. Approval of an action is not only retrospective, but prospective. To approve an action as right in certain circumstances, is to provide a rule or precedent for the future. Here is something which (if the relevant circumstances ever recur) must be done again. And such an imperative can hardly apply to the motives of an action, since it is not within the agent's power to act from a given motive when the occasion arises. The most that he can do is to carry out the action from whatever motive he may have.

This discussion suggests a further question of the grammar of ethics. A right action is one which I ought to do; and I can hardly be said to have an obligation to do it unless I can do it if I so decide. Can I do the *right* thing if I so decide? Only, it would seem, if I can *identify it as right*. How do I judge that an action is right? Mill's answer is that I must judge by a consideration of the consequences of the action, and since I am to judge before I act, this must mean that I am to weigh up the *probable* consequences of the various alternative possible actions which the situation allows. It is a familiar objection that I cannot in fact foresee the consequences of possible actions; that

man has not foreknowledge to trace the consequences of a single action of his own; and hence that utility (in the highest sense of which the word is capable) is, as a test of right and wrong, unfitted to his understanding, and therefore worthless in its application.[13]

13. Sedgwick's *Discourse*, quoted by Mill, *Dissertations and Discussions*, I, p. 142.

To this, Mill replies that the whole course of human life is founded upon the fact that (even outside the scope of scientific investigations) we can roughly predict the consequences of actions in familiar circumstances. As we eat and drink, buy and sell, think and speak, we employ our foresight, our knowledge or our habits, acquired by experience. In all these contexts the principle of judging consequences is well enough fitted to man's capacity. 'Our foresight of consequences is not perfect. Is anything else in our constitution perfect?'

But even this view depends upon limiting our considerations in some way. For it seems highly unplausible to say that I can form even a reasonable opinion about the more remote consequences of my actions. The hedonistic principle itself introduces a most important limitation: the only consequences to be considered are the pleasures and pains of individuals. If any deed of mine were to start a chain of physical action which resulted in the destruction of an unobservable and uninhabitable planet, this would be without any moral significance. Nevertheless, the world of individuals is a very large one: am I to consider the welfare of everybody before I make up my mind how to act?

To this, very sensibly, Mill replies that 'the welfare of the persons concerned', in most actions of ordinary people, means simply the welfare of the few members of their acquaintance who enter into the original intention of the act, or are immediately affected by it.[14] Ordinary people seldom have to consider the affairs of whole societies or nations, except in ways for which there are already well-established traditional rules.

What is the value of all these limitations and reassurances? A man's choice may be as rational as it is well-intentioned, and yet it may be disastrous to himself, or to his acquaintances, or to mankind. And Mill sees that there is no escape from this conclusion. It would seem, then, that the only imperative that we can reasonably wish our approval to convey is that a man should choose the action which will *probably* produce the greatest amount of good. To seek to give the imperative:

14. *Utilitarianism*, ch. ii.

'Choose the action which *will in fact* produce the greatest possible amount of good' is indeed 'not suited to man's capacity'.

This modification of Utilitarianism makes a distinction, then, between the *right act* (assessed by rational probability) and the *most fortunate act*, a final verdict upon which can never in fact be given. Mill often writes as if he had this distinction in mind: a man must judge as well as he can – the merely accidental is not his responsibility. It is, no doubt, the more *inward* view, since it considers the dilemma of the agent as well as the cash-value of his external action. But Mill sometimes seems to take the other view: the imperative to give is, 'Do the best, somehow, anyhow!' Here the achievement, rather than the inner principle, is regarded as the example or precedent to be followed. But if we ask how the achievement is to be achieved we are at once thrown back upon the inner principle.

5. MORAL RULES AND THE MORAL TRADITION

Utilitarians profess to hold that there is one and only one basic *moral law:* that it is right to promote human happiness. They are bound to question the use of subordinate or derivative maxims or rules of morality. For to discover the right action a fresh calculation of consequences would seem to be necessary on each occasion.

I think this conflicts with common sense views of morals. For it is commonly held that we can decide what is right in a given situation by applying a general rule of a comparatively simple kind. 'Lying is wrong'; if, then, we can identify an action as having one very simple property (it is a deliberate untruth calculated to deceive), we know at once that it is wrong. To begin to calculate would perhaps be taken as a sign of moral weakness: as Professor Sedgwick said, 'To hesitate is to rebel.'

Bentham is untiring and unsparing in his denunciation of all codes or rules of morality. Their chief use, he held, was to bind men in obedience to their masters, whether lay or clerical;

some rules could perhaps be interpreted as extremely vague and confused expressions of the principle of utility; more often they expressed nothing more than the sentiments, super-stitions, and interests of different groups. As moral principles they were useless and inapplicable.

In regard to this question, Mill compromises in a typical fashion. On the one hand, he insists that practical maxims and rules of conduct cannot be applied to actual situations without new observation and reflection.

No one needs flatter himself that he can lay down propositions sufficiently specific to be available for practice, which he may after-wards apply mechanically without any exercise of thought. ... Let us envelope our proposition with what exceptions and qualifica-tions we may, fresh exceptions will turn up, and fresh qualifications be found necessary, the moment any one attempts to act upon it.[15]

We are to reflect whether we are prepared to accept any maxim as valid without exception, in all circumstances. Are we never justified in lying or stealing? If we are inclined to accept a maxim in this unconditional sense, then it seems to me that we shall be obliged to hesitate and to cavil as to *whether this be lying or no*. And even if we admit some such maxims, shall we not find that their application is limited to the less important problems of morality? Such maxims deal with my relations with anybody-in-general, but cannot begin to determine what my relationships ought to be towards those bound to me by ties of acquaintance, family, and private obligation.

On the other hand, Mill recognized that there is guidance to be found in a tradition. He is prepared to defend even the vague generalities which Bentham had dismissed:

He (Bentham) did not heed, or rather the nature of his mind pre-vented it from occurring to him, that these generalities contained the whole unanalysed experience of the human race.[16]

15. 'Aphorisms' (1837), in *Dissertations and Discussions*, I.
16. 'Essay on Bentham', *Dissertations and Discussions*, p. 351.

Mill inclined rather to Coleridge's view:

> The long duration of a belief ... is at least proof of an adaptation in it to some portion or other of the human mind.[17]

Now this recognition that the experience of the past can provide us with guidance for the present has significance on different levels. There is first the obvious point that our circumstances are near enough to those of our ancestors to enable us to apply their general conclusions with profit, provided we do so with a full awareness that there may be novel features in the situation. Mill calls these rules 'secondary principles', and remarks that moralists whose first principles are altogether at variance, may yet agree to a considerable extent in incorporating the same secondary principles into their systems. But this is not all that Mill intended in his defence of traditional moral wisdom.

It sometimes happens that, in a moment of moral perplexity, I appeal to a precedent – to a previous decision of someone I know well, or to a course of action adopted by a character in a novel. I regard this as a precedent because my situation seems to be nearly the same as that of the previous agent in all relevant respects, or to differ from it in relevant respects which I feel I know how to 'allow for' in my application. But what respects are relevant? The pleasures and pains of the persons concerned, and (beyond them) of mankind in general. But obviously these must be placed in an order of importance; and in fact, in trying to decide upon what I ought to do, I am trying to place them in an order of importance. I feel, then, that the precedent is a guide, because there is a parallel between the various interests and claims that I have to consider, and those which faced the previous agent, close enough to permit me to take his decision as appropriate to my problem. His decision is an evaluation of the different interests and claims that confronted him, and if I adopt it, is likewise an evaluation of the elements in my own situation. This act of

17. 'Essay on Coleridge', *op. cit.*, p. 395.

evaluation itself determines what is relevant and what is not, and the order of importance in what is relevant.[18]

Now the earlier Utilitarians tried to decide this order of importance by reference only to the general happiness principle, and to the facts of social life. A friend must receive more consideration than a stranger simply because my opportunities of benefiting a friend, and being benefited by him, are more extensive and intensive than my opportunities with a stranger. To this was added a doctrine of the utility of contracts and general rules of behaviour – the Utilitarian doctrine of justice which derives from Hume.

Mill introduces – or rather re-introduces – an altogether different principle for determining what is relevant and what is important in deciding these questions. He affirms that the most important of all the possible consequences of an action are those which affect the inner life of the agent and of the other persons concerned. And he is not thinking so much of the feelings which the action will arouse at the time, but of the long-term effects upon habits of feeling, that is to say, upon character.

It often happens that an essential part of the morality or immorality of an action or a rule of action, consists in its influence upon the agent's own mind: upon his susceptibilities of pleasure or pain, upon the general direction of his thoughts, feelings, and imagination, or upon some particular association. Many actions, moreover, produce effects upon the character of other persons besides the agent.[19]

The effect of an action upon a person's character cannot be predicted without a deep understanding of the person concerned: it may, indeed, depend upon 'some particular association'. And the only valuable guidance here will have to come from those who have what we call 'a wide experience of life'; who have mingled much in the world and have made a good

18. Compare the parallel problem of determining what is relevant and what is important in an inductive inquiry (ch. v (3)).

19. 'On Professor Sedgwick's Discourse', *op. cit.*, p. 131.

use of their opportunities, or who have 'a large share of human nature in their own breasts'.[20] It was on account of his reverence for human character and for fallible human wisdom, that Mill so highly esteemed Coleridge; and in another essay he says that the most valuable guidance in dealing with our fellows is to be found, not in the writings of the moral philosophers, but in 'those poets and novelists, who have spoken out unreservedly any true human feeling'. This view of the poet's task is, of course, pure Wordsworth. It is to our experience of 'real life', rather than to scientific experiment, that Mill is obliged to turn for guidance upon the most difficult and searching moral questions.[21]

6. THE SPRINGS OF MORAL ACTION

The last two sections of this chapter have been occupied with the question: How do we know what is right? This is the principal question of the logic of morals. We have now to consider a fundamental question of the psychology of morals: How are we able to do what is right? What inner impulses lead to right conduct?

Mill's answer to this question is derived very largely from his study of Hartley and of Bentham and rests upon his acceptance of the doctrine of Associationism. Hartley's exposition is an attempt to refine upon Hume's, and to give it a frankly physical basis which Hume's sceptical account of mind and body had avoided. At the time of writing his *Treatise*, Hume regarded the association of ideas as a primitive force not altogether unlike gravitation:

a kind of *attraction*, which in the mental world will be found to have as extraordinary results as in the natural, and to show itself in as many and as various forms.[22]

20. 'On Aphorisms', *op. cit.*, p. 206.
21. Wordsworth's doctrine is found in the Preface to the *Lyrical Ballads* and in his letter of June 1802 to John Wilson: *Letters* (ed. De Selincourt), I, No. 130.
22. *Treatise*, Everyman Edition, I, pp. 19–21.

But Hume's enthusiasm for this mode of explanation waned before he came to write his *Enquiries;* and his disappointment seems, on the whole, to have been justified by the later attempts to apply it. In the writings of Mill it appears very much as an *a priori* principle without detailed evidence in its support. He makes no attempt to defend the principle against the destructive criticisms of Coleridge.[23] James Mill is master here.

How do we do what is right? The Utilitarian answer is that we may do what is right from any motive, good or bad. Man is born with various desires and he acquires others by education. Infants desire food: children refuse food and desire sweets and stories: grown men refuse sweets and stories in favour of tobacco and philosophy. But whatever may be the external 'lure', or object of desire, we are always moved towards pleasure or the prospect of pleasure, and away from pain or the prospect of pain. Bentham's *Table of the Springs of Action* shows a great variety of desires, some self-regarding, others for the welfare of other people. Of the altruistic desires, it is important to distinguish sympathy from general benevolence. Sympathy is directed towards the happiness of particular persons – whose pleasure will normally be shown to the agent and be itself a pleasure to him. General benevolence is the desire to do good to anybody and everybody. Both these may well give rise to right conduct. But since neither of them desires the right as such (but only contingently), they are likely to be capricious, partial, and unjust in their operation. It was for this reason that Bentham always recognized the necessity of external sanctions: the law and public opinion, the educator and the patron. For these provide artificial rewards for right conduct and artificial penalties for wrong conduct. In other words, they supplement the other-regarding desires of men, by appeal to their desire for rewards, for peace and security, and for reputation.

It would no doubt be hypocritical to overlook the importance of these external sanctions. But clearly their sphere of influence is limited. Their existence cannot explain how a man

23. *Biographia Literaria* (1817), chs. vi and vii.

sets himself to do the right thing by his wife and children in the privacy of his own home; nor how he tries to do justice to the claims of his friends in matters towards which both the law and public opinion are indifferent. What Bentham lacked (or, rather, what his theory lacked) is a conscience, or a free and rational will which can make its own choices *sub specie boni* and without regard for private interest.

The freedom of the will, in the sense of the independence of the will from outside influences, is a doctrine which Mill never seems to have considered seriously; although there were times in his early life when the doctrine of necessity oppressed him. He held firmly to the conviction that the predictability of human conduct is an essential postulate of the science of human nature. And he came to see that an important distinction must be made between freedom of conduct and freedom of desires. 'The will' is not simply a name for the desire from which a man acts: for we often say that a man has been moved by desire to act against his will. Nor, on the other hand, is 'the will' a name for a single faculty of the soul. Mill follows Locke in regarding the will as a power or causal disposition of the self; but he recognizes that the same man may have a number of different 'wills', or inclinations more or less permanent, towards different aims or objects. Thus a man may have a will to achieve power over others, a will to remain respectable and sober, a will to knowledge or to reputation. Such a will is shown in the regularity with which he chooses what seems to him likely to bring about one or other of these aims, and in the hesitation and distress which he shows whenever he is 'led away by desire' to act in a way likely to defeat one of his aims. If, then, we use the term 'will' in the singular, we must mean by it the permanent character of a man in so far as this is revealed in his deliberate conduct; it is, Mill says, character as an 'active phenomenon'.

In its earliest phase, a will is *a habit of desire*. But Mill remarks that a man of firm purpose will continue to pursue his object, even at times when he desires other things, apparently more strongly; even at times when he has altogether ceased to find any considerable pleasure in contemplating his object. Will now appears as *a habit of action*. Does this action not now result from any desire at all? Mill considers that it might be the case that the man is now acting from blind habit – that is to say, in a way as obviously mechanical as the way in which he puts his clothes on in the morning. But are we to accept this as an account of the way in which a virtuous man acts, when he chooses pain and disgrace rather than abandon his principles? Mill tried to amplify his explanation by adding that a habit of action itself generates a secondary desire – the desire to do what we have always found pleasure in.

A man of firm purposes finds his chief pleasure in being firm to his purpose. His reward, in short, is the pleasure of being consistent.[24]

If this is the way in which the will is formed, we have to ask: What sort of objects can become the aim of a habit of action? The answer to this question depends upon what sort of objects can be found pleasant or can be presented in a pleasurable light, whether directly or indirectly. As we have already seen in Chapter One, the theory fully explains how an educator can encourage habits of desire for one's own good, and for the good of one's friends, and even for the good of mankind in general. What the theory has now to show is how the will to virtue *as such* can arise in men. Can justice, honesty, personal independence, and dignity be represented in a pleasurable light? Mill always regards our inclination to virtue for its own sake as less 'natural' than our inclinations towards prudence, sympathy, or benevolence. The inclination to virtue, for instance, is not found in very young children:

> Young children have affections, but not moral feelings; and children whose will is never resisted, never acquire them.[25]

Mill's view is that we have no native desire to virtue as such. Like speaking, reasoning, living in cities, and cultivating the

24. See *Utilitarianism*, ch. iv, and *Logic*, VI, iv.
25. 'On Professor Sedgwick's Discourse', *Dissertations and Discussions*, I, p. 138.

soil, the moral faculty is not a part of our nature, but it is a natural outgrowth from it. The principle which subordinates our natural inclinations to care for ourselves and our friends, and to give pleasure to others; which subordinates these to the principle of the greatest happiness of the greatest possible number (each counting as one and none for more than one) can only be the result of education.

This will to virtue (which now appears as very nearly the same thing as a will to justice) is presented to us in a pleasurable light, indirectly, by attaching artificial rewards to its exercise. The will to do what is right because it is right, must therefore be either a habit of desiring artificial rewards which cannot otherwise be obtained, or it must be a desire to continue acting consistently in accordance with a habit engendered in this way.

Mill is able to add, however, that this is to take too abstract a view of virtuous action. For, on any given occasion, the will to do what is right because it is right may be reinforced by other habits of desire – by benevolence, for example, or by personal sympathy. It is because a good character includes other wills besides the will to virtue as such that good men commonly find lively pleasure in right conduct. Conflicts may, of course, sometimes arise between a will to do one's duty and a will to please others: but if a man is benevolent and sympathetic, as well as of a strong sense of duty, he will commonly find that his righteous intention is supported by his other impulses:

> So feeling comes in aid
> Of feeling, and diversity of strength
> Attends us, if but once we have been strong.[26]

Mill thus attempts to mitigate the arbitrary character, or artificiality, of the will to virtue by associating it with the wholly natural impulse to benefit others. There are, he admits, certain moral associations which are *wholly* artificial and which

26. Wordsworth, *Prelude*, Book xii. For Mill's discussion of the peculiar nature of our inclination to the right as such, see *Utilitarianism*, ch. iii.

can be dissolved by reflective analysis; and the utilitarian notion of duty would appear equally arbitrary, and be as likely to be 'analysed away', did it not so completely harmonize with sympathy and benevolence. This connexion with sympathy and benevolence renders virtue at least more stable if not more 'natural' than the will to power or to gain.

This argument does not seem consistent with what is said in the *Autobiography* of Mill's own experience. He there describes a time in his life at which 'analytic habits' served to dissolve his own inclination towards the greatest good of the greatest possible number: and more than this, he found those habits capable of undermining 'all desires and all pleasures which are the effects of association, that is ... all except the purely physical and organic'.[27] And surely this is what one would expect. Mill's pleasure in what he conceived to be his supreme duty in life was undermined when he thought he could see the various stages by which external influences had built up this sentiment in him. It was finding an *explanation* which derived the habit of pleasure from circumstances outside himself that made him feel that the pleasure was 'artificial' and 'unreal'. In Mill's particular case, the explanation seemed to show him as the mere creature of another mind: and this made the discovery all the more dramatic and unwelcome. But the same associationist psychology provided explanations of a parallel kind for *all* habits of feeling except the purely physical and organic. And Mill clearly says that he became for a time insensible to all these pleasures, or at best, sensible to them in a less degree. If explanation is to bring *disillusionment*, then certainly the discerning psychologist is going to be a man of very few pleasures.

In his own experience, Mill found that this disillusionment was only temporary. He learned to accept himself as a being with a certain character, the result of his experiences and education, just as throughout his disillusion he had accepted himself as a being with certain inherited, organic sensibilities. He learned to be grateful for all his pleasures, including even

27. *Autobiography*, p. 138.

the pleasure he had learned to take in what he conceived to be his duty. But in this process of confirmation subtle changes took place. He saw that the sentiment of duty is not the only sentiment of value in itself; it has a place in a character which includes benevolence, sympathy, intellectual pursuits, and the love of natural beauty. And this character is to be judged as a whole. And in these reflections Mill was, in effect, confirming by his own free judgement and with his own original modifications, the notion of duty which he had, up till that time, professed only out of a desire to win his father's approval.

This personal confirmation seems to indicate an important difference between a sense of duty and other sentiments. The sentiments of sympathy and benevolence seem to be common to all men: but different notions of duty are proper to the different traditions of the human race. How the notion of duty begins we do not in fact know, but that only means that we are free to speculate. It is at least clear that particular notions of duty are transmitted through the family and the society in which the family is placed. Notions of duty are transmitted as imperatives: they are *to be done* because the doing of them wins artificial rewards, and the neglect or violation of them, artificial punishments. But surely there comes a stage in a man's life when he is able to resist them or accept them by his own judgement. (This may be only when he has to teach them in turn to his own children.) And to accept them (whether modified or not) is to have an inclination to perform them for their own sakes. Mill's account of the formation of habits of duty omits this crucial stage, and misrepresents this positive inclination as a mere desire to persist in a habit – an empty desire for inertia. Mill recognizes that there is a stage of education at which a child becomes able to correct and modify received opinions upon matters of fact: and he is right in saying that this is done by means of analysis and observation. To correct received opinions upon morals, something more than 'analytic habits' is necessary: another kind of reflection is required, not purely intellectual.

7. FREEDOM AND NECESSITY

It is possible to judge freely what is right and what is wrong. But it does not necessarily follow that a man will act in accordance with such judgements. Deliberate actions arise from habits; and a man may act from any habit comprised in his character. Is it possible for a man to change his habits, to alter his character, in such a way as to strengthen his inclination to act rightly, and weaken his tendencies to act wrongly? This can, of course, be done by increasing a man's knowledge of his situation, and of the connexions of causes and effects. Can it also be done by strengthening the will to do what is right for its own sake, or the will to please others?

In the *Autobiography*, Mill describes a time in his life at which he believed that determinism was incompatible with any notion of a man's freedom to alter his character. He is referring to the period after his illness or mental crisis of 1826:

... during the later returns of my dejection, the doctrine of what is called Philosophical Necessity weighed on my existence like an incubus. I felt as if I was scientifically proved to be the helpless slave of antecedent circumstances; as if my character and that of all others had been formed for us by agencies beyond our control, and was wholly out of our own power.[28]

It seemed to him that he found a way out of this debilitating belief by his doctrine that 'will is the child of desire':

I saw that though our character is formed by circumstances, our own desires can do much to shape those circumstances; and that what is really inspiriting and ennobling in the doctrine of free will, is the conviction that we have real power over the formation of our own character; that our will, by influencing some of our circumstances can modify our future habits or capabilities of willing. All this was entirely consistent with the doctrine of circumstances, or rather, was that doctrine itself, properly understood.

Does this doctrine really contain *all* that is ennobling and inspiriting in the doctrine of freedom? If we try to state Mill's

28. *Autobiography*, p. 168.

view as a doctrine of freedom, it is, of course, a doctrine of conditional freedom. I am free (within limits) to be virtuous, if I desire to be virtuous with a strong enough desire. But am I free to desire virtue, or to desire virtue more strongly? There is here, also, a conditional freedom: I am free to strengthen my desire for virtue, my permanent inclination to virtue, if I desire to do so strongly enough. Mill makes no attempt to go behind this conditional freedom: his doctrine is that (within certain very important limits) I can become what I *in fact* desire to become: I am not always obliged to let myself become the kind of person I do not desire to be.

The key to Mill's doctrine is his concern for individual character. A doctrine of the efficacy of desires for *objects* would leave man the creature of external lures. Mill is asserting the efficacy of a desire to be a certain kind of person. If I desire money, then of course I really do desire it, and this desire may serve to make me richer. But a man may desire money, and yet at the same time *wish* that he did not desire it so strongly. And Mill's doctrine is that *this* desire also may be effective: it is a desire for a certain state of character and it may serve to bring that state of character into being. The practical question of money-getting begins with a man who in fact has this desire: and the practical question of becoming more virtuous begins with a man who has this desire. In both cases, the *origin* of the desire is irrelevant to the practical question. If I do indeed desire money, what does it matter how that state of mind came about? If I do indeed desire virtue, what does it matter if some psychologist has a theory as to why I desire it? This is not to deny, however, that the question how I came to be so very fond of money might be relevant to the question (which the man with a desire for greater virtue might put to himself) of how I should seek to correct and modify the desire for money. And, of course, if any one felt that he wished to cure himself of virtue, he might reasonably ask how he came to suffer from this habit. 'How did I come to desire virtue?' might also be a relevant question for a man who wished to strengthen that desire: but it would be relevant only to the choice of ways and means of carrying out this desire: it would in no way alter *the fact* from which his questions of ways and means arise – the fact, namely, that he does desire virtue.

Mill insists, then, that if I desire anything whatever, the practical question is '*How to get it?*', and 'How did I come to desire it?' is always irrelevant. In judging that I desire it, I must not be supposed to be making any judgement whatsoever on the question of how or why I came to desire it. This doctrine seems to me to be sound: it is only highly necessary to add to it a corresponding account of the irrelevancy of psychological analysis to judgements that something is right or wrong, good or bad, beautiful or ugly, and to judgements upon matters of fact, or analysis. 'This is what I want', 'This is right', 'This is in fact the case', 'This follows logically from that', are all 'autonomous' in the sense that they are unaffected in their validity by any theory of the mechanisms by which such judgements are formed by the mind.

8. THE UNITY OF CHARACTER

In connecting duty with benevolence and sympathy, Mill was insisting upon the unity of the individual. The will is the character in action, but the character is something more than its manifestation in action; it includes dispositions of thought and feeling in the most delicate state of equilibrium. 'The maintenance of a due balance among the faculties now seemed to me of primary importance,' he wrote of the period after 1826; and since his own life had been unbalanced towards speculation and moral action, he from this time on made the cultivation of the feelings, the passive susceptibilities, a cardinal point in his ethical and philosophical creed.[29] And it was from Wordsworth that Mill derived his notion of the cultivation of the feelings: Moral life can be affected by our enjoyment of nature.

29. *Autobiography*, p. 143.

> ... feelings too
> Of unremembered pleasure: such, perhaps,
> As have no slight or trivial influence
> On that best portion of a good man's life,
> His little, nameless, unremembered, acts
> Of kindness and of love.

And, conversely, the moral experience affects our attitude to nature:

> For I have learned
> To look on nature, not as in the hour
> Of thoughtless youth; but hearing oftentimes
> The still, sad music of humanity.

Nothing more clearly marks the advance of John Stuart Mill upon the moral philosophy of James Mill and Bentham than this turning away from the purely intellectual disciplines to 'the internal culture of the individual' as understood by Wordsworth. It was not, in Mill himself, anti-intellectual. He found nothing to *abandon* in the science of psychology: he continued to believe in its relevance for morals, for he believed that upon it might be based a 'science of human character' which should enable men to understand more clearly what would be the most important consequences of their actions, i.e., the effects produced upon the inner life of themselves and others. What Mill enables us to see is not the irrelevance of analytical psychology, but its inadequacy. Even if pleasures could be weighed or counted, psychology could not tell us what consequences would be good, and hence what actions right; and even if we could learn from psychology what actions are right, this would not enable us to carry them out.

In considering the 'inner consequences' of actions, both upon oneself and upon others, it is of the utmost importance, Mill held, to remember that what is good for one may not be good for others. For 'there is no reason that all human existence should be constructed on some one or some small number of patterns'.[30] Different kinds of excellence of character

30. *On Liberty*, p. 125.

are possible, and they are also desirable, both because this permits an experimental way of living, and because variety is itself a thing to be enjoyed. Mill's ethical teaching here leads on into his politics. And in his ethical and his economic teaching the value of the individual character is his first consideration:

Among the works of man, which human life is rightly employed in perfecting and beautifying, the first in importance surely is man himself.

The Utilitarian morality of doing has given way to an inward morality of being. This morality is based upon a direct study of the inner moral life, by reflection, and by experience of human society at large, and by the interpretation of imaginative literature. Mill's method turns out to be very much the same as that which Coleridge had applied to history; a personal, intuitive, morally discriminating method, a method of direct observation, but not the method of the experimental sciences.

9. NATURALISM IN ETHICAL THEORY

We have now to ask what is of permanent value in Mill's conception of ethics. We may take it that his first aim was to give an account of right and wrong, good and bad, duty and obligation, in *naturalistic* terms; that is, to explain how we come to understand and to apply these predicates without referring to a divine order, or to innate ideas, or to any faculty of *a priori* intuition; to show that we derive them from ordinary human experience under the discipline of ordinary logic. Secondly, Mill wished to show that ethics is a part of an observational science, the 'science of human nature'; that its methods are analytic and inductive; and that we may expect progress in our ethical knowledge, parallel with the progress that has been made in the other natural sciences. As we have seen, it was in pursuit of his second aim that Mill found himself committed to hedonism. The English empiricists had already concentrated their attention upon the simpler organic desires of man. Here, apparently, was a mechanism whose working could be traced far and wide in human conduct, and one which, in itself, was understandable by the help of mechanistic analogies. They therefore took the organic desires as a model of all the inclinations of the soul, and the organic pleasures as a type of all human satisfactions. By reference to them, and to the association of ideas and desires in accordance with definite principles, they attempted to explain all the variety of man's volitions and passions, and to test all the laws and maxims of morality.

Mill attempted to build his system of morals upon the same narrow but definite basis. He admits two fundamental ethical principles: that pleasure and pleasure alone is intrinsically good, and that the right action is that which secures the greatest possible pleasure of the greatest possible number. Mill often writes as though these propositions contained in themselves the sum of purely ethical truth, all other principles of morality being concerned with the different ways of securing the maximum possible pleasure for the greatest possible number of persons. So that there is a sense in which Mill looked for no new *ethical* truths: the progress which he hoped to see in the science of ethics was concerned wholly with the 'secondary principles' – with new means of securing happiness, whether in new circumstances or in existing circumstances.

Let us consider the first proposition. Mill's view is that our desire or inclination for what is good, is *a kind of desire for pleasure*. In any narrow meaning of the word 'pleasure', Mill evidently does not believe that all pleasures are good, or that all good things are pleasures. He plays upon the vagueness and ambiguity of the word until his notion of pleasure includes the full range of human inclinations, and the relation to the basic model of physical pleasures is altogether lost. Mill's 'pleasures' are not, after all, phenomena which can be exactly identified and measured; and the propositions he makes about them cannot be shown to rest upon any process of induction.

75

What he has to rely upon is experience – the discriminating experience of an educated mind.

There is a second, and fundamental, sense in which the hedonistic model proves to be irrelevant. The hedonist takes the organic pleasures and pains as a model, not only because they seem to be open to exact observation, but also because they seem to be *intelligible*. Why is food good to the hungry, rest to the weary? Why is the one sex attracted to the other? Such pleasures seem to be *explained* by our knowledge of the body and its working, and of the nature of life. And this biological explanation is mistaken for a vindication or *justification* of the pleasures. Surely men ought to feel these organic pleasures, for unless they did the race would come to an end. This comes very near to saying that the principle that pleasures (or the organic pleasures) are intrinsically good can be deduced from a more fundamental principle – and, moreover, a principle of natural science.

If we reflect on this argument, we shall see that it provides neither a justification nor an explanation even of the organic pleasures. To say that food or sexual intercourse is necessary for the continuance of the human race is not to explain why it is *pleasant*. Locke could offer an explanation on these lines because he could appeal to the arrangements of a beneficent Providence; to a Natural Law, established by God, which so generously connects the fate of the race with the pleasures of its members. Neither Hume nor Mill could link the two in this way. Locke's Natural Law may also be said to provide a *justification* for such pleasures by showing that, as a general rule, to enjoy them is to serve the grand designs of the Deity. This, of course, is not to appeal to a biological law: it appeals to the implied moral principle that God's aims are always right and good. In the absence of such a postulate, we have to accept our feelings of pleasure (however caused) as *data*.

Nevertheless, we have also to judge them. We have to compare one pleasure with another, and (since the meanings of 'pleasure' and 'pain' are so greatly extended) we have to sort out the pleasures from the pains. Upon what principles do we discriminate? Mill has very little to say on this crucial question. He appeals to 'the wise', to the traditional wisdom. This is his Naturalistic account of 'good' and 'bad': he distinguishes these ethical predicates from 'pleasant' and 'painful' only by referring to systems of preference which exist in the reflective judgements of experienced men and women in a given society.

If we now turn to the second of Mill's basic principles, we see that he was anxious to insist that statements about what is right or what is wrong are *genuine statements*, and that they are based upon a calculation of the pleasures and pains that different actions are likely to bring. This was to permit him to say that the inclination to do what is right as such is in fact an inclination to pleasure.

No doubt judgements about right and wrong display a far greater variety than Mill (or our discussion of Mill's views) has allowed for. But it seems to me that in many cases such judgements are based, at least in part, on calculation in a broad sense of the word. What factors enter into such calculations? Do we merely add up the amounts, or weigh the preferences, of the pleasures and pains that we expect? I have argued that we never merely do this; we also take into account the distribution of the pleasures and pains. And the *inclination* we feel is surely an inclination to maintain certain principles of distribution – to regulate our actions by reference to the existing needs and claims of ourselves and others. So that the inclination to do what is right is never an inclination towards pleasure as such, but towards pleasures *justly* distributed. And by a just distribution we do not mean one determinable by simple arithmetic. For our notion of justice here we have once again to refer to tradition.

Mill may be said to offer us a theory of the natural origin of the *content* of obligations: what he does not do is to explain the *ground* of our obligations. In a parallel fashion, he can explain how we come to have a scale of values, but not what we mean when we say that one pleasure is better than another. We have duties and obligations: but this fact cannot be explained as *a natural product of society*. Mill cannot show how original ethical judgements are made: moral wisdom remains intuitive and traditional and in no determinate relation with the logic or the truth of science.

NOTE.—Since this chapter was written the importance which Mill attached to moral rules (mentioned in paragraph 5) has been emphasized by Mr. J. O. Urmson in the *Philosophical Quarterly*, January 1953. His interpretation has been challenged by other writers, but seems to me in the main fully justified.

Mill asserts very definitely that one should usually be guided by those *general rules* which have been formulated as a result of the long experience of men in society. The philosopher is entitled to test traditional rules; to ask whether the general observance of a rule makes for greater happiness than the general observance of any alternative rule or than leaving the matter outside the scope of rules. And in applying such a test, preference must be given to the 'higher' kinds of pleasure. The place assigned to rules is a notable departure from the view of Bentham: Mill actually defines morality as 'the rules and precepts for human conduct'. Where there is a clash of duties (where one and the same action is required by one rule and forbidden by another), one should choose simply by reference to the probable consequence of the action individually considered. Mill seems to commit himself to the view that in all other cases the right act is the one which is in accordance with a valid rule. A rule is valid only because it passes the utilitarian test: and it is difficult to believe that Mill meant us to follow such a rule where it is *known* that on this occasion it will bring more harm than good. Perhaps this is meant to be covered by his remarks on conflicting duties.

CHAPTER THREE

Politics

His Satanic free-trade Majesty, John Stuart Mill.
HENRY ADAMS

*

I. METHODS IN THE SOCIAL SCIENCES

WHAT is the 'science of society' and what is its relation to that branch of philosophy traditionally known as 'politics'? In his 'political' writings, Mill by no means confines himself to the study of *governments*. The *Essay on Liberty* begins by stating that the problem of individual liberty cannot be conceived in the narrow sense of 'freedom from government interference': for liberty in England is restricted far more by public opinion than by laws or government action. And Mill held that the problems that arise concerning governments are generally involved with problems about the behaviour of men in society, and in all sorts of institutions. There is, then, a study of society and of institutions, including all the departments of state. It is this study which occupied Hume, Bentham, Coleridge, Comte, Tocqueville, and John Stuart Mill.

Mill's predecessors had engaged in the attempt to show that a science of society is possible. Their methods had been rejected by the Empiricists. In the Sixth Book of the *Logic*, Mill attempted to analyse the correct methods of such a science: and he came to the conclusion that Bentham and his own father had been mistaken in their whole 'conception of philosophical method, as applicable to politics.' In the first two sections of this chapter we shall consider Mill's own doctrine of the logic, or fundamental mode of enquiry and reasoning, suitable to sociology. In the subsequent sections we shall consider Mill's views on political questions.

The study of society, as Bentham clearly saw, must have two aspects. There is first an enquiry into the nature of the

79

laws that govern it, and of the forces at work in different societies at different times; and secondly 'censure' or criticism of the different forms of society, the different kinds of institutions, and kinds of governments. John Stuart Mill was aware of these two aspects. He asserts that the philosopher's first business is not to frame universal precepts, but to ascertain universal laws: society must be contemplated 'in the point of view characteristic of science' before the philosophy of society can make progress. This is the necessary preparation for any framing of policies.

All phenomena of society are phenomena of human nature, generated by the action of outward circumstances upon masses of human beings: and if, therefore, the phenomena of human thought, feeling, and action, are subject to fixed laws, the phenomena of society cannot but conform to fixed laws, the consequence of the preceding.[1]

The causes that operate in society combine and modify each other: so that they certainly cannot be identified by a series of specific observations or experiments. For in all such cases what is observed will be an intermixture of the effects of a wide variety of causes. Hence 'empiricism', or a purely observational science of society, is impossible. So much for Macaulay and his so-called 'Baconian' methods. There must be analysis of facts and explanation of what happens in society, by reference to independently known principles.

These 'principles independently known' must include the laws of individual psychology. This was for Mill a matter of great importance: for only by reference to these laws could justice be done (both in theory and in practice) to individual freedom. But Mill cannot accept the theoretical basis of the Benthamites: the attempt to explain *all* social facts by one simple principle – that of individual self-interest. What goes on in society, he holds, is the result of a diversity of causes. It follows that a 'geometrical method' is inapplicable in sociology. The right method must rather resemble that of the

1. *Logic*, VI, vi (2).

physical sciences: it must attempt to explain complex phenomena by something like a composition of forces in mechancs.
Some of the ultimate causes would be physical facts of
geography, events of a purely physical kind. But the characteristic determinants would be human: and Mill looked to
individual psychology to provide a set of simple basic laws
of human conduct, known independently of the social context
under investigation. These laws of individual psychology
were to stand to sociology in the same relation as the laws of
mechanics to the physical sciences generally. Mechanics provides us with types of connexion which we regard as self-
evident: we think that we have understood a physical change
if we see how it could have come about by the mechanical
operation of hidden parts. Similarly, Mill hoped that sociology
would explain an observed connexion by showing how it
might have come about through the operation of the desires,
habits, passions, of masses of individual people.

Mill says that there are two kinds of deductive argument,
both of which are used in the explanation of social changes.

(1) We begin with abstract laws which are already known
to hold of human conduct, although we know that wherever
they hold they are likely to be modified in their operation.
E.g.: The love of gain. From the love of gain, we deduce
what would happen if certain changes were made – if, for
instance, the duty on corn were to be repealed. If such a
change were actually made, we should expect events to provide us with a verification of our deductions. But often the
effect is so overshadowed by quite independent factors (such
as a blight on potatoes), that we have to be satisfied if we can
show that the effect we deduced may well have been one of
the causes which brought about the situation actually observed. But in either case, the economic explanation *makes
sense:* for we know that the love of gain is a *vera causa:* it
actually influences human conduct.

(2) We may begin with some connexion of facts in history,
and try to show that there is a causal connexion between them
by working out a progression from one to the other in accord-

ance with basic known laws of human conduct – and physical laws. It is, for example, a fact that the divorce rate has increased during and since the last war; and that the same phenomenon was observed in the case of the previous war. But it is only because we think we can see a psychological connexion between the two phenomena that this repetition is of any significance.

Mill remarks that the first method can be applied with advantage only where the 'general state of society' can be assumed to be constant, and it is desired to estimate the effect of a limited social change in that society. This leaves untouched the grand question, How does the 'general state of society' itself come about? Are there any general laws governing the relations between its constituent phenomena? The 'general state of society' comprises the degree and distribution of knowledge, industrial development, moral standards and moral conduct, artistic achievement, class-structure, religion, forms of law and of government. Everyone supposes that these are somehow connected. They may vary, to a great degree, independently of each other, but there are stages in history at which we see that they have all entered a new phase: a new 'general state of society' has resulted. Society progresses – not necessarily for the better. Is there any kind of law governing these great epochal changes?

If there is, it is evident that we cannot hope to infer it from our knowledge of psychological principles, even with the help of our knowledge of the laws of physical changes. Knowledge of what Mill calls 'Individual Human Nature' is not enough. Our method can only be *historical:* it must begin with sequences which have already been accomplished. This is the so-called 'Inverse-Deductive Method'.[2]

Mill says that it is possible to distinguish certain repeated sequences on the grand scale. He is thinking, no doubt, of what he had learned from Saint-Simon and Comte: there are, at the least, periods of stability and periods of transition. History, when judiciously examined, does afford certain

2. *Logic,* VI, x.

empirical laws of the succession of general states of society:

And the problem of general sociology is to ascertain these, and connect them with the laws of human nature, by deductions showing that such were the derivative laws naturally to be expected as the consequences of those ultimate ones.[3]

Mill's fundamental contention is, then, that there can be no ultimate sociological laws; that in observing society we are observing only the actions of human beings, and the consequences of those actions. Therefore any regularities and connexions we may see in the mass must be derivable from the principles of individual psychology – whether by deduction (and prediction), or by explanation *ex post facto*.

What is the cash value of the statement that we can understand what goes on in society only when we reflect how man in society might be led, or used, or forced to act, and ask what would be the consequences of those actions?

If we understand by Mill's principle that what men do and suffer in society can be inferred from what man would do and suffer *if he were isolated*, then it is self-contradictory. And Mill again and again refuses to speculate about what sort of creature man would have been if he had not been brought up in society.

Does Mill mean that what goes on in society can be understood by reference to what individuals *intend*? Here indeed we have a limited and definite principle which is as misleading as it is untrue.

The life of institutions (of the State, of the Church, of marriage, or of private property) is a feature of what goes on, what is done and what is said, in society. All this is clearly *the result* of the actions of individuals. But (i) not all those actions are deliberate and purposeful; men have not always reasons in mind when they act, even if they are able to think of good reasons after the action is done. And (ii) whether or not an action has a purpose, and whether or not it fulfils that purpose, it has, as a general rule, many other important conse-

3. *Logic*, VI, x (4).

quences which never formed part of anyone's purpose. And surely it is wise to consider whether it may not be the case that what goes on in society is far less the result of changes deliberately willed by many men, than of changes caused but not willed by men. At all events, this mixture of the results of purposes (often conflicting) and of the unpurposed consequences of actions is to be seen in the life of institutions new and ancient. It can be observed in the life of a council or committee. Sometimes, perhaps, a resolution is passed which indicates that a majority of the members share the same intention; and sometimes such a resolution may be carried out as the supporters intended. But these are rare events. Most often resolutions reflect accidental overlappings of conflicting purposes – or the simple fact that no one has any purpose at all. And in any case, beyond all these purposes, the acts of institutions have effects on individuals and on other institutions which no one ever foresaw or could have foreseen. Where these effects meet *a need*, the Utilitarian philosopher at once proclaims that they are serving a purpose, and that the existence of the purpose is part of the explanation of the existence of the institution. Mill is liable to do this. Institutions exist to serve purposes: if they did not serve these purposes they would wither away: they are sustained in existence from day to day, by the intentions of those who make use of them. They live because they are *wanted*. As if it were necessary for inflation, that anybody should *want* it!

Are we to say, then, that Mill's fundamental contention is a truism or a *falsism? All that goes on in society is to be explained by the laws of the nature of individual men*. This is a falsism if it be taken (as sometimes it must be) to refer to deliberate intentions; and I think it is also plainly false if it means that as a general rule we are able to explain large-scale social changes by reference to facts established by the observation of individual men.

This is seldom the case. The really useful hypotheses that have to some extent enabled us to explain social changes have been those which correlated one social fact with another social fact. Marx, for example, tried to show that the character of social and political relationships in a given society depends upon the stage reached in the exploitation of nature. Of course, we might press our enquiry further, as Mill would have us do, and as Marx was himself sometimes inclined to do, and say: Men work together in society for the exploitation of nature, because each man has appetites and ambitions which he plans to satisfy. But this adds nothing, for our evidence that men in general have such appetites and ambitions is simply that they work together for the exploitation of nature. And it is easy to see that the mechanical, egotistic psychology by which Marxists sometimes feel obliged to augment their social theory, and which is in truth based only on social facts, has proved a source of irrelevances and embarrassments. The fruitful hypothesis is the connexion of the social facts themselves.

Mill's own theory of social change was, of course, altogether opposed to Marx's: it is the theory of an idealist and an intellectual. He believed that the fundamental determinants of social change are developments in human knowledge. It was the change from a theological conception of the world to a rationalistic conception that overthrew the power of the Church and the Divine Right of kings, allowing men of worldly power and rational wisdom to undertake the government of the nation and the village. And Mill, in his day, saw signs of another great intellectual crisis: the change from metaphysical to positive and scientific ways of thought. This change had already broken the great establishment of the Age of Reason – the Squirearchy, the ancient Universities, the great Corporations, and Parliament itself in its eighteenth-century shape. The way was being prepared for the rule of democracy and the sociologists.

Such were the views that Mill derived from his French predecessors and contemporaries; and although they were modified in the course of his life the fundamentals remained unchanged. And no doubt Mill supposed that this intellectualist view of the causes of social change required him to hold his reductionist thesis about the laws of sociology: the thesis, namely, that the ultimate explanations of social theory must be framed in terms of 'individual psychology'. At all costs it was necessary to avoid the admission of a 'collective mind' or a 'collective person'. But it can be doubted whether there is indeed any difficulty in claiming that 'what happens in society' happens to individual men and women, without holding this reductionist thesis. It is interesting in this connexion to compare Mill's views on the relation of psychology to physiology. Here it was Comte who maintained a reductionist view, holding that all the laws of psychology must find their ultimate explanation in terms of bodily changes. This Mill refused to accept. Whatever the theoretical reasons for supposing that reduction ought to be possible (he argued) it will still be practically necessary to keep the study of mind independent of the study of the minute processes of the body; for our sources of information, and our methods of investigation, are in fact independent. It seems to me that Mill might very well have been content to take the same view of the relation of sociology to psychology: for what happens in society commonly depends on ways of individual behaviour which are never observed in any other context, and on effects of human conduct which would be completely trivial were it not for the fact that they are multiplied a million-fold in the lives of the masses.

2. THE METHODS OF POLITICAL ECONOMY

The very existence of the science of Political Economy was something of a challenge to Mill's view of the method appropriate to social studies. For Political Economy seemed to rest upon postulates which defined 'human self-interest' as though it operated without any modification in human society: the method employed seemed to be purely deductive. Mill's apologia (in *Logic*, Book VI) succeeds in showing that the 'science' can never give a complete account of what happens in society: Political Economy is 'abstract' – but is not Mill himself committed to the view that every science must be abstract? In effect, Mill admits that an important set of deductions can be drawn from these postulates, but denies that they constitute a science: they must be corrected and modified before they can be applied; and Political Economy is a part (although a singularly independent part) of a science of society which is genuinely empirical and historical and dynamical.

The 'human self-interest', from which Political Economy derives, is analysed by Mill into three associated desires: man's desire for wealth, and two other desires which are in perpetual conflict with it, namely, the aversion to labour and the desire for the present enjoyment of commodities. Under the influence of these desires, men are led to produce rare commodities by their own labour and the bounty of nature, and to exchange them in such a way as to secure the greatest possible gain to themselves. The laws of industry and of distribution, the operation of a free market, are deduced from the laws of these desires, together with laws governing men's varying physical circumstances. The economic laws describe how men would act *if* the operation of these desires were unaffected by any others. The result is a deductive system which is 'abstract' in the sense appropriate to a science. The basic laws of the system of economics define a set of causes or 'forces' which are properties such that: (i) if anything possesses one of them, it will almost certainly possess others within the set; and (ii) it will almost certainly possess others outside the set, by which the operation of the basic principles will be modified. Thus, in buying and selling we see a set of economic properties illustrated; what happens can be calculated only by the help of economic laws. But in any actual situation, we often also observe the operation of other non-economic forces, and this may well materially affect the result. That in certain spheres of social life (e.g., the Stock Exchange) the economic motives operate in comparative isolation, is the justification for demarcating economics as a separate science.[4]

4. *Logic*, VI, ix (3); which quotes from Mill's *Essays on Some Unsettled Questions of Political Economy*, written in 1830–4 and published in 1844.

Mill's *Principles of Political Economy* makes a distinction between the laws of production and the laws of distribution. The former, he thought, were everywhere valid: the latter depend upon political arrangements within a given society made in the interests of the dominant class. If the balance of active power in the society were to alter, different arrangements for distribution would be made. It seems that the science of economics must incorporate some principles of a purely non-economic character: all the more reason, therefore, for insisting that political economy is a branch of sociology. But the *reasons* which incline a society to pass (for example) from free trade to protection cannot themselves be understood without a consideration of the working of the purely economic motives.

The laws of Political Economy can be used in making predictions as to what would happen within the same general state of society if certain changes (affecting economic motives) were introduced. For in such cases the extent to which the economic motives are modified by general factors (such as stupidity or superstition) is assumed to remain unaltered; and if a 'deviation' can be calculated from existing data, this will also be applicable to the prediction. The same is true of the operation of such special factors as tariffs, dislike of trusts, etc., where these can be assumed to be independent of the contemplated changes, or dependent in a known way. But economics cannot enable us to predict the effects of a given change in a society whose general state was not the same as that on which the prediction was based; nor to make predictions where the operation of non-economic motives is relevant, but in an unknown way.

Marx inherited from the Classical Economists a notion of 'economic necessity' which Mill had abandoned. Mill fully recognizes the way in which men's non-economic motives may set at naught the inferences of economists. He also explicitly states that there are many fields of human conduct in which wealth is not the principal object; political economy does not pretend that its principles are applicable here. Nor is there anything in Mill's account of economics as a science to support the view that the prediction of economic changes, in a concrete situation, is easier or more certain than the prediction of other social changes.[5]

We must now leave questions of method, and turn to Mill's own diagnosis and censure of social trends and political institutions. We shall notice that Mill displays a considerable flair for discovering existing tendencies and suggesting possible causes. But it will not be very easy to see that he does this by an application of the Inverse-Deductive Method. Indeed, the effect of his own political views on his conception of the correct method of sociology is more obvious than the effect of his method on his views and policies.

3. POLITICS

The institution of government serves as a check upon the conflicting actions, emotions, and intentions of men. This fact was made the cornerstone of the Benthamite theory of politics. But their view of human conflicts was narrow, over-emphasizing conscious reasoning and deliberate will. They thought of men as each pursuing his own ostensible greatest interest, and they saw that the result of such a situation would have been intolerable if government had not existed. But all this had somehow to be related to purpose. To acquiesce in government as an existing institution was repugnant both to the practical and the theoretical aims of the Benthamites. They had to raise the question: What are the purposes of government? What is the nature and working of government? Does not any government in fact consist of a group of men, and have not these men private interests of their own? And in what, after all, does their authority consist? It is of human origin – a consequence of the coming together of men in society. Hence the paradox, that, although governments are set up to serve common interests, they in fact are used to serve the interests of the rulers. And the remedy for this situation

5. Cf. *Autobiography*, pp. 236–7.

is, of course, the device of representative government, which secures, over a period, an *identity of interests* between rulers and ruled. Given this identity, government will in fact serve the greatest happiness of the greatest possible number. Its results will be good: and therefore men should act in such a way as to maintain it in existence.

This account of government is due to Bentham and James Mill, and tries to avoid the difficulties which Hume had pointed out in Locke's theory of contract. The classical exposition is to be found in the article on government which James Mill wrote for the supplement to the *Encyclopaedia Britannica* in 1825. This became, we are told, the bible of the younger Benthamites and was expounded week by week at the Cambridge Union Society by Charles Austin and other friends of John Mill. But in due course John Stuart Mill himself came to regard it with great suspicion. He had also to expound it at the fortnightly meetings of the London Debating Society – to expound it and to defend it against the Coleridgeans with whom he half-sympathized. These conflicts, and the experience he there gained of other schools of political thinking, made him aware of many things which the doctrine, professing to be a theory of government and not merely a defence of Parliamentary Reform, ought to have made room for, and did not. When, therefore, Macaulay attacked the essay on government in a famous article in the *Edinburgh Review*, John Mill was obliged (he tells us) to admit that there was truth in several of Macaulay's strictures. First came the admission that 'my father's premises were really too narrow, and included but a small number of the general truths, on which, in politics, the important consequences depend'; and (later on) that his whole method of political philosophy was mistaken.[6]

The criticism of the method has already been undertaken, and I have already tried, in Chapter I, to trace some of the

6. See *Autobiography*, p. 158, etc, and *Edinburgh Review*, March 1829. Mill's 'Speech against Sterling', of the same year, is printed in the *World's Classics* edition of the *Autobiography*, and is of great interest.

many influences which led Mill to add to his father's premises. The most important of John Mill's political writings are *The Spirit of the Age* (1831), 'Civilisation' (1836), the 'Essay on Tocqueville' (1840), the *Essay on Liberty* (1859), and *Representative Government* (1861). To these must be added ' The Claims of Labour' (1845), and the chapter on 'The Future of the Labouring Classes', added to the *Political Economy* in 1847. From the very first, we see that quite new currents of opinion were at work: the Coleridgeans, the Saint-Simonians, Comte, Carlyle, Tocqueville, and (later) Humboldt. And Mill was prepared by his own experiences and character to take a wider view both of individual human nature and of society and of governments. It is true that in his later works he sometimes seems to contract again in certain respects, and to re-assert some of the narrower views of the Benthamites; yet it is always with a significant difference. James Mill's essay on government has all the bold crudity of a mechanic's drawing: every line in it is designed to serve a single purpose through the means of a single set of laws; John Mill's essays are long and rambling and are sometimes inconsistent with themselves; a multitude of subtle and conflicting considerations lead to various conclusions. But in these considerations of Man, Society, and the State, it is possible to recognize, if obscurely, the men and the societies we know, and the governments that have the rule over them.

4. REPRESENTATIVE GOVERNMENT

Governments ought to promote the general happiness. Mill believed that the form of government which best promotes this end is a popular form of Representative Government. This, therefore, is 'the Ideally Best Form of Polity'.

Mill fully recognizes that representative institutions are not suited to all peoples. The type of government suited to a people depends upon the balance of active powers that exist, or can immediately be called into existence, in the society. James Mill had tried to show that representative government was in the *interest* of this or that group of people. But interests are not active powers unless those to whom they belong are willing to act upon them. Representative institutions will not work unless each man is capable of conducting his own affairs and is disposed to stand up for himself. This requires a certain standard of education or intelligence: but neither government nor being governed is simply a matter of intellect. Each requires self-reliance and courage combined with a spirit of moderation and compromise and many other qualities of character. Obviously, then, the ideally best form of polity is not suited to all. However, Mill holds that other forms of government may be judged by the degree to which they educate their peoples towards a completely popular government. And here he has a word to say for various forms of paternalism as well as for enlightened despotisms: they are the best polity for a given nation if they tend to prepare it for the next step forward towards the Ideally Best.

It is, then, impossible to understand the question of the adaptation of forms of government to states of society without taking into account not only the next step, but all the steps which society has yet to make.[7]

Mill attaches more importance to the political education which a government provides than to the day-to-day efficiency with which it carries out its agreed tasks. The two are of course inevitably connected, but Mill here shows so strong an interest in progression towards Representative Government that he runs the risk of substituting Progress, for Human Happiness, as the ultimate test of political institutions. 'John Stuart Mill was concerned with the advance of "Civilization"; but Bentham was ... simply concerned with making people as he found them more happy.'[8] Such apocalyptic strains are apparently one of the dangers which beset any theory of historical development.

7. *Representative Government*, Everyman Edition, p. 201.
8. W. Harrison: Introduction to Bentham's *Fragment on Government*, Blackwell, Oxford (1948), p. xli.

Mill believed that a popular representative government inevitably makes for progress. There is, he held, a great releasing of human energy; democracy makes men discontented and 'nothing is more certain than that improvement in human affairs is wholly the work of the uncontented characters.'[9] The industry and commercial prosperity of the British Middle Class, the go-ahead expanding economy of the Northern States of America, are (as Mill saw in reading Tocqueville) in part the result of freedom from government interference, in part also of the address and decision of the governments themselves. This Mill could fully admire. 'Not what is done by a democratic government, but what is done under a democratic government by private agency, is really great.'[10]

That government should itself directly promote the happiness and virtue of its individual citizens was something for which Mill here offers a somewhat oblique justification. (And indeed the doctrine is a two-edged sword.) He seems to assert that Representative Government has a tendency to promote nothing less than the general mental and moral advancement of the whole people, and yet to call this a *merit* merely because, as a consequence, the character of the *government* will be improved. I think Mill may be confused sometimes as to whether Representative Government is to be preferred because it is an improving, or a self-improving, type of constitution. But the two are quite compatible, and no doubt he means to assert *both* grounds of preference. He thought that representative institutions would tend to make a people wiser in the arts of government, more progressive, more hardworking and far-seeing, more prosperous; collectively greater and individually sharper. Mill also hoped that, if certain safeguards were provided, popular government would allow a new flowering of individual life and inner character. And all these things he was, by this time, accustomed to call elements in human happiness.[11]

9. *Representative Government*, p. 211.
10. Tocqueville, quoted by Mill, *Dissertations and Discussions*, II, p. 29.
11. *Representative Government*, p. 195.

5. POPULAR GOVERNMENT AND MAJORITY RULE

How far were Mill's expectations and hopes of democracy wise, and how far were they well-founded?

Coleridge had insisted that Permanence, as well as Progress, is an element in the social good. Mill now rejects this distinction. He describes it as 'plausible and seductive' but unscientific, being based upon the difference between the sentiments to which the two make their appeal. (As though this difference were not here relevant!)

'If there is anything certain in human affairs, it is that valuable acquisitions are only to be retained by the continuation of the same energies which gained them. Things left to take care of themselves inevitably decay.' All that is necessary in any form of government is to make provision for *progress*.[12]

This strenuous doctrine shows how far Mill was now prepared to admire the 'all-pervading and restless activity', the 'superabundant force' which Tocqueville had seen in America. We may well believe that any forward step in the spiritual life of a people (in education, respect for the law, or in private morality) is liable to be lost again: but surely what is immediately needed is a breathing space in which the new achievement can become effortless and habitual. This can certainly be helped by institutions of a static type, imposing a steady, not an accelerating, pressure. It is also a fact that the very effort that has been expended in one direction may lead, as a consequence, to a regression in some other field. The most superficial observation shows that every *reform* is itself a menace to other achievements. In the period that follows a reform, therefore, it is necessary for zeal to be abated and balance restored. To expect that the same kind of methods and institutions as make the new advances will also suffice for the conserving of those already made, can hardly be called political wisdom.

Something of the same over-emphasis on improvement is

12. *Representative Government*, pp. 186–8.

seen in Mill's admiration for the uncontented type of person. We may agree with Mill that democracy tends to encourage the active, dissatisfied type of life, and that it has proved eminently suitable to expanding capitalism. What we have to examine with more care is the view that democratic institutions are generally able to muster the best existing energies and powers of the people for the determination of day-to-day questions of government; and at the same time to raise the general moral, intellectual, and 'active' life of the whole people.

The first question is possibly less complex than the second. Tocqueville commented with some asperity on the low level of efficiency reached by the state governments and by the Federal Government in America. They fell far below the level of those European countries in which affairs were left in the hands of the professional servants of the Crown – very far indeed below the level of those in which there was still an hereditary official class. In America (according to Tocqueville) very few of the most able citizens attempted a political career: men of education and refinement could not stomach the methods of party politics; men of the greatest energy and ambition were otherwise engaged in making their private fortunes. To this Mill replied that a political career in America could hardly amount to very much in any case, because 'America needs very little government'. And this would naturally be the case in any advanced community, for in proportion as men become more and more self-reliant, there is a certain 'withering away of the state'. But Mill's real answer is that Tocqueville himself points to the remedy. The public are learning all the time by *their own* mistakes and failures; when things go wrong, they elect new officers of state and start again with a new policy. It may well take longer for a whole people to learn the arts of self-government than for a bureaucracy to learn the arts of government – to reach that standard above which (as Mill held) a bureaucratic state cannot rise. In the long run it is the popular governments that must be the most efficient, because they can be replaced over-

95

night by new men if they fail to stand up to the criticism of the people whom they govern. And the men to carry out the new policy can be chosen from any class and any walk of life.

There is clearly a great deal to be said for Mill's view. Under a popular government, decisions are taken (or may be taken) after full and peaceful discussion in which all citizens may be represented. The wise may bring their wisdom, the paid officers of the state may bring their files. Those who might be victimized may air their potential grievances; existing powers, which could hinder the success of a measure, can reveal their intentions and can perhaps be placated. A public opinion can be formed on the basis of revealed facts and stated prejudices. And the opinion of the majority at the end of these consultations will become the act of the state.

It is this transition from the 'enlightened public opinion' to 'the opinion of the majority' that has often seemed painful to philosophers of Mill's type. For it is a transition which it is very hard to display in purely rational disguise. Are we to say that there is greater wisdom in the opinion of the majority than in any of the minority views? Let us suppose that the minorities have the fullest freedom to express their opinions and to produce their evidence. Are we to say that their views are mistaken merely because they have failed to convert a majority? Have we even any right to say that *in the long run* the views of the majority are likely to be right? We may say that if the majority show average reasonableness they will not wish to make enemies of minorities, and will try to avoid doing them injustice. But there may be equally reasonable minorities, anxious (for the most obvious reasons) not to antagonize the majority. May not the reasonable minority be right and the reasonable majority be wrong?

It is in accordance with the tradition which Mill inherited to claim that all political disputes could be settled by a long-enough conference of reasonable men. If so, the reasonable majority and the reasonable minority would agree in the long run; and a deadlock could not arise 'in an advanced community'. But we have no example of such an advanced community.

Should we say, then, that the view of the majority ought to be carried out, not because it must be the wisest, but because it is the view of the majority? Tocqueville himself sometimes expresses such a view, but he vindicates it by appeal to the workings of Providence – to a natural law, in effect, which guarantees that the majority-opinion will coincide in the long run with the greatest good of all.

Should we say that it is bad for men to be governed against their convictions, and (by arithmetical deduction) worse if the many are so governed than if the few are?

In fact, Mill makes the transition, or makes a way for it, in his argument that in any society the institutions of government are in the hands of the 'active powers' in the society.[13] This is a hard fact, a condition under which all government is carried on. And in a democracy the majority party in the legislature normally represents the dominant power in the society, and they *will* have their way. Indeed, the very possibility of peaceful discussion rests on the assurance that the majority in the assembly *does* represent the leading *active power* in the community. And the virtue of the discussion is that, in the long run, both majority and minorities will learn from experience.

6. DOES DEMOCRACY EDUCATE THE PEOPLE?

We now turn to the second, and wider, argument in favour of Representative Government: that it tends to raise the intellectual, moral, and active powers of the people.

Tocqueville was confident that this occurred in the American States, and above all in the townships of New England, which had since colonial times enjoyed an independence which was totally strange to a French observer. In these small communities it was evident that the practice of self-government exercised an ennobling influence. A man who had to

13. *Representative Government*, p. 182.

serve on a jury or on the local bench, or to act as the unpaid officer of the corporation, was confronted with problems and issues which could not be decided by any consideration of private interests. He was obliged to consider the general good and to hold an opinion on matters of public interest. And he was obliged to act in the full view of his personal friends and enemies.

The native of New England is attached to his township because it is independent and free: his co-operation in its affairs ensures his attachment to its interest; the well-being it affords him secures his affection; and its welfare is the aim of his ambition and of his future exertions: he takes a part in every occurrence in the place; he practises the art of government in the small sphere within his reach; he accustoms himself to those forms which can alone ensure the steady progress of liberty; he imbibes their spirit; he acquires a taste for order, comprehends the union or the balance of powers, and collects clear practical notions on the nature of his duties and the extent of his rights. ....[14]

Education at this local level would no doubt provide men of character to take part in the government of the County, the State, and even the Union. But it is doubtful whether Tocqueville or Mill fully understood the power of the mass-parties, with their professional bosses and their national funds; or even the power of the professional civil servants. These were already in existence, and their powers have been growing ever since. In all the great democracies, as in all great states, there has been a steady decline of local institutions, and a steady increase in the power of the nation-wide authorities.

Nevertheless, Tocqueville was obviously right in his view that democracy tends to diffuse political experience more widely than any other form of government; and that democracies have a definite interest in general education. And there seems to be justice in Mill's conclusion that whatever other disadvantages there may be in popular government, the people who take part in it must feel themselves to be more grown-up than is possible under other kinds of rule. Whether there is

14. *Democracy in America,* trans. Henry Reeve, World's Classics, p. 66.

always *a tendency to improvement* in political wisdom will presumably depend in part on the stability of the general state of society. For something which we call 'learning from experience' there surely must be: a people learns not to make in the future the same mistakes as it made in the past. But the extent to which this wisdom is retained from one generation to another, and the extent to which it is relevant, depend on considerations which differ from one society to another. These advantages, such as they are, provide Mill with his decisive argument in favour of Representative Government. It is no longer a matter of 'identity of interest between government and governed' : the decisive thing is that democracy makes men of character.

But to this favourable view Mill had to face a most formidable objection. It was well enough if popular government served to educate men, but how if it were to educate them all to be alike – sheep nibbling side by side in the same pasture?

7. THE TYRANNY OF THE MAJORITY

Tocqueville held that democratic institutions tended, of themselves, to produce a tyranny of the majority – a tyranny exercised not by violence but by the social pressure of a vast mass of indistinguishable citizens. Mill ventures to correct this opinion. He thinks that Tocqueville has confounded the effects of democracy with the effects of a progressive commercial civilization.[15] But this was cold comfort: and Mill was profoundly shocked by Tocqueville's chapters on the Unlimited Power of the Majority in the only existing example of a democratic country.

Tocqueville gives a short and simple demonstration that in a democratic country there will be no real freedom of opinion or of action. Democracy asserts the right of private judgement: on every question, every citizen has the right to think and say what he will; and within the limits of the law he may also do what he will. But in fact the vast majority of

15. *Dissertations and Discussions*, II, p. 62.

citizens cannot, and know that they cannot, make up their minds for themselves. They must follow some authority. But the only available authority is the will of the majority. The ordinary man, therefore, adopts what he takes to be the opinion of the majority: he cannot bear to be opposed to it or to see it opposed. So long as no opinion on a given question can claim to express the will of the majority, discussion may be carried on freely. But as soon as an opinion is, or is successfully represented as being, the opinion of the majority, then at once it becomes the opinion of the overwhelming majority. A submissive silence follows, and most of those who expressed views of their own now join their voices in concord with the majority. Are they afraid of violence or of legal penalties? In America this is not normally the case. They are afraid of being different, of being regarded as aliens by their own people. They are impressed (as the unthinking multitude are impressed) by the *mana* of the majority.

There is an amazing strength in the expression of the determination of a whole people, and when it declares itself the imagination of those who are most inclined to contest it is overawed by its authority.[16]

And more: experience has taught them that obstinate opposition is universally condemned. Tocqueville draws a moving picture of the American with views of his own, who, after many vain attempts to gain a hearing, 'subsides into silence, as if he were tormented by remorse for having spoken the truth'.

This account of the America of his day is no doubt exaggerated and is not consistent with other things that Tocqueville himself says. For example, local loyalties, and local authorities survived in rural America, as he himself saw: and there were also religious authorities to which the ordinary man, if a believer, might appeal, and which were not seldom flatly opposed to the dominant trends of majority opinion. Moreover, the very vacillation of this majority view (on which

16. Tocqueville, *op. cit.*, p. 173.

Tocqueville remarks very unfavourably) must give a hope to
the faithful remnant in any minority: their turn may come.

But whether the picture is a faithful one or not, the argument must be taken seriously. It is claimed that, to the degree
that other authorities (religious, local, cultural) decay, the
power of the opinion of the mass-majority becomes tyrannical
and irresistible. The argument depends upon the premise that
ordinary men and women are unable to make up their minds
for themselves, without the help of an authority. Mill was
well aware that this was *to a great degree* true.

8. LIBERTY

In 1840, Mill was prepared to argue that the tyranny of the
majority sprang from the undue growth of commercialism,
rather than from the development of political democracy; and to
maintain that there was no *essential* connexion between the two.

The free enterprise of commerce and industry in Northern
America had very largely absorbed the older landed interests;
the spirit of commerce had captured the workers in the towns,
and even farms were being run on industrial lines. So that the
whole population presented the appearance of one class. Of
course, within this one class the many were employees and
the few were employers. But the employees hoped to set up
in business for themselves, or to prepare the way for their
sons. The commercial interest, as Tocqueville showed, had
become, or was in process of becoming, the only powerful
interest in the community.

In 1840, Mill feared that the British middle class might in a
similar way absorb the whole life of this country. But by the
time he came to write the *Essay on Liberty* (in the 1850's), Mill
was convinced that the workers would have an independent
future and was already looking forward to the more remote
day of their coming to power in a democratic Britain.

In the *Essay on Liberty* Mill wrote:

In England, from the peculiar circumstances of our political
history, though the yoke of opinion is perhaps heavier, that of law

is lighter, than in most other countries of Europe; and there is considerable jealousy of direct interference, by the legislative or the executive power, with private conduct; not so much from any just regard for the independence of the individual, as from the still subsisting habit of looking on the government as representing an opposite interest to the public. The majority have not yet learnt to feel the power of the government their power, or its opinions their opinions. When they do so, individual liberty will probably be as much exposed to invasion from the government, as it already is from public opinion.[17]

That day is our own day. Evidently the great majority have come to believe that government is a suitable instrument for guaranteeing a certain minimum (and ever-growing) standard of living for everyone in the country. But the 'spirit of improvement is not always a spirit of liberty'. As a means to this end legislation interferes at every turn with economic activities; and as a means of protecting children it interferes more and more in private and family life. The precedents so established provide all kinds of opportunities for further government interference.

So completely has history falsified Mill's earlier prophecy of a 'withering away' of the democratic state. The change is no doubt due in part to human greed or appetite: some of us hope to catch up with others by the help of free meals or free beauty treatment, and all of us want to make sure that we secure the tea-crop from Ceylon and the beef-crop from Australia. But, in part, the change of outlook is due to an expanding sense of sympathy and sense of justice. We feel that the government alone is capable of dealing with suffering and poverty on the mass scale which these present in a mass-state. We cannot return to the freedom of enterprise and initiative which we have lost, without the strongest feelings of guilt, as well as feelings of frustrated appetite. It is, then, for our time that Mill wrote his *Essay on Liberty*.

The problem which he here discusses is that of maintaining the life of the individual against the pressure of a huge

17. Everyman Edition, pp. 71–2.

urbanized society. In the essay, Mill tries to lay down a line of demarcation to show where society may rightly interfere and where it may not. He divides the activities of an individual into a 'social sphere' and a 'private sphere'. Mill's view of the division is to be found in Chapter IV.

> As soon as any part of a person's conduct affects prejudicially the interests of others, society has jurisdiction over it, and the question whether the general welfare will or will not be promoted by interfering with it, becomes open to discussion. But there is no room for entertaining any such question when a person's conduct affects the interests of no persons besides himself, or needs not affect them unless they like (all persons concerned being of full age, and the ordinary amount of understanding). In all such cases, there should be perfect freedom, legal and social, to do the action and to stand the consequences.

It is notable that, amongst the consequences which a person may quite properly be expected to stand, is the disapproval and dislike of his fellows. Mill tries to draw a difficult (but surely very necessary) distinction between these feelings, and their expression in conduct *calculated* to intimidate or penalize. A man who becomes roaring drunk every night cannot expect his neighbours to cultivate his company or to defend his reputation: but he can expect that they will not try to have him turned out of his home or out of his job.

Mill defends the right of the individual in the private sphere on considerations of utility. But his chief argument is the very dubious one that if society interferes at all in this sphere, it will do so at the wrong moment and in the wrong way. Mill's real opinion on the question could, perhaps, be more openly stated: 'Every man has a natural right to the full expression and development of his own character, whether other people like it or not.' The doctrine of the full development of individuality is Mill's version of the Natural Right to Happiness; and this, in its turn, is precisely the suppressed ethical premise of Utilitarianism.

Since almost anything of importance that a man does affects the welfare of others, and may affect it prejudicially, the principle does not seem absolutely to restrict the interference of society in any significant way. But of course Mill does not say that society *should* interfere throughout the social sphere: he merely says that society should do so if this would promote the general welfare. So that every actual application of the principle has to be justified on its own utilitarian grounds.

The last two chapters of the *Liberty* contain discussions of actual and possible applications, and the *Letters* contain many more. Mill objects, for example, to restrictions on the sale of drugs, poisons, or alcohol; to compulsory anti-smallpox vaccination; to the enforcement of 'go-slow' by the trade unions in the factories; and he naturally objects to legislative defence of the Sabbath. On the other hand, he approves marriage laws in so far as they protect the children of the marriage or rights that come into existence with the children. He considers that parents are (like legal guardians) acting in the interests of society in carrying out their duties to their children, and that it is for society to see that they do their job properly. The state (not the family) should see that education is provided: but the parents, being responsible for the existence of their children, must pay for that education; and fathers may be put to forced labour if they are unable to pay in any other way. The state should also see that parents do not have more children than they can support. It is, says Mill, a mischievous act to add to the numbers of the poor, and a serious offence against all who live by the remuneration of labour.

It will be seen that Mill's social and political reflections did not lead him to attach any importance to 'family rights'.[18]

Mill concludes with a warning: there will always (he says)

18. Bain says that Mill's *Essay on Liberty* was written with the relation of the two sexes very much in mind. This is not very obvious to the reader: but Mill certainly held that society was inclined to interfere quite unnecessarily in this matter – as witness, Mill's own declaration on the eve of his marriage. (See Chapter I above and *Letters*, I, p. 158; Bain, *J. S. Mill, A Criticism*, p. 108.) The views of Mill and of his wife on this subject are given at length in Professor Hayek's *J. S. Mill and Harriet Taylor*.

be spheres where the state can undertake a task with far better promise of success than private enterprise; but in reaching a decision on any question of nationalization, it is always to be remembered that every new task which is assigned to the state adds to the general power of the state and diminishes the power and independence of the individual.[19]

In considering this doctrine of the social and the individual spheres, we must take account of the famous defence of freedom of thought and expression which is given in the second chapter of the essay. Mill holds that neither society nor the state is ever justified in restricting this liberty. The state forbids certain actions and the direct solicitation to such actions: this is inevitable. But the state is never justified in forbidding the expression of opinions.

Mill's argument rests on the view that anyone who forbids the discussion of an opinion must be assuming the infallibility of his own contrary views. Mill agrees that men and governments may act with confidence upon their own opinions, even though they know that those who dispute them and oppose them *may be right*. But, according to Mill, this very confidence which a government may feel in acting can be a *rational* confidence only where their own view has been open to complete liberty of contradiction. 'On no other terms can a being with human faculties have any rational assurance of being right.'

Here, surely, we do well to call nonsense by its name: to claim to be right is not the same thing as to claim to be infallible. Imagine the civilized ruler of a primitive and barbaric people: can he never have *any* rational assurance that his public actions are right? There is no one to understand them, no one to contradict or disprove. We may admit that his confidence, in the case of many public acts, would be fortunately increased if they had run the gauntlet of a parliament or a free press: but so also would his confidence be increased, very likely, if he had been able to take twice as long over making up his mind. It is not a question of absolute assurance: no public debate, however long-drawn-out, can provide that. It

19. *Essay on Liberty*, p. 165.

is a question of a degree of confidence: and surely a ruler could achieve this alone – and, very often, that degree of confidence appropriate to the action in question. And it is easily possible to imagine or to recall circumstances in which the rulers of civilized peoples would be right to trust their own judgements even so far as to prohibit the entry and the discussion of certain opinions. That the right is very commonly abused is a further factor which should never be forgotten.

Mill rightly castigates the view that persecution of opinions is always doomed to failure:

> It is a piece of idle sentimentality that truth, merely as truth, has any inherent power denied to error of prevailing against the dungeon or the stake.

But he underestimates the harm done by false and mischievous opinions, especially when these happen to be minority opinions. And we have to add that it is no less sentimental to suppose that truth must prevail over the ridicule, slander, provocation, bogus philosophizing, and vituperation, of minorities. Mill overlooks the great tactical advantage of being in opposition, with no other immediate end than the discredit of authority. He remarks that invective, sarcasm, personal vilification and unmeasured vituperation are of little if any use to a minority. How much better all demagogues have known their own business!

9. LIBERTY AND INDIVIDUALITY

The day has now come when the majority have learned to think of the power of government as their power; and (as Mill prophesied a century ago) individual liberty is no doubt exposed to invasion from the government as well as from public opinion. Is it perhaps a little disconcerting not to find this state of affairs as uncomfortable as Mill would have wished us to do?

It is true that in one important respect the invasion has hardly begun. In Britain, the freedom of thought and expression has hardly suffered through government action. Indeed, the development of a mass-society (middle class in its standards of living but without any of that individual initiative which Mill admired in the middle class), has provided a market of immense size for every kind of opinion *capable of expression in popular terms.* The result has hardly been one which Mill would have wished to see : a mass-public bewildered, blasé, and exhausted by variety; the crowding-out of difficult and more profound thought.

But this is only a part of the story. We cannot deny that freedom of economic enterprise has diminished enormously, and that the existence of the family as a centre of personal loyalties is endangered. Mill cared a great deal for the former and nothing at all for the latter. Freedom to express one's individuality in a personal style of living has also suffered greatly through economic legislation. Possibly the relations of the sexes are less restricted by opinion to-day than they were a century ago: they are certainly freer at law. But this must be offset by the increasing tendency to impose a uniform standard of outward conduct as a condition for the holding of more (and more humble) kinds of employment.

And so the tale might go on. What are the lessons that we should draw from it?

It seems to me that Mill was correct in thinking that the tyranny of public opinion arises from the wearing away of those institutions which, in an earlier day, stood between the individual and the mass of society, as well as between the individual and the great nation-state. He was right also in seeing that this process was the result of economic changes in society – though he predicted wrongly the course those changes would take, and was probably mistaken in thinking them entirely independent of the progress towards political democracy. Nor did Mill take seriously enough, in his later writings, the implications of his own view. For if a mass-state is to be avoided only by preserving or renovating or improvising intermediate institutions, then the relation of these to individual liberty is a problem of the greatest importance.

The fact of the matter seems to be that the growth of the

individual to maturity is furthered by the existence of institutions of different kinds which incorporate and express different aspects of traditional wisdom, knowledge, and skill. The state itself includes many such institutions – the Courts of Justice, for example – and the action of the state is never simply and directly responsive to the switchings and changings of public opinion. But it is important that the state should have many formidable rivals. Such institutions limit individual liberty, but they stimulate a definiteness of response. The individual gradually learns to decide between them where they disagree, and so to make up his own mind and to go his own way. But the life of an individual is many-sided, and a man whose independence is established in the sphere of pure speculation may still need the discipline of his church to make him or to keep him a good father. So that a whole range must at all times be in existence: and all must be social powers to be reckoned with by their members – even by those no longer in tutelage. That there should be limits to their powers is obviously essential. Complete departures from traditional ways must always be possible: but it is arguable that such departures should not be made too easy, lest they should appear to be trivial.

It is to some such view that we may be led by re-reading Mill's earlier letters and papers, in the light of his later, more fully developed, doctrine of personality. What men do in society arises out of their whole character and not merely out of reasoned purposes. Mill, in his later works, does less than justice to the educative value of non-political institutions. And at the same time he somewhat misconceives the way in which democratic institutions do their work of education and of government. He over-emphasizes the importance of rational argument. Political differences are not merely differences of opinion which can be settled by debate: they commonly involve differences in moral judgement of an ultimate kind: they are conflicts of will and feeling and character. And the purpose of deliberation, in democracies of the British model, is less to reach a 'solution' than to show exactly where the lines of division lie, and what sort of compromise will in fact be accepted by all the different parties in a peaceful manner. In his later years Mill was inclined to the view that a more perfect method of representation might enable his country to avoid the coming struggle for power between labour and capital. He became a zealous advocate of a form of Proportional Representation, and hoped that it would be adopted at the moment when Labour was still without a majority and Capital suitably alarmed. This scheme is typically rationalistic: the perfectly-chosen representatives would reach a solution of the dispute, and this would be incorporated once and for all into the law of the land. But if political disputes are conflicts of personality and interests, then a 'settlement' of a dispute is no more than a temporary compromise which, for the time being, both belligerents are willing to accept.

It has in fact proved the case that wisdom has come to Capital and Labour (in so far as it has come at all) through experience of conflicts. This shows the real value of that perpetual, but (in the main) peaceful, conflict which goes on in a democratic state. The wisdom is largely a matter of good judgement, sense of proportion, moderation, respect for opponents, and grasp of unifying interests and sentiments. It includes also knowledge gained by trial and error in a variety of fields of government. But even this kind of knowledge cannot be incorporated into a constitution: it is eminently practical and pragmatic.

10. INDIVIDUALS AND INSTITUTIONS

Before Mill died, the influence of his political writings had begun to wane before the rising power of English Idealism. T. H. Green was English in character and Hegelian in training, and contrived to unite a doctrine of individual freedom with a belief in the independent (or almost independent) existence and moral value of the state and other institutions. And in appealing to an unintellectual loyalty and reverence towards government and establishment, he by no means overlooked the iniquity of corruption and the necessity of reform. He thus had his own doctrine of improvement, to which (like Mill) he devoted all his own great powers. And he had (what Mill lacked) a faith that could determine that institutions shall be real and have positive moral value in themselves. Green had also a deeper and truer sense of the unique position of the state. For the state is not merely a useful device: and even as a useful device it cannot be separated from moral conflicts and loyalties; for it is useful to different movements for different and incompatible ends. In their long histories, governments have been used to do a bewildering variety of things: to persecute heretics, or to protect them; to abolish open-field farming; to change the reigning dynasty; to collect income-tax; to provide free schools and free milk in the schools. But no government came into existence, or continues in existence, to perform any of these things: and, indeed, many of the things which a government does would be entirely unnecessary if there were no government. Nor could we imagine anyone inventing government to do any of these things. For beyond its uses for conflicting movements, the state exists as a reality – as a real social phenomenon – to be reckoned with by all movements, institutions, and individuals. The Utilitarianism of Bentham, even when expanded by Mill, cannot altogether succeed in taking the state seriously.[20]

It might also be added that Mill could not succeed in taking the church (or the family) seriously. In his Coleridgean period he attempted to outline a reformed Establishment: but there was too much of Comte and too little of Coleridge in it. The miscellaneous body which he describes would (if it could ever have made up its mind) have proved highly serviceable to society. But it has nothing to do with the Body of Christ or the Everlasting Gospel. Surely neither the sociologist nor the social reformer can afford to ignore a mystique merely because he disbelieves it.[21]

20. See Rush Rhees, *Science and Politics*, Aristotelian Society, Supp. xxiii.
21. Mill's account of his new Establishment is given in brief in his letter to Sterling of 22 October, 1831, to which reference has often been made in this book. It is the second of Elliot's collection.

CHAPTER FOUR

Deduction and Demonstrative Science

Mine professes to be a logic of experience only.
MILL TO STERLING, 1839

*

I. INTRODUCTION

How did Mill understand the phrase 'a logic of experience only'? As he explains clearly enough in his *Autobiography*, one aim of the *Logic* was to refute the view that there are necessary truths which can be known by direct intuition of the mind and which need not be tested by sense-experience. He regarded this view as the great intellectual support of false doctrines and bad institutions. 'And the chief strength of this false philosophy in morals, politics, and religion, lies in the appeal which it is accustomed to make to the evidence of mathematics and of the cognate branches of physical science. To expel it from these is to drive it from its stronghold.'[1]

It was in this crusading spirit that Mill put forward his view that the principles of mathematics and of physics are alike derived from observation by means of inductive inference; and introduced James Mill's doctrine of 'inseparable association' to account for their appearing necessary. Mill hoped to do for his own age what Locke had done for the eighteenth century: to conduct a fundamental inquiry into *the sources of our knowledge*. His own general view had already been outlined in his essay on Coleridge in 1840:

... the truth, on this much debated question, lies with the school of Locke and of Bentham. ... We see no ground for believing that anything can be the object of our knowledge except our experience, and what can be inferred from our experience by the analogies of experience itself.[2]

1. *Autobiography*, p. 226.
2. *Dissertations and Discussions*, I, p. 409.

The *Logic* does not undertake the whole of the task which Mill set himself. For in the *Logic* he professes to confine himself to an inquiry into modes of inference – into the means by which we acquire such knowledge as comes to us otherwise than by single observations or perceptions of the mind.

Logic is not the science of Belief, but the science of Proof, or Evidence. In so far as belief professes to be founded on proof, the office of logic is to supply a test for ascertaining whether or not the belief is well grounded. With the claims which any proposition has to belief on the evidence of consciousness, that is, without evidence in the proper sense of the word, logic has nothing to do.[3]

The *Logic*, then, avoids (or almost succeeds in avoiding) the fundamental questions about the nature of those judgements which we make upon the objects of our immediate experience. The inquiry into such judgements is undertaken in a much later book, the *Examination of Sir William Hamilton's Philosophy*. In that work he gives his own doctrine of 'consciousness'. In the meantime, we can see the point of Mill's 'logic of experience', at least in its negative intention.

By 'experience', Mill evidently meant perceptions, memories, pleasures, pains, and other feelings : and not any so-called **noetic** experiences unassociated with sensuous content. Mill is opposed to the mystical Intuitionism of the 'Germano-Coleridgean Philosophy' and to the mathematical *a priori* Rationalism which derives from Descartes and Leibniz.

But Mill was obliged to fight a war on two fronts. In the field of mathematics and the physical sciences, his emphasis is all on experience, as against the appeal to 'necessary truth'. In the field of politics and sociology he was willing for a time to attack the doctrinaire, *a priori* methods of his father, and even to claim Coleridge as an ally. But here he found himself upon extremely dangerous ground. For an attack against Benthamism in politics had already been launched by Macaulay, in the name of *experience*. That Mill should find profit in Coleridge's political writings and none (or precious little) in Macaulay's

3. *Logic*, Introduction. The edition is the eighth, the latest.

no doubt does him credit. But it is somewhat bewildering to follow the manoeuvres by which he condemns the empiricism of Macaulay, while at the same time defending an empirical view of science. In fact, Mill never doubted his father's main premise that politics can become scientific; what was needed was an altogether new model for the science of politics; this would rescue politics from 'empiricism and unscientific surmise', and base it firmly upon the notions, not of Bacon but of Newton.[4]

This war on two fronts helps to show the peculiar nature of Mill's philosophy of experience. It is nothing if not systematic. Mill never underestimates the importance of deductive inference, or 'ratiocination', in the building up of our knowledge. He is as much concerned to preserve reasoning as to oppose theoretical Rationalism. And when, on the other hand, he attacks the Empiricists for their indifference to theories, he never fails to insist that the test of all theory lies in an appeal to experience.

The logical doctrines which I shall try to convey and to criticize in the present chapter have therefore a double aspect, experiential and systematic. The purely philosophical interest of Mill's logic is still immense. Its controversial and polemical interest is at the present time diminished, but it has not vanished. (Every age gives rise to some form of the Intuitionism which Mill opposed, and in every age it has its special appeal for those who 'by backward steps would move.') The *Logic* remains one of the greatest expressions of what, on the Continent, would be called Liberalism – meaning by a Liberal one who (in Mill's words) is 'on the movement side in philosophy, morality, and art, as well as in politics and socialities.'[5]

2. MEANING

Mill begins his treatise on logic by insisting on the necessity of a preliminary analysis of language. Of this he had been con-

4. *Autobiography*, p. 160; *Logic*, Book VI, ch. vii and ch. x.
5. *Letters*, I, p. 104 (to Lytton Bulwer).

vinced by his study of Hobbes and of Locke's 'immortal third book' of the *Essay on Human Understanding*. But in fact Mill's interest in language is not very wide. His theory is a means of dealing with analytical propositions and does not really give more than an account of the use of descriptive words and of proper names. There is no view of language as a structure embodying purely formal elements. The workings of the vital logical signs, such as *not, and, or, all, some, if – then –*, is not explained in such a way as to show their connexion with the basic principles of logic. Nor is any special syntactical account given of the terms of arithmetic and geometry. As we shall have many occasions to see, Mill's theory of language is deficient, and leads him to an incorrect view of mathematics and an inadequate view of science.

Mill writes as if words had their meanings independently of each other and of their context of utterance: as if discourse consisted in putting words together in a certain order, very much as bricks are put together in a wall. This of course will not do. The meaning of a word is the meaning that it has in its context. What, for example, does 'members' mean in the sentence 'members only admitted'? The other words in the sentence, the sentences before and after, the speaker, the place where the words are spoken, all these may have to be taken into consideration.

It is true that some words, for example technical terms, and some sentences seem to be used only in certain sorts of context; and in so far as these conditions of utterance are constant, they can, of course, be disregarded. This regularity gives rise to the common-sense view (shared by Mill) that words have a fixed proper meaning which can be learned in isolation from contexts, or in relation only to minimal contexts. But to generalize from such words is to fall into the 'Proper Meaning Superstition'.[6]

Mill begins with what he calls *general names*, i.e. descriptive words such as 'red', 'man', 'rational'. He supposes that a general name is applied anywhere and everywhere in accord-

6. See I. A. Richards, *The Philosophy of Rhetoric*, p. 11.

ance with a rule. The rule is that 'red' shall be used to describe only those things which have a certain colour quality; 'man', to describe only those things which have a certain subtle combination of properties, some perceptible at a glance, others discoverable only by prolonged observation. These necessary qualifying properties are called the *connotation* of the general name. They are not properties which a man may have and many men do have (e.g. being six feet high), but properties in the absence of which it would be improper to call the object 'a man' at all. These properties themselves have general names, e.g., a certain property in the connotation of 'man' we call 'rationality'. Now 'rationality' connotes various other properties: and of course all that 'rational' connotes is connoted by 'man' (but not *vice versa*, since there might be rational angels). To give a rule covering the connotation of 'man' is to give a verbal expression which will be substitutable for 'man' in all contexts (or rather, in those contexts where 'man' has the sense or meaning we are discussing). Such a rule is a definition of 'man' (in this sense of the word).[7]

Now the connotation of 'man' is, in a sense, the *meaning* of the word 'man'. But there is already implicit another sense of the word 'meaning'. For it is also true (according to Mill) to say that 'man' means 'Peter, Jane, John, and an indefinite number of other individuals, of whom, taken as a class, it is the name.'

This relation of 'man' to John, is called by Mill, *denotation*. The word 'man' connotes rationality and animality, and denotes Peter, Jane, and John, and any other creatures who have these properties.

Mill holds that certain words denote without connoting:

Proper names are not connotative: they denote the individuals who are called by them; but they do not indicate or imply any attributes as belonging to those individuals.[8]

7. See *Logic*, I, v (2). Mill agrees with Hobbes that the word 'red' when *first* applied, must have been applied arbitrarily, or at the choice of the speaker. 'This is red' was then a purely verbal proposition, equivalent with 'I give the name "red" to this'. But once a procedure has been adopted for the use of 'red', then 'This is red' becomes descriptive, true or false.

8. *Logic*, I, ii (5).

John is so called, perhaps, because that was the name of his father: but in speaking of John, I am not implying anything whatsoever about his father: and a man does not have to have a father called 'John' in order himself to qualify for the name. In this, proper names differ from definite descriptions: these also refer (if they refer to anything at all) to one individual. 'The first Emperor of Rome', 'the only son of John Styles', are obviously connotative and have *meaning* whether or not there is a person to whom the description applies. A proper name, on the other hand, is meaningless unless it refers to someone.

The distinction between names and descriptive phrases is no doubt an important one. We can refer to an individual by means of a predication which applies to him; or by means of a mere name or a demonstrative pronoun (this, that); and it would be sensible enough to say of both kinds of expression that they 'have denotation'. But Mill does not confine himself to general terms used in definite descriptions: he says that all general terms have denotation, even when used *as predicates;* general terms *are* 'general names'. Now when we use a general term as a predicate, we most certainly do not use it to make reference to some particular thing. 'Mill was not a great scientist' refers, of course, to Mill, but does not refer to any great scientist. *Which* great scientist could anybody suppose it refers to? Why then did Mill say that general terms, when used predicatively, 'have denotation'? Because, in the same sentence, the predicate 'was not a great scientist' *applies to* Mill; and these two quite different logical relationships are confused by Mill and are both called 'denotation'. No doubt he was misled by considering the special situation where a general term is used in a definite description. For a definite description both refers to the individual to whom the terms of the description *apply*, and (of course) describes it. Mill saw that names do their referring without any description: names merely denote – definite descriptions denote and connote. From this position he slips into saying that *all* general terms do both, thus passing over the really fundamental distinction between expressions that merely refer and expressions that merely describe.[9]

3. ANALYTICAL PROPOSITIONS

The doctrine of meaning – of denotation and connotation – is used by Mill to provide a basis for his distinction between genuine propositions and propositions merely verbal; which, in turn, leads to the distinction between real inference and merely apparent inference, a distinction absolutely fundamental to his account of deduction and induction.

The proposition 'every man is a rational creature' might be regarded, and had in fact been regarded, as conveying an insight into the real essence of a natural kind. We know which creatures are men, and we know that they are all rational: and this is seen not to be *accidental*. The proposition is universal, necessary, and certain; we know it by insight and not by observation.

Locke rejected this view. He said that such statements convey no information whatever about real essences, but only about nominal essences. They are all trifling, barely verbal, propositions. Mill avoids saying that they are trifling, but agrees that they are purely verbal; for the predicate merely repeats a part of the connotation of the subject term. An essential proposition 'either gives no information, or gives it respecting the name, not the thing.'[10]

There is a dilemma here which Mill never faces. Are we to say that analytical propositions convey *no* information, or are we to say that they convey information about words only?

In my view these analytical or essential propositions are technical expressions by which rules of definition get themselves applied in argument. There is a well-known *device*, widely employed, by which a rule of language (in these cases the definition of a descriptive term) is itself used *as a premise* in the argument. Consider the following inference:

9. See P. T. Geach, 'Subject and Predicate', *Mind*, October 1950.
10. *Logic*, I, vi (2) and (4).

John is a man, therefore he is rational.

This inference might be tested by expansion in either of two ways. We might say:

(1) 'John is a man' is asserted as true. But the word 'man' connotes the meaning of the word 'rational'. Hence we may also assert 'John is rational'.

or we might resort to a syllogism and say:

(2) All men are rational and John is a man: therefore John is rational.

Both procedures are regularly used. The first is easy enough to follow, once we realize that words are used in accordance with a definite procedure and that rules can be drawn up to cover particular points in the procedure. It is (2) that ought to puzzle us. Why should we offer as a statement of fact what is (by the very procedure of the language we are using) incapable of being false, and at best interpretable only as vain repetition?

There are two explanations to be offered. First, that a rule of inference can often be shown to depend upon other rules of inference; and the simplest way of doing this is to take the *other* rules of inference as premises and derive the dependent rule as a conclusion. And, of course, the premises and conclusion of an argument must look like propositions.[11]

The other explanation is somewhat less creditable to us all. It is often uncertain whether or not a given predicate is a part of the connotation of a subject term. (Is a unit specific gravity a defining property of water or not?) Hence in an argument we incline to the propositional form, hoping that our con-

11. The inference is itself conducted by means of rules which do not appear as premises. It is only in recent years that the real nature of this procedure has been made clear. Carnap and others have now shown that it is possible to construct a system of rules for a given language L, through the means of a quite different language, L' (the 'meta-language'). In such a system, the rules of L are nowhere used as *statements* in any discourse which also includes statements in that language.

nexion of the predicate with the subject will be accepted as a true generalization even by those who do not regard it as a proper part of the connotation.

It seems to me that, unless they are intended as empirical (in which case they are not 'essential' propositions at all) we should say that such expressions as 'All men are rational' are rules of language used as premises. We have to regard this special procedure as a device for getting the rule applied in an argument. It should be noted that even an *explicit* tautology, such as

All rational beings are rational

can be viewed in the same way: for such expressions secure the application of the rule of language that a class-name, when used as part of a subject-term, is itself a *kind* of predicate. This rule is not a definition of any particular descriptive term, but is a general rule about the construction of statements of all kinds. Its importance for logic is immense: for logic is an attempt to formulate all the *general* principles of statement-construction and inference. Our solution therefore has the advantage of applying to implicit tautologies (or essential propositions) and to explicit tautologies; and of showing the connexion between the two.

4. IMMEDIATE INFERENCE

The doctrine of merely verbal propositions is closely connected with Mill's doctrine of merely apparent inference. The exact connexion was stated by the late Reginald Jackson in the following way:

'p, therefore q' (the inference of q from p) is a merely apparent inference, where 'not – p or q' is a merely verbal proposition.[12]

Let us consider two of Mill's examples:

1. 'All men are rational, therefore no man is incapable of reason.' This is only apparent reasoning, for the proposition

12. See *An Examination of the Deductive Logic of J. S. Mill* (1941), chs. v and vi.

'Either it is not the case that all men are rational, or no man is incapable of reason' is merely verbal, and is an application of one of the rules of 'Immediate Inference'.

2. 'Socrates is a man, therefore he is a living creature.' Here 'living creature' is a part of the connotation of 'man', and hence the proposition 'Either Socrates is not a man or he is a living creature' is merely verbal.

In such cases, Mill says that the inference is apparent and not real. We are not proving our conclusion: but only 'appeal-, ing to another mode of wording it'; the conclusion contains no new truth, nothing which was not already asserted in the premises. In cases of genuine inference, on the other hand, 'we set out from known truths, to arrive at others really distinct from them.'[13]

As we have seen, there is a sense in which Mill's objections are perfectly valid. Tautologies cannot ever justify a transition to a *new* proposition: the conclusion drawn cannot be *distinct from* the premises, cannot be (in this sense) anything more than a new expression. This is not to belittle the importance of the transition to a new expression: for the new expression may be needed to show a part of the meaning of the premises which would otherwise pass unnoticed. We should add that the rules we are applying are objective conventions, not private whims: that these rules have to be *learned*. When I meet a term whose connotation is incompletely known by me, a 'necessary proposition' which interprets it will show me a fact about language which 'is to me as much an external fact as a presentation of the senses can be.'[14]

This is seen, of course, if instead of a necessary proposition the rule itself is formulated. That the word 'man' connotes animal is in no sense an 'apparent proposition'. It is a hard fact.

Granted that immediate inferences do not enable us to arrive at a conclusion distinct from the premises, are we to

13. *Logic*, II, i (3).
14. *Examination of Sir William Hamilton's Philosophy*, 2nd ed., p. 371.

agree with Mill that they are not really entitled to be called inferences at all? This is a matter in part of choice of terms and can best be settled after we have discussed the more elaborate forms of deduction known as syllogisms.

5. THE SYLLOGISM

(a) Is the Syllogism a Question-begging Argument?

The whole of the second book of the *Logic* is devoted to the distinction between real and apparent inference. It is not, as the arrangement of the books might suggest, an independent study of deduction, or 'ratiocination'. For in the first chapter we are concerned with 'Inference or Reasoning in General', and induction is introduced as being 'without doubt, a process of real inference'. And in the subsequent chapters the formal development of the syllogism is a mere perfunctory outline. What concerns Mill is the great question whether the syllogism itself be real or merely apparent inference.[15]

Mill begins by recalling the view of former logicians that 'a syllogism is vicious if there be anything more in the conclusion than was assumed (asserted?) in the premises'; that 'a syllogism can prove no more than is involved in the premises.' If this were true, it should (he thinks) lead us to regard the syllogism as useless and frivolous and not as a means by which we infer new truths. And Mill explicitly dissociates himself from this view. He holds that the syllogism *contains* genuine inference to new truth, although he states 'that the argument from the premises of a syllogism to its conclusion is merely apparent inference.'[16]

Where then is the genuine inference to be found? Mill answers: in the generalization which leads us to formulate the universal premise. When we have formulated this premise 'the inference is finished'. This inference is, of course, not deductive but inductive. Induction is the only valid method of inference to new truth.

15. See Jackson, *op. cit.*   16. See II, iii (1) and (2).

Let us first consider Mill's *negative* thesis. We cannot draw a syllogistic conclusion r, from known premises p and q, by pure deduction, unless the proposition 'not (p and q) or r' is a merely apparent proposition, or tautology.

It would be difficult to over-emphasize the importance, in philosophy, of this thesis. In its contemporary form it is the view that in all valid deduction, the connexion between premises and conclusion is tautological; that wherever p necessarily implies q, the transition from p to q never gives us new truth. And the thesis had the same broad implication for Mill himself: for he held that all valid ratiocination can be expressed in syllogistical form. The thesis which Mill thus indirectly applied to all deduction is to-day regarded by many philosophers as the key to the understanding of all forms of necessary connexion. Indeed their only quarrel with Mill is that they still speak of deductive *inference* from known premises, while he refused the name of inference to any form of pure deduction.

Let us consider the celebrated *Dictum de omni et nullo*, the maxim on which the syllogisms in First Figure rest. The maxim is: 'That whatever can be affirmed (or denied) of a term distributed, may be affirmed (or denied) of whatever is included in the distributed term.' In the following example the minor term is a class-name:

> All merchants are prosperous,
> All salesmen are merchants;
> All salesmen are prosperous.

Given the pair of premises, what exactly does the dictum permit us to extract from them? We are now to assert that somebody is prosperous – but who? Only salesmen, because it is only salesmen who have been stated to fall within the class of merchants. In other words, we are merely permitted to state that *salesmen* belong to the class of the prosperous – the class to which they (in common with all other merchants) have already been assigned in the major premise. We cannot say anything whatever about shopkeepers or stockbrokers. It is clear enough that we gain in our conclusion only a new expression for something already said in other language in the premises. And this is admirably shown in the Venn diagrams, where, having plotted our two premises, we see our conclusion by a mere re-direction of attention: it has already been plotted on the diagram.

Mill also considers in detail a celebrated syllogism in which the minor premise concerns a particular individual:

> All men are mortal,
> Socrates is a man;
> Socrates is mortal.

Here, again, we are permitted to infer that somebody is mortal. But who? Only a particular member of the class of men, all of whom have already been consigned to mortality in the major premise. But here Mill *objects:* we could not know that all men are mortal unless we had first made sure that Socrates is himself mortal.

The general principle, instead of being given as evidence of the particular case, cannot itself be taken for true without exception, until every shadow of doubt which could affect any case comprised with it, is dispelled by evidence *aliunde.*

He concludes that

no reasoning from generals to particulars can, as such, prove anything, since from a general principle we cannot infer any particulars, but those which the principle itself assumes to be known.

There are two points in this objection. First that the universal premise could not possibly be *true* unless the conclusion were true. This is, of course, the case in virtue of the *minor premise* which assigns Socrates to the class which forms the subject of the universal premise. So that either the conclusion is true or the premises cannot both be true.

But Mill is saying something more than this: he is saying that the major premise could not be known to be true unless the conclusion were already *known not to be false.* This is another matter altogether, and we need to make clear what we mean by *inference* as distinct from *implication*.

Strictly speaking, no inference takes place at all where we merely note a relation of implication between premises and conclusion. 'If wishes were horses, then beggars would ride' does not pretend to establish the conclusion as true. In order to do this we must be in a position to assert the premise as true: 'Wishes are horses, therefore beggars do ride.'

(b) The Universal Premise

We have seen that 'not (p and q) or r' shows us a connexion between premises and conclusion, which is a necessary condition for the validity of a deduction. But we cannot actually infer our conclusion as true, unless we can assert our premises as true. If both premises were *singular* propositions we might claim that mere observation enabled us to assert them. If both were 'Some ——' propositions, we might say that successive observations enabled us to assert them. But in the syllogism at least one premise must be *universal*. Hence the complete understanding of the syllogism depends upon an understanding of the procedures by which we establish the truth of universal premises. And the question Mill raises is, 'Can I come to know the truth of *the universal premise* without actually knowing the truth of the conclusion?'

Mill first suggests that the universal premise contains the results of particular observations.

Now, all which man can observe are individual cases. From these all general truths must be drawn, and into these they may again be resolved; for a general truth is but an aggregate of particular truths; a comprehensive expression, by which an indefinite number of individual facts are affirmed or denied at once.

But is the general proposition a conjunction of singular propositions, re-expressed in a convenient abbreviation? Clearly this will not do. As we have seen, Mill says 'all men' *denotes* all men; but the denotation is not in any sense an *indication* of the individual men; nor is there any means of resolving a statement about 'all men' into a conjunction of truths about individual men. It must therefore be misleading to call 'All men are mortal' a re-expression of an aggregate of particular truths.

Mill saw this clearly enough. His first account of the universal premise is that it is itself a conclusion inferred from a limited selection of the cases which fall under it.

Generalization is not a process of mere naming, it is also a process of inference. From instances which we have observed, we feel warranted in concluding that what we found true in those instances, holds in all similar ones, past, present, and future, however numerous they may be. We then, by that valuable contrivance of language which enables us to speak of many as if they were one, record all that we have observed, together with all that we infer from our observations, in one concise expression; and have thus only one proposition, instead of an endless number, to remember or to communicate. The results of many observations and inferences, and instructions for making innumerable inferences in unforeseen cases, are compressed into one short sentence.

Having made our generalization, our genuine inference is finished. When we then make a new observation and say:

The Duke of Wellington is a man, therefore he is mortal,

it is misleading (according to Mill) to say that we are making a new inference; our knowledge that the Duke is mortal comes from the knowledge which we have already expressed in general notation in our universal proposition. This is done before we begin to syllogize: in the syllogism we are registering a new case, not coming to know a new fact.

The first account, then, is that the universal premise is inferred from individual cases, but goes beyond them and covers an indefinitely numerous class. But Mill is not satisfied with this account. He notices that animals act as if they made inferences without ever employing general propositions. Human beings do so too:

All our earliest inferences are of this nature. From the first dawn of intelligence we draw inferences, but years elapse before we learn the use of general language.

The village matron who is asked to diagnose a child's illness, 'pronounces on the evil and its remedy simply on the recollection and authority of what she accounts the similar case of her Lucy. We all, where we have no definite maxims to steer by, guide ourselves in the same way.'

And many great intellects have been able to choose means to their ends 'without being able to give sufficient reason for what they did', i.e., to express the general propositions which they were applying.

These considerations led Mill to a second account of inductive inference. It is essentially inference from certain observed particulars *to other particulars of the same class*.[17]

The stage by which we express a general rule determining the class is thus seen not to be essential to the validity of the argument. It is useful for communicating our views to others; highly useful to ourselves as an aid to memory. But it is no real part of the argument: inductive inference could and does proceed without it.

All inference is from particulars to particulars. General propositions are merely registers of such inferences already made, and short formulae for making more. The major premise of a syllogism ... is a formula of this description; and the conclusion is not an inference drawn *from* the formula, but an inference drawn *according* to the formula; the real logical antecedent or premise being the particular facts from which the general proposition was collected by induction.

On this view, a factual syllogism would be no less valid if it omitted the 'memorandum' or general proposition altogether:

Peter, John, and a limited number of other individuals were all men and all mortal;
The Duke of Wellington is a man;
Therefore the Duke of Wellington is mortal.

Can we accept this as a complete account of the syllogism? Manifestly not: it is only because we are prepared to adopt the

17. *Logic*, II, iii (4). The first account of the general proposition is given in paragraph 3 of the same chapter.

first of these propositions as a rule or formula for making new particular inferences, that the syllogistical conclusion is one which we are prepared to assert. As Mill himself says, the inference must be made according to the formula. In a full account of the syllogism, therefore, the formula cannot be omitted.

(c) The Syllogism: Two Stages in the Inference

We return therefore to Mill's first account of the universal premise. Is Mill correct in saying that this premise could not be *known* to be true, unless we already knew the conclusion to be true?

It is obviously the case that the premises could not *both* be known to be true unless we already knew the conclusion to be true. We could not know that all M is P and also know that S is an M, unless we already knew that S was also a P. However, Mill very frequently omits all reference to the *minor* premise in his discussion, and what he really has in mind in insisting on the value and use of the syllogism, is the point in which the syllogism does indeed differ from an immediate inference.

For the universal premise in any syllogism is such that it can be known (in some sense of 'know') to be true, although a given conclusion, together with its appropriate minor premise, were altogether unknown. We can know the general rule without knowing all the cases that fall under it: and this in spite of the fact that, given a minor premise introducing a particular case, or group of cases, the major could not be *true* unless the appropriate conclusion were true.

Our 'knowledge' of this universal premise derives from observed particulars which fall under it, but what we claim to know goes beyond these particulars and embraces all of a given description. Mill sometimes says that we know the examined instances and resolve to make use of them as a rule for making further singular propositions; and he thus raises doubts as to whether we can really be said to *know* the universal proposition in the sense of 'knowing' appropriate to singular propositions. But at all events this 'knowledge' is what is essential to our inferring the conclusion.

In making new inductions in this way we certainly add to our knowledge. The conclusions we draw are in no sense re-expressions of what is stated in the evidence. Always something more is asserted in the conclusions than is contained in the evidence. This then is the constructive stage in the syllogism. But Mill says that in adding our minor premise and drawing the appropriate conclusion we are merely deciphering, or re-expressing, what is already expressed in the major premise: 'The inference is finished when we have asserted that all men are mortal.'

It seems to me perfectly just to distinguish these two stages of inference. But it is no less important to see the difference between the second stage as it occurs in immediate inference and the second stage as it occurs in the syllogism. By inductive inference I reach the proposition 'All acids turn litmus red.' To make the deduction 'Therefore some acids do so' is valid enough, but we can learn nothing from it except the purely verbal rule about 'all' and 'some'. If, instead, I make the observation that what I have in this bottle does not turn litmus red, *I have introduced a third term* and can at once conclude that the complex properties of acidity do not belong to this liquid. 'The use of the syllogism is in truth no other than the use of general propositions.' The key to the understanding of the syllogism is the minor premise, i.e., the relation between general propositions and singular or less general propositions which fall under their subject or predicate term. Mill somewhat obscures this by his neglect of the minor premise. It is only in virtue of this premise that the connexion between the major and the conclusion is tautological: and it is because I can know the universal without knowing all the minor premises that together analyse its subject-term that I can know the universal without already knowing the conclusion.

In this exposition Mill has raised fundamental issues for the first time in the history of logic, and it would be superfluous to object that he is not able to solve them all.

(1) Philosophers are still divided upon the question of the nature of general factual propositions. F. P. Ramsey, the Cambridge logician, boldly proposed not to call them propositions at all: and this would seem to be the natural development of Mill's hints that they occur in syllogisms, not as premises, but as formulae according to which particular conclusions are derived.

(2) Few philosophers to-day would wish to avoid calling deduction a kind of *inference*. For even if we accept Mill's view that such inference is valid only where the connexion between premises and conclusion is tautological, we may still insist on its historical rights. Moreover, pure deductive inference serves a vital purpose in communication – the explication of the meaning of the statements being made, the terms being used. To know what an expression means is to know the procedures for its use in connexion with actual situations, and with all the other signs in the language. So that *understanding* an expression is not an event which takes place at a moment: it is a process which is never finally ended. Deductive inferences assist this process by providing models for the correct use of expressions.

Let us then admit two kinds of inference, deductive and inductive. Whenever we speak of inference we should strictly mean an argument which leads to the assertion of a conclusion. But the primers of deductive logic are naturally concerned to formulate the implications which hold between propositions, and are therefore inclined to be content with setting out a purely conditional argument: 'If p and q, then r.' Upon such an implication, an inference *might* be based, but this is not itself an inference. Mill addressed himself to this missing stage: he showed that every syllogism with a *factual* conclusion must rest upon the inductive inference contained in the major premise. We shall not at the moment pursue further the nature of inductive inference, but shall consider in the next section those systems of reasoning which derive, or seem to derive, conclusions from *non-factual premises*.

6. ARITHMETIC

(a) Mill's Rejection of Nominalism

Mill's discussion of the syllogism hardly touches the greatest triumphs of Reason. These are to be found in 'Demonstrative Sciences', that is, in mathematics and logic. Here deduction begins with premises which are themselves supposed to be known *a priori*, that is to say, to be necessary truths not based upon experience.

It might seem obvious that these premises should be treated by Mill in the same way as the 'essential propositions'; that is to say, they might be shown to be merely verbal. This he resolutely refuses to do. It is impossible, he thinks, to regard such statements as '2 + 1 = 3' as merely 'a statement that mankind have agreed to use the name three as a sign exactly equivalent to two and one.' This Nominalism will not explain the applications of arithmetic and algebra in empirical propositions. 'All numbers must be numbers of something; there is no such thing as numbers in the abstract. *Ten* must mean ten bodies, or ten sounds, or ten beatings of the pulse.' And in more tortuous language he expresses the same conviction to the students of St Andrews University:

> It is chiefly from mathematics we realize the fact that there actually is a road to truth by means of reasoning; that anything real, and which will be found true when tried, can be arrived at by a mere operation of the mind.

It was this firm conviction that led Mill to hold his celebrated doctrine that the axioms of arithmetic and geometry are laws of nature known to us by experience.[18]

18. See *Logic*, II, v (Geometry) and vi, and III, xxii and xxiv. Also *Address to the Students of St Andrews University*, p. 46.

The substance of this paragraph appeared in the *Proceedings of the Aristotelian Society*, 1947, and is here reproduced with permission of the Editor.

(b) Outline of Mill's Views of Arithmetic

Number is a property of groups of objects; it is the characteristic way in which the group is made up of, and may be separated into, parts. Number-properties can be seen and felt and we identify them by general names. Addition and subtraction, multiplication and division, are physical operations. We can, for instance, take one object from a group of three, and the result is a group of two and a group of one: and these two groups look and feel different from the original group of three. This operation can be carried out on any triad, whether of pebbles, men, printed marks, etc., and the result is in every case the same. If we have already assigned the general names '1', '2', '3', to denote anything having the sensible appearance that such groups present to us, then we discover by repeated observation that the property of being physically divisible into a one and a two is always associated with the property of being a three. This property is therefore incorporated into the connotation of these number-signs, in much the same way that the property of being composed of oxygen and hydrogen is incorporated into the connotation of the sign 'water'. So that, from the statement 'Here is a group of three' we infer 'Here is a group that can be divided into a two and a one.' By similar procedures we discover all the different 'modes of formation' of the different number-groups, and so can establist systematic *definitions of the numbers*. These are given in terms of the operations upon other numbers.

But the series of numerals we use is indefinitely extensible: so that we cannot exhaust the possible experiments along these lines. It is a further stage of observation to notice that in fact the equations we formulate are all illustrative of certain general laws. The only laws given by Mill are three *axioms of equality:* these are not in fact sufficient to ensure that the arithmetical operations are all carried out as we expect them to be: but some set of general axioms is evidently possible and necessary. By our inductive knowledge of these axioms, Mill says, we are able to predict the results of operations upon numbers which we have never met with in experience.

The truth of these laws and of the laws underlying the definitions is known by observation and induction. They have the status of uniformities which have been found to hold in nature and exceptions to them are possible, even if not clearly conceivable by us. It is, for example, possible that I might find a group of three pebbles which did not divide into a two and a one. And it is possible that our laws of arithmetic might not have held at all. If we are unable to conceive this, it is because our minds are limited by the narrowness of our experience – by the inseparable associations we have in fact encountered.

(c) Two Important Presuppositions

In fact, Mill says, we find that the axioms and definitions of arithmetic are 'true of all objects whatever'. But here he becomes cautious, for this seems to prove too much. He goes on to introduce an important qualification or condition: and there is another condition, no less important, implicit in his whole account of arithmetical laws. I will first discuss the implicit condition.

The laws of arithmetic are laws of nature, but not causal laws. They are principles of co-existence and not of temporal sequence. When I drive three cows into a field where there are five already, the resulting group of eight is not a consequence in the temporal sense: it is there the moment the two groups coalesce. If we allow time to intervene, then causal laws may operate in such a way as to upset the calculated result. In a year's time, for instance, there might be seven cows or nine cows or no cows at all: and we can imagine cows multiplying or disappearing in shorter intervals than that. In making the calculation we abstract from all the causal properties of cows: hence our inference must be understood as dealing only with instantaneous associations and dissociations of physical groups.

It is usual to see in this doctrine – that the laws of arithmetic are non-temporal – a dim (but welcome) recognition by Mill that mathematics is not a branch of physics. We can see that the net result of the doctrine is that the laws of arithmetic hold only if we assume that the groups we are dealing with *remain stable*. This assumption, then, is implicitly recognized by Mill.

The other qualification he himself introduces with the help of an example. He says (very justly) that if I were to add one pound troy to one pound avoirdupois, the result is not two pounds of either, or of any weight. Why not? Because the units I am adding do not satisfy the first of the axioms: they are not really equal. And Mill says very solemnly that it is a condition of applying arithmetic correctly, that all the numbers be numbers of the same or equal units.

I suggest that by 'equal' Mill really means no more than 'all members of the class to be counted'. If this interpretation is correct, Mill is here introducing a fundamental condition which always attaches to applied arithmetic: the calculations are not reliable unless the objects are first *correctly counted*. To mistake a pound troy for a pound avoirdupois is comparable with mistaking a bullock for a cow when it is cows (not cattle) that are to be counted. This is one way of getting a miscount. There are many others which Mill passes over in complete silence.

We have then two fundamental conditions which must be satisfied if arithmetical calculations are to be used for inferring empirical propositions: the systems counted must remain stable and the counting must be correct. And I think that it is statements made under these conditions that Mill calls 'purely numerical inferences'. Given these conditions, he says, the laws of arithmetic are exactly true of all objects whatever without mixture of hypothesis.

(d) Comment: The Application of Arithmetic

In attempting to apply an arithmetical rule, are we ever led to regard the rule itself as *overthrown*? In the case of an empirical science there are definitions which could be overthrown by evidence gathered in attempting to apply them in their proper field. For there are definitions which are founded upon, and which embody, experimental generalizations: and if new evidence appears which must be accepted as genuine and which contradicts the generalization, then the definition is rendered useless and mischievous and is abandoned. Could this happen in the case of arithmetical definitions or axioms?

Suppose that I count the cows in one meadow and find that there are 25; and count the cows in another meadow and find that there are 26; and that the cows are then all driven into the same field. I now calculate that there are 51 cows altogether. But it might happen that, on making a new count, I find that there are only 50, or that there are 52 cows. And we can imagine that the discrepant result would be obtained however often the whole procedure is repeated from the beginning; and that it is obtained in counting other objects besides cows. But it seems clear that no evidence collected in this way would ever be admitted as evidence against the principle that $25 + 26 = 51$. And this, in one sense of the words, is to say that it is *inconceivable* that the principle should be overthrown by such evidence. And if such evidence cannot falsify or weaken the principle, then it cannot serve to verify it or help to establish it either. The principles of arithmetic are not based upon generalizations about the results of counting and adding and recounting.

What, then, do we say if (as sometimes happens) the calculated result is not the same as the result of a new count? We say either that the counting must have been incorrect, or that the group has not, after all, remained stable throughout our operations. In other words, we explain the discrepancy by reference to the failure of one or other of the two general conditions which Mill himself half acknowledges, and tries (as I think) to formulate in his account of 'purely numerical' propositions.

What Mill hoped to define in his 'purely numerical' propositions were statements about the numbers of actual objects, which should have the absolute certainty which we associate with the principles of arithmetic. It was necessary to exclude from his class, therefore, propositions which could not be relied upon, either because of physical changes in the groups, or because of oddities in the counting. But *all* statements about the numbers of actual objects are made on the basis of somebody's counting, and are made about objects exposed, for however short a time, to the hazards of change and chance. We can never in fact be *certain* that a given proposition fulfils the conditions required by Mill for absolute certainty: hence we can never be absolutely certain that a given proposition is 'purely numerical' in his sense. All that we can do is to take precautions which will tend to increase the probability that a given statement is 'purely numerical': but no care will ever guarantee that a statement about the numbers of actual objects in a group is true. The only absolutely certain numerical propositions are those of pure arithmetic, and our 'knowledge' of these is of just the same kind as the knowledge we have of the definitions of a system. For what the principles of arithmetic give us are the connotations of the different arithmetical expressions. It is true that we should not call these 'numbers' or 'functions of numbers', unless they also had denotation. But the identification of what the numerical expressions denote is itself a procedure carried out under certain physical conditions: and error may occur.

(e) Could Arithmetic Fail to Apply?

What is implied in Mill's doctrine is this: If the world were different in some (perhaps not clearly conceivable) way, the laws of arithmetic would not hold of objects. He recognized that this consequence of his views was highly paradoxical and likely to be rejected out of hand by most philosophers.

What Mill has in mind has nothing to do with changing the names of numbers (or the signs for them): he is concerned with a change in part of their connotations – in the axioms and definitions which correlate the different modes of formation of the several numbers. He supposes, I think, that there is an original part of the connotation which does not change – one of the manners in which an agglomeration is made up of parts (or members) and may be separated into parts (see III, xxiv, 5). In the case of the triad, he may be thinking of the fact that it consists of *three groups of one*. By reference to this original part of the full connotation of '3', we identify a triad. Might we find that it cannot be separated into a group of one and a group of two, as its full arithmetical connotation implies? This, he thinks, *could happen*. For, as he says in Book II, the definition '3 = 2 + 1' presupposes an arithmetical theorem (or rather, an empirical generalization) 'that collections of objects exist, which while they impress the senses thus, $^\circ_\circ{}^\circ$, may be separated into two parts thus, $^{\circ\circ}$ $^\circ$.'

It is, I think, only by this appeal to the senses that we can give any meaning at all to the notion that the equivalence of different 'modes of formation' of the different numbers is an *accidental* matter. For it is only because their members happen to be arranged in different patterns that the two groups are distinguishable. They are certainly not distinguishable *in number*, that is to say, from the point of view of a person engaged *in counting*. Mill wants to say that a group may be identifiable as a triad, in virtue of being arranged thus, $^\circ_\circ{}^\circ$, *whether or not* it can be re-arranged thus, $^{\circ\circ}$ $^\circ$. But have such sensible patterns anything whatever to do with the application of arithmetic? Surely they cannot have. For all sorts of things can be counted which do not 'impress the senses' in any way. Locke says: 'Number applies itself to men, angels, actions, thoughts; everything that either doth exist or can be imagined', and Mill often takes an equally comprehensive (and optimistic) view.

It seems to me, therefore, that the sensible appearances of the groups of objects that we count are entirely irrelevant to the application of arithmetic by counting, and that the so-called 'uniformities of co-existence' with which we are concerned are no more than a feature of the calculus and of the procedures we employ in applying it. They are to be found wherever our numbers have been correctly applied to stable objects: and, if they fail, it is a sign that the counting is incorrect, or the objects unstable.

7. GEOMETRY

(a) *Outline of Mill's View*

There exist in the visible world, points, lines, plane surfaces, circles, squares: these are properties and relations of actual physical things, and of the images of them which we form with such notable accuracy. From our observations of these properties we form approximate generalizations, such as: that if two lines are straight then they enclose no space; that if a body is round, all the lines drawn from the centre to its edge are equal. From these generalizations we build up the technical definitions of 'circle', 'point', 'straight line', etc. Such definitions are based on experience of the physical world in much the same way as the definitions of chemical substances. There is no question, therefore, that they have application. But in constructing them we introduce an element of abstraction, simplification, and idealization. We define a straight line as having no thickness: the straight lines we can identify all have thickness, but for the purposes of measuring distances or angles, we usually overlook it. It is, therefore, more convenient to adopt the idealized definition. Similarly, we define a circle in such a way that its radii are equal, in spite of the fact that the measurement of all round bodies shows only that the radii can be very nearly equal. Our definition is

true of all circles, so far as it is true of any one: but it is not exactly true of any circle; it is only nearly true: so nearly that no error of any importance ... will be incurred by feigning it to be exactly true.

This feigning is a well-understood feature of the application of geometry: 'We formally announce in the definitions that we intend to proceed on this plan.'

In spite of this precaution, the truths of geometry have been supposed to be absolutely precise, certain, and necessary. Mill holds that they are never precise or accurate, and could not be so simply because the definitions of geometry cannot be taken literally. (A straight line with *no* thickness is nonsense.)

They are, however, certain in their approximate acceptation. For the observations upon which they rest extend to all kinds of measurable objects, and have in fact been supported by all correct (approximate) measurements since observation began.

What of their necessity? The theorems follow by logical necessity once the definitions are granted: but the definitions and axioms themselves are (of course) not necessary in this sense. Their necessity is, indeed, merely our subjective feeling that we cannot conceive any alternatives to them. Like an isolated and unreflective people, we cannot conceive exchange value except in terms of our own currency.

(b) Comment

Mill rejects traditional Nominalism on the grounds that it fails to show how the definitions and laws of geometry apply to the world. What distinguishes a calculus for geometry from a mere sign-language is the fact that 'straight lines', 'circles', can be used in empirical statements, such as 'This is a straight line', 'This is a circle'. And the link which connects the calculus with our empirical statements is the procedure of measurement. We have found by measurement that if the sides of a triangle are equal then the angles are also equal; that the three interior angles of a triangle are equal to two right angles, etc. Mill insists on the unbroken regularity with which such results have been confirmed by approximate measurements; and holds that we have based our definitions of 'triangle' and 'angle' on these results. To the original connotation of the word, presumably a visible shape, we add all these relational properties, simply because we have never met anything that looked triangular of which these general laws failed to hold. Logical analysis has reduced these definitions to an elegant and economical system. Therefore to *deduce* from 'This is a triangle', the further theorems about it, is a highly safe ratiocination. But the new truths we reach are applications of the inductive generalizations which now appear as axioms or definitions in the system.

This view over-simplifies: for if the definitions and first

principles of geometry were based on experience *in the same way* as our definition of 'man' or 'water', then they would be liable to be overthrown by new observation. Can this happen in the case of definitions of 'straight line', 'triangle', etc.?

It cannot happen. Because what we now mean by *correct* measurement is one which conforms to these definitions. And incorrect measurement is, of course, unable to establish an exception to the principle. Suppose that I measure the sides of a triangle and find them to be equal, and proceed to measure the angles and find them unequal, what do I do? I say that *either* my measurements have not all been correct, *or* the figure has changed during the course of the measurements. I say that, provided the figure remains stable, my measurements cannot all have been correct, because I do not regard the operation of measuring sides as independent of the operation of measuring angles. Each is a check upon the other. I can, of course, have evidence *against* the correctness of one set of measurements, which is independent of my view of the other set. But to prove either to be correct, I must consider both. This is a matter of procedure, and it is *not* the procedure we should adopt in discussing whether a liquid having the physical properties of water has, or does not have, the chemical properties. For here the ascertainment of the physical properties is, as a matter of procedure, independent of the ascertainment of the chemical properties. In the case of a triangle there is no such independence: there is, therefore, no procedure for identifying an exception to the rule that an equilateral triangle has equal angles. This is a perfectly definite sense in which an exception is inconceivable.

This argument must not be taken to suggest that the applications of geometry depend upon some kind of trick. There are actually cases where there seems to be a discrepancy between angles and sides; but in such cases we are normally able to find independent evidence that the measurement has been wrong or that the object measured has been unstable. This is, of course, a generalization from the facts: and Mill was quite right in saying that a wealth of evidence stands in support of our principles of geometry. We have indeed found that we can apply them successfully. My point is not that exceptions do occur which cannot be explained, but simply that if they did occur we should still say that they must be explicable in the one way or the other.

8. THE NATURE OF LOGICAL TRUTHS

(a) Logical Necessity

Logic is 'the science of Proof, or Evidence' and *The System of Logic* is concerned with the methods of inference used in the various sciences – physical and psychological, mathematical and moral. But we have also to consider that logic is itself an enquiry, employing its own methods of inference; and is a branch of knowledge regarded by many philosophers as the most certain, and by some philosophers as the most complete, of all branches of knowledge. We must, therefore, examine here the sources and nature of our knowledge of logic itself. This Mill did in his *Examination of Hamilton* (Chaps. vi and xviii–xxiii) and in certain controversial chapters in the *Logic*.

Mill considers as examples of fundamental logical truths, the three laws of thought: Identity, Excluded Middle, and Non-contradiction; and (in another place) the *Dictum de Omni et Nullo*.

What strikes us about these laws is that they seem to be necessarily, and not accidentally, true. The statement that *all propositions are either true or false*, seems to be necessary in the same sense as a proposition in arithmetic or geometry. It is not like *all animals are either male or female*, which is universally true and may have the necessity of a definition. This is not necessary in the mathematical sense because we can easily imagine that different definitions would have been needed to describe a different world.

Mill examines this notion of necessity and decides that to say a proposition is necessary is to say that any contrary to it is inconceivable. He distinguishes two senses of the word.

(i) A proposition may be such that we cannot conceive any contrary of it to be *true:* any contrary is *incredible.* (ii) A proposition may be such that no contrary of it can be represented to the mind as a *possible* state of affairs. Mill holds that it is the second sense that is relevant to the nature of logical necessity:

We cannot represent anything to ourselves as at once being something, and not being it; as at once having, and not having, a given attribute.

It is to be noticed that this is, on the face of it, a psychological statement: there is something (A and not-A) which we are *unable to represent* to ourselves. Is this not, perhaps, a contingent limitation? Mill wishes to strengthen his first statement, but he does so by a further psychological proposition. A contradiction, he says:

is not only inconceivable to us, but we cannot conceive that it could be made conceivable.[19]

Mill regards the inconceivability of a direct contradiction as 'primordial': nothing can make me conceive an object both white and not white. But how is it that I cannot conceive an object red and not coloured, or an object both white and red? Mill argues that these inconceivabilities are derivative: *red* and *coloured* cannot be separated in representation because they have never in fact been separated in my experience. From the idea of *red* my mind inevitably passes to the idea of *colour*, and hence by a primordial incapacity cannot proceed to *not-coloured*. Again, whatever in my experience is red is not white: but from not-white I cannot pass to white: hence my incapacity to combine red and white.

The epithet 'primordial' seems to suggest that our incapacity to represent simple contradictions is *innate*. But elsewhere Mill hesitates to affirm that this is an original part of our mental constitution.[20]

19. See *Examination,* ch. vi.
20. *Examination,* p. 418. For Mill, as for Locke, there could be no question of innate principles: but neither Locke nor Mill wish to deny that the *tabula rasa* has innate capacities.

As for the other inconceivabilities, they are held to rest upon inseparable association in all our experience. The Law of Inseparable Association (constant conjunction without contrary associations), invented by James Mill, is held to be 'the key to the phenomenon of inconceivability', and hence of logical necessity. (Just as uniform association had been taken by Hume to be the key to the problem of causal necessity.)

This psychological account of logical necessity might give rise to different views of the nature and status of the propositions of logic.

(b) Psychologism

We might say: The principles of logic are binding upon all discourse because whenever we violate them we are describing in language a state of affairs which we are unable to represent to ourselves in thought. In fact, we often make use of expressions which, upon analysis, we can see to be contradictions. It is a question therefore whether we ever really understood the expressions when we used them: presumably we did not. The study and application of the precepts and rules of logic help us to keep discourse within the bounds of what we can understand.

In Chapter xx of the *Examination*, Mill allows himself to write as though this were a complete account of logic. He says that logic is inseparable from psychology, and that the only way to understand the validity of logical rules (such as the Square of Opposition) is to study the psychology of our beliefs. Logic

is a part, or branch, of Psychology; differing from it, on the one hand, as a part differs from the whole, and on the other, as an Art differs from a Science. Its theoretic grounds are wholly borrowed from Psychology, and include as much of that science as is required to justify the rules of the art.

He, therefore, accepts Hamilton's view of the province of logic which makes it a collection of precepts or rules for thinking, grounded on a scientific investigation of the requisites of valid thought.[21]

This proposal for the complete psychologizing of logic must surely end by abandoning altogether the claim that logic settles questions of validity of arguments. For in what way could an enquiry into our habits of belief have any bearing on their truth or falsity? The view that we accept the law of non-contradiction only because we find it impossible to think a contradiction, seems to allow no way back, through any psychological investigation, to the statement that contradictions do not exist in nature.

(c) Logical Truths are Inductive

Fortunately Mill also puts forward a different view as to the nature of logical principles.

We might say: These principles are binding because they are inductions resting upon past experience; and because that experience is all-pervasive. The test of the *validity* of logical principles lies, not in their inconceivableness, but in the uniformity of experience.

In such cases the inconceivability of the negative, if real, is accounted for by the experience; and why . . . should the truth be tested by the inconceivability, when we can go farther back for proof – namely, to the experience itself?[22]

This view is an extension to logic of Mill's account of mathematical truths. The laws of logic and mathematics are natural laws of co-existence: they are assimilated to the laws

21. *Examination*, pp. 388–9. See also two remarkable letters written by Mill to W. G. Ward, one in 1849 and the other in 1859. In the former, Mill says that perhaps two straight lines can enclose a space, for all that we cannot conceive it. 'Our not being able to conceive a thing is no evidence of the thing being in itself impossible.' In the later letter, Mill explains that where (in the *Logic*) he has spoken of inferences following *necessarily* from their premises, he means simply that the reasoning is *conclusive*, and this is a psychological matter. *Letters*, I, pp. 146 and 227.

22. *Logic*, II, vii (4).

governing Natural Kinds and the connotations of empirical terms. Just as we observe that certain properties (e.g. volume and mass) always occur together in what we call a material substance, and others with these, in an animal or in a species of flower; so we also observe that the property of having three straight sides always occurs along with the property of having three interior angles equal to two right angles. And, more generally still, we observe that what is red is always not-white and that what is not-white is never also white. Even the laws of syllogism are interpreted as laws of co-existence:

'Things which co-exist with the same thing, co-exist with one another'; 'a thing which co-exists with another thing, with which other a third thing does not co-exist, is not co-existent with that third thing.'[23]

All that distinguishes the so-called Necessary Truths of mathematics and logic from other laws of co-existence is their all-pervasiveness and the absence from experience of anything which could even suggest a contrary instance.

(c) *Comment*

This view assures us of the *truth* of logical principles, but makes next to nothing of their alleged necessity, which (for Mill) is purely subjective. Logical principles will, of course, have the same necessity as any analytical statement, e.g. 'All men are rational'. But plainly the necessity of propositions of logic and mathematics is something more than this. As we have seen, there is no procedure for saying that a figure has three straight sides, all equal, but not equal interior angles. Similarly, there is no procedure for identifying an object as red and yet not coloured. For the question of its redness is not independent of the procedure by which we determine whether or not it is coloured. And when we pass to purely formal principles of logic, the overlapping of procedures is even more striking. We cannot decide that x has the property A by any procedure which will not also settle the question whether or not x has the property not-A. An object both A and not-A

23. *Logic*, II, ii (3).

is *inconceivable* because it is excluded by our fundamental procedures of description and predication.

I conclude, therefore, that it is false to say that the propositions of logic are necessary merely in the sense that they mark the limits of our imagination, or that they are definitions based upon all-pervasive features of experience. It is, however, possible to find in Mill's writings traces of a theory which pays more serious attention to language as a structure. I shall build up this theory with the help of various hints given in the *Logic* and the *Examination*.

(d) A New View of Logic

First let us seize on Mill's notion that logic is a set of rules for properly conducting any kind of discourse. This he accepted from Hamilton. According to this view, the law of non-contradiction would be a rule of inference: from 'x is A' we can infer the statement 'It is not the case that x is not-A'. And the syllogism would be a set of rules for drawing inferences from certain pairs of statements. 'Laws now no longer mean necessities of nature: they are laws in a totally different sense; they mean precepts.' To break such a precept is to utter syllables which have no use or meaning: as Mill himself states in Chapter VI:

That the same thing is and is not – that it did and did not rain at the same time and place, that a man is both alive and not alive, are forms of words which carry no signification to my mind. ... The word *is* has no meaning, except as exclusive of *is not*.

And Mill compares this case with the meaninglessness which arises through the use of subject and predicate terms not in general use, e.g. 'Humpty-dumpty is an Abracadabra.' Here we may imagine the speaker to attach some meaning to his sentence, although we don't know what it is. But a *formal* contradiction casts doubt on the meaningfulness of predication itself.

The case is more hopeless than that of Humpty-dumpty, for no explanation by the speaker of what the words mean can make the assertion intelligible. Whatever may be meant by a man, and whatever may be meant by alive, the statement that a man can be alive and not alive is equally without meaning to me. I cannot make out anything which the speaker intends me to believe.[24]

According to this view, logic is not concerned with the use of terms which have connotation or denotation, but with signs used to indicate the way in which the descriptive terms are being employed; signs integral to the very existence of the language. The rules of logic are given in *standard forms of expression*. They apply to any sentence whose meaning either is, *or can be*, expressed in a given standard form. These standard forms are not always actually used in discourse, but we can always translate what we have said into standard form and test its validity by reference to the logical rules which define the use of these forms.

The sole purpose of any syllogistic forms is to afford an available test for the process of drawing inferences in the common language of life, from premises in the same common language.

Mill also recognizes the difficulties of translating from ordinary discourses to standard discourse. This is a procedure; but there are no rules (other than rules-of-thumb) for carrying it out. But if the procedure is correctly done, we can, with the help of logical rules, go on to 'think in symbols'. That is, to make inferences mechanically with attention directed, *not* to the full meaning of the signs, but only to those features which have purely formal significance. Hence the 'symbolical thinking' of Leibniz's *Ars combinatoria;* thinking which plays such an important part, not only in mathematics and logic, but in any science whose descriptive meanings are rigidly controlled by definitions.[25]

24. See *Examination,* p. 73.
25. On standard forms of expression, see the *Examination,* pp. 429, 439, 444–5; on symbolical thinking, see Mill's account of algebra in *Logic,* III, xxiv.

CHAPTER FIVE

Induction and Scientific Method

If there is any science that I am capable of promoting, I think it is the science of science itself, the science of investigation, of method.   MILL TO STERLING, 1831

*

I. THE PROBLEM OF INDUCTION

IT is the great achievement of John Stuart Mill to have found logic deductive and to have left it both inductive and deductive. That there are *general* methods of induction, Bacon had shown. But it was the defects rather than the merits of his thesis that had remained current. Hamilton and Mansel held that scientific enquiry is a matter in which a few tricks are to be learned, but everything really depends upon familiarity with a special field – 'a patient habit of attention to details'. They deny any *general* theory of the proof or establishment of factual generalizations. Hamilton thought that once the evidence was collected, nothing remained but to frame a universal law:

> Generalization is usually so easy that there is little exercise afforded to the higher energies of Judgement and Reasoning. ... Science has, by the Inductive Process, been brought down to minds, who previously would have been incompetent for its cultivation, and physical knowledge now usefully occupies many who would otherwise have been without any rational pursuit.[1]

Mill repaired and advanced the work of Bacon. In opposition to Hamilton, Mill claims that it is only under a discipline that reason is productive of new truths, that methods of enquiry and tests of validity can be framed which apply to all fields of enquiry without restriction, and which are therefore an essential enlargement of logic. In logic viewed as a whole,

1. Quoted by Mill, *Examination of Sir Wm. Hamilton's Philosophy*, p. 401.

deduction is only a part and the smaller part. What distinguishes Mill's attempt from Bacon's is that he sees the two as one. The problem of induction, as Mill views it, is essentially the question of how we establish (or defend) general factual propositions. Mill has particularly in mind those universal propositions which occur as premises in a syllogism. In his account of the syllogism, as we have seen, Mill has demonstrated that the connexion between the premises and the conclusion is tautological. The logic of the syllogism is a logic of mere consistency. Nevertheless, it is Mill's view that the syllogism *contains* genuine inference as well as apparent inference. This discovery of new truth in a tautological argument had been a stumbling-block to the formal logicians:

> But what the Logic of mere consistency cannot do, the Logic of the ascertainment of truth, the Philosophy of Evidence in its larger acceptation, can. ... It is therefore alone competent to furnish a philosophical theory of Reasoning.[2]

In other words, deductive logic is concerned with the question whether the conclusion follows from the premises and not with the question of the truth of the premises. But unless we are prepared to assert the truth of the premises we cannot be in a position to *infer* anything whatsoever. It is, therefore, necessary to supplement the logic of consistency by 'a logic of truth'. Mill does not fall into the trap of supposing that *every* premise is inferred from something previously known (*ex praecognitis et praeconcessis*). He is content to suppose that we know particular premises by observation. In effect, therefore the 'logic of truth' is concerned with the question of how we come to know universal propositions.

There are, of course, all sorts of universal propositions; indeed, any sentence in which 'all' occurs as a quantifier is a *prima facie* universal. Many such propositions, which we should at once dismiss as being irrelevant to the problem of induction, were not excluded by Mill. We might, to make a brief review, consider the following unsorted collection:

2. *Examination*, p. 405.

Definitive propositions; e.g., 'All mammals are animals';

Mathematical propositions; e.g., '5 + 7 = 12', which could certainly be used as a universal premise in a syllogism;

Laws of Perspective, and other apparently necessary principles of very wide generality, such as 'If A is longer than B and B is longer than C, then A is longer than C';

Generalizations from experience such as 'All swans are white';

Finite Enumerations, e.g., 'All the people in this room are under 40';

Universal connexions in fact, such as 'The further a body falls the harder it hits';

Generalizations about causes producing effects, such as 'If the rain fails then the harvest will be small';

Scientific Laws, such as the inverse square law of gravity.

Mill sets aside the finite enumerations (or Perfect Inductions) and universals used purely hypothetically. He is convinced that in all cases where we have an existential statement, the universal proposition contains a genuine inference, and that in all cases the inference is *inductive*. From a sample we proceed to make an assertion about the whole; from what is present we make inferences about what is remote; from what is past, to what is present or future. And in his chapters on the syllogism Mill indicates that the inference in all these cases passes from a finite sample to an infinite or open class – or at any rate to an indefinitely numerous class.

An inference may be correct or incorrect. In what circumstances is the inference justified? Clearly the connexion between the evidence and the generalization is not 'logical' at all in the old sense of the word. That is to say, according to Mill's interpretation, it is not a tautological connexion. In the case of a syllogism, to assert the premises and deny the conclusion is to talk *nonsense;* but it is never this *kind* of nonsense to assert the evidence for a generalization and yet to deny the generalization itself. Nor is it *in every case* unreasonable to be prepared to assert the evidence and not to be prepared to assert the generalization. The problem of induction, as Mill sees it at its widest, is to determine what kind of connexion justifies this transition from evidence to generalization.

To this question, Mill makes a characteristic answer: the

transition is justified when there is a uniformity of nature – a law, a universal fact. This answer is characteristic in that it shows Mill's extreme preoccupation with the business of objective enquiry and the achievements of science; his opposition to all forms of conceptualism. It is not a philosophical answer, for it seems to suggest that we can test the validity of such transitions by some further observations – by finding out in some independent fashion whether or not such a uniformity exists.

There are, according to Mill, two kinds of uniformity:

>   (i) Uniformity of coexistence;
>   (ii) Uniformity of succession.

In asserting that all S is P on the basis of certain evidence, we must mean to assert that one or other of these kinds of uniformity exists. Otherwise we should say that the S's that had been observed to be P, were so 'merely by accident'. This then, in Mill's view, is what we *mean* when we assert a genuinely universal premise. Of course, the question of validity has not been answered but re-stated: In what circumstances may we know that a uniformity exists?

2. MILL'S DOCTRINE OF DEMONSTRATIVE INDUCTION

(*a*) *Co-existence*

Mill attempts to answer this question in respect of both kinds of uniformity. Uniformities of coexistence, such as the laws of arithmetic and the laws governing the coexistence of properties in natural kinds, are known through experience on a vast scale; experience in which no exceptions have been detected, and in which (very commonly) it is a psychological impossibility for us to *imagine* an exception. The induction here in question is induction by simple enumeration – admittedly a precarious procedure. But Mill holds that:

the precariousness of the method of simple enumeration is in an inverse ratio to the largeness of the generalization. The process is delusive and insufficient, exactly in proportion as the subject-matter of the observation is special and limited in extent. As the sphere widens, this unscientific method becomes less and less liable to mislead; and the most universal class of truths, the law of causation, for instance, and the principles of number and of geometry, are duly and satisfactorily proved by that method alone, nor are they susceptible of any other proof.[3]

This is Mill's statement: inductive argument in which the evidence is collected just as it turns up, is in general unsatisfactory: but it is not unsatisfactory where the evidence is very extensive, occurs in a very wide variety of circumstances, and is without exception. As it turns out, Mill's objection to 'simple enumeration' is in fact rather different: he holds that it is *inadequate* as a means of identifying *causal* uniformities. And his real point is that in examining causes, we can (and should always) have recourse to other methods which depend upon a principle which applies only to causal uniformities.

We have seen in the previous chapter that there is good reason for rejecting Mill's doctrine that the propositions of arithmetic and geometry are known by observation and induction. I have tried to show that it is misleading to say that we have found no exception to these laws: the point is that our procedures always enable us to avoid identifying anything as an exception, never (indeed) permit us to say that we have established an exception. These 'Uniformities of Co-existence' may therefore be excluded from the problem of Induction.

But others remain. Mill recognizes 'ultimate' laws governing Natural Kinds as non-causal. Where, in a given substance, property A is always found associated with property B, we do not say A causes B or B causes A. For both co-exist. We may say that X precedes and causes both: but Mill always supposes that there are some uniform co-existences which do not thus derive from causal uniformities. Some laws governing natural kinds are of fundamental importance in explaining what goes on in the universe. Our very notions of the different categories of physical objects depend upon the uniform

3. *Logic*, III, xxi (3).

association of properties perceived through the different senses, e.g. the manifold correlations of size, shape, and weight, of temperature and colour. At a more analytic level we notice the correlation of large-scale properties (colour) with small-scale structure (crystal-shape). These laws are certainly not merely formal: divergence from them can be imagined and could be identified. The enquiry into microscopic conditions was distinguished in pre-Baconian logic as the enquiry into *material causes*. It is most certainly inductive and rests broadly on the collection or 'enumeration' of positive instances. Its *justification* is part of the 'problem of Induction'.

The distinction between the two kinds of Uniformity is not a fundamental one. Induction is concerned with the methods by which we establish the existence of various kinds of contingent uniformity in nature: some of these uniformities involve a temporal sequence, others do not. For example, *the further an object falls the harder its impact*. This generalization from experience is refined into a scientific law which is not really a law of sequence at all. Mill was inclined to regard such functional laws as causal; perhaps because the logical relationship is an asymmetrical one. Strictly speaking, the whole important body of laws of mechanics is excluded from the scope of Mill's uniformities of sequence; so also are many other principles of the physical sciences, such as physical constants, functional relationships, laws governing the association of properties. Many of the things which Mill says about causes have application to these principles also, but not all.

(b) Sequence

What does Mill mean by a uniformity of sequence? Uniformities of sequence are Mill's name for laws of cause and effect: and (in his view) all such laws connect two phenomena or characteristics in an asymmetrical manner. This asymmetry may be seen as temporal:

> 'If you put down fertiliser the fruit will be larger';
> 'If you light the fire the explosion will follow';
> 'If you press the switch the light will go on.'

In each case one phenomenon comes first and – the cause being completed – the effect immediately follows.

There is also an asymmetrical logical relation. The inference from the cause to the effect is unconditional, i.e., given A, B will follow no matter what else may or may not be happening in the universe at the same time or previously. (If this inference were not possible, A would not be a *sufficient* antecedent cause.) On the other hand, an inference from effect to cause is only sometimes possible; it is in fact possible where A is both sufficient and necessary for B, and indeed where A is merely necessary for B, without being sufficient. In the examples above, the fruits may wax fat, the explosion may occur, the light might go on, without the 'cause' being operative at all. There might in fact be an alternative cause.

We might suppose that the asymmetry is due simply to the way we phrase the questions and the answers to our questions. If A puts a bullet into B's heart, can we infer that B will die? Yes, unconditionally. But if we begin with B and say 'B is dead' does it follow that anyone shot him? Obviously not. But if we begin differently with B and say 'B has a bullet through his heart' does it follow that somebody shot him? And now the answer is yes.

Where the cause is precisely stated and the effect described only in more general terms, then it appears that there are many alternative causes for the same effect. But if the effect itself is stated very precisely, may it not be the case that there is one and only one cause both sufficient and necessary to produce it? Mill thinks that alternative causes are possible *in nature*. By 'cause' then Mill means *a sufficient cause*, not a necessary and sufficient cause. A is the cause of B in Mill's sense, if A being given, B follows in all cases immediately and unconditionally.

The notion of sufficient antecedent cause cannot be made precise. We *can* say precisely what we mean by the necessary cause or factor: A is a necessary causal factor for B if it is true that 'if not A, then not B'. We might suppose, therefore, that A is a sufficient cause of B in those cases where 'if A then B'.

But were we to adhere strictly to this definition, it would be difficult to know what could be *omitted* from the sufficient cause of anything. It would be nearer to Mill's meaning (and to ordinary usage) if we were to say that A is the sufficient cause of B in cases where A *added to the ordinary course of events in the world* is sufficient to produce B.

Mill's conception of 'cause' is a narrow one and excludes many enquiries which would usually be regarded as *causal*. In ordinary life we are concerned to know both necessary conditions and sufficient conditions. We are interested to know what, if anything, will be sufficient to cure a headache; but we are also anxious to cure it as *economically* as possible, that is, to do only what is *necessary* to effect a cure. We make universal propositions about necessary conditions as well as about sufficient causes: both give rise to 'prediction' (backwards or forwards in time), both are used in systematic explanation.

(c) *The Law of Universal Causation*

In what circumstances can we know that a uniformity of sequence holds? By what procedures can we *justify* the assertion of such a uniformity? What kind of evidence would be conclusive evidence of the existence of a uniformity? In what cases is an inductive argument demonstrative?

As we have already hinted, Mill is not here prepared to accept mere enumeration or collection of positive instances without contrary instances. But fortunately it is precisely in the field of causal enquiry that arguments of an altogether different logical kind are available. For we *know* that every event whatever has some sufficient antecedent cause: we know, in respect of *any* event X, that some selection of its antecedents A B C D ... constitutes a sufficient condition for X. If therefore, by observation, we can come to know all the antecedents of X, we know that some of these must be the cause of X: it may be A or A B or A C or A C D, etc., etc. We have a set of alternative suggestions, and Mill's *Methods of Induction* are procedures for testing these alternatives and eliminating those which do not hold in all cases. If it is not true in all cases that *if A then X*, we can eliminate A as not sufficient for X. In this way we can eliminate all accidental (non-universal) connexions, leaving us with a sufficient cause of X, or with a number of alternative sufficient causes of X. So we build up a proof of a causal proposition by elimination: the connexion between the evidence (the facts about particular instances) and the conclusion (the causal universal) is shown to be a kind of syllogistic connexion after all. For in certain favourable cases we can say that the evidence is conclusive, the premises are demonstrative; only one thing *can* be the cause of X. This is possible because we include amongst the premises, not only the 'evidence' relative to X, but also a general principle which applies to all events whatsoever. This is the Law of Universal Causation – a principle which is acknowledged as the keystone of his doctrine of demonstrative induction about causes. But how are we to distinguish cases where proof is possible from cases where it is impossible? As later writers have shown, we really also need another general premise – to the effect that we have in this case assembled all the relevant facts about X and its antecedents. For evidence cannot be *conclusive*, unless X is 'perfectly known'; the *favourable cases* in which we have a proof of a causal proposition must be cases in which we *know* that we have sufficiently examined and analysed X's antecedents. Both these principles must be knowable if we are ever to say that we have *conclusive* evidence that A is a sufficient cause of X. Both are also involved in causal arguments which are not regarded as demonstrative – the inferences which we tentatively make from evidence which we do *not* regard as decisive. We say 'It looks as if A is sufficient for X.' We are (according to Mill) prepared to go so far because we know that something must be a sufficient cause for X; and we have made an examination of X's antecedents. But we are not prepared to go further because (presumably) we do not feel sure that we have *fully* examined X's antecedents and eliminated all but one.

This, then, is the broad outline of Mill's account of Induction. We can, in causal enquiries, use *negative* or eliminative methods, because (1) we can know enough about X to pick out all those antecedents of X which might cause it; and (2) we know that one or other of them must cause it. And these methods in some cases serve to demonstrate the truth of a causal proposition; in others, to give us that rational belief or 'probability' (in Locke's sense) which is typical of a growing science.[4]

3. MILL'S METHODS OF INDUCTION

(a) The Possibility of Proof

It is now time to fill in the outline of Mill's doctrine by pursuing some of his arguments. The most important passages are in the Third Book of the *Logic*, Chapters III, IV, V, VIII and XXI. Mill begins with the general thesis that whenever we argue from particular instances to a universal we presuppose that *some* kind of uniformity exists in nature: the difficulty is to know when we are justified in saying that this particular type of uniformity exists. It is here that he first says that simple enumeration is inadequate:

> Popular notions are usually founded on induction by simple enumeration; in science it carries us but a little way. We are forced to begin with it; we must often rely on it provisionally, in the absence of means of more searching investigation. But, for the accurate study of nature, we require a surer and a more potent instrument.[5]

Mill takes as an example the proposition 'All swans are white'. This statement implies that what has been true of all

4. In the sequel it will appear that Mill is sometimes confused and mistaken as to the working of his two principal Methods of Induction – the Method of Agreement and the Method of Difference. He sometimes writes as if they were *simply* methods of elimination. They can indeed show conclusively that certain connexions do not hold: but they are of course also enumerative – they serve to accumulate instances. And the evidence they collect (whether positive or negative) is in some cases evidence about *necessary* conditions – not about sufficient causes at all.

5. *Logic*, III, iii (2).

observed swans is not an accidental property: there is some kind of causal connexion between being a *swan* and being *white*. Mill supposes that statements of this type can be proved true by reference to evidence: 'The great generalizations which begin as Hypotheses must end by being proved.' There must be some way of coming to *know* a universal proposition, if we are ever to be in a position to use it as a major premise in a syllogism.

Mill remarks that the induction that all swans are white 'cannot have been a good induction, since the conclusion has turned out erroneous', meaning that the universal had in fact been accepted as proved when no proof had been accomplished.

How did Mill imagine that the crisis of proof occurs? In the case of the white swans, a naturalist might have observed that all swans he had recorded came from certain known parts of the globe. Might there not be causes at work in the unknown regions, to produce red swans or black swans? In this way he would have come to regard the generalization as merely tentative (not *known*), and would in due course have contrived its disproof. At the same time he would have exhibited the marks of a superior mind:

The observation of nature by uncultivated intellects is purely passive: they accept the facts which present themselves, without taking the trouble of searching for more: it is a superior mind only which asks itself what facts are needed to enable it to come to a safe conclusion, and then looks out for these.

It is not enough to find by chance experience that all observed S's are P: we need also, for a proof, some assurance that if there were in nature any contrary instances we should have known of them.

How can this assurance be obtained? Mill says that there are methods employed by scientists, and that these provide a test of the validity of inductive reasoning, 'similar to the syllogistic test of ratiocination'. The Methods of Induction are thus offered as if they provided an independent check upon mere observation and enumeration. 'My treatise contains ... a reduction of the inductive process to strict rules and to a scientific test, such as the syllogism is for ratiocination.' Do the methods somehow enable us to know, not merely that all the S's we have observed are P, but that nature could not produce an S that was not P? [6]

(b) *Analysis of the Four Methods*

I shall give four of the 'Canons', or regulating principles, in Mill's own words and then go on to discuss, in an independent fashion, the methods which are supposed to derive from them. I shall omit altogether the Method of Residues.

First Canon. If two or more instances of the phenomenon under investigation have only one circumstance in common, the circumstance in which alone all the instances agree is the cause (or effect) of the given phenomenon.

Second Canon. If an instance in which the phenomenon under investigation occurs, and an instance in which it does not occur, have every circumstance in common save one, that one occurring only in the former ; the circumstance in which alone the two instances differ is the effect, or the cause, or an indispensable part of the cause, of the phenomenon.

Third Canon. If two or more instances in which the phenomenon occurs have only one circumstance in common, while two or more instances in which it does not occur have nothing in common save the absence of that circumstance, the circumstance in which alone the two sets of instances differ is the effect, or the cause, or an indispensable part of the cause, of the phenomenon.

Fifth Canon. Whatever phenomenon varies in any manner whenever another phenomenon varies in some particular manner, is either a cause or an effect of that phenomenon, or is connected with it through some fact of causation. [7]

The methods are illustrated by means of letters. The letters on the left side represent features of the antecedent event; the letter X represents 'the phenomenon' whose cause (or effect)

6. *Autobiography*, p. 209.
7. *Logic*, III, viii. See von Wright, *The Logical Problem of Induction*, Helsinki (1941); and Professor Broad's comments in *Mind*, 1944.

is being investigated. We may begin with the case where enquiry is being made into the *effect* of a given phenomenon X. Let us suppose two positive instances have been observed:

(1) X is followed by ABC.
(2) X is followed by ADE.

Here we may make a decisive inference, viz., that X is not sufficient for BC nor for DE: or, in Mill's sense of the word, X is not the *cause* of BC or of DE. This is a decisive step, a negative step, an elimination. But the two instances offer something more; we have two instances of X followed by A and no case of X without A. We have, therefore, *enumerated* certain evidence that X is the cause of A, although, of course, this is not in the least decisive.

If we take a different example, where we are trying to find the *sufficient conditions* for a given effect X, the situation is altogether different:

(3) ABC is followed by X.
(4) ADE is followed by X.

Here the elimination which can be made is not really relevant to the search for a sufficient condition. We can infer conclusively that neither BC nor DE is *necessary* for X: but for all we know, ABC and D, or any selection of them, may be sufficient for X. We have (it is true) two instances of A followed by X, but that does not give A any significant advantage. Hence, when applied to the task of finding sufficient conditions, the Method of Agreement is not in fact a method of elimination at all. It is simply a method of enumeration. Mill failed to see this important point, and in fact says that the argument proceeds 'in a similar manner' whether from effect to cause or *vice versa*.[8] His summary account of this method, as being a method of elimination, also slurs over the same point. He re-states the First Canon as follows:

The Method of Agreement stands on the ground that whatever can be eliminated is not connected with the phenomenon by any law.[9]

8. *Logic*, III, viii (1).   9. *Ibid.* (3).

The truth is, that if 'cause' means sufficient conditions, then BC may be the cause of X *although X occurs in its absence*. Clearly, then, no decisive eliminations of candidates for the position of *cause* can be made by this method. At best, if we knew we had two positive instances which differed only in one respect, we could infer that the circumstance once present and once absent was not *necessary* to the phenomena. And if we have a mass of instances, all including A, we infer tentatively, by enumeration, that A is necessary to X. Information about necessary conditions may, of course, be interesting or may not. What the Method of Agreement enables us to infer is that 'all possible causes of X contain A'. If X is prize marrows and A is planting the seed, the information would be disappointing.

The Method of Agreement is confined to the study of positive instances; clearly our enquiries into causes will have to consider also negative instances, i.e., instances in which X is absent. There is some difficulty in the meaning of the phrase 'negative instance' – a phrase not actually used by Mill, but here employed as the equivalent of his 'instances in which the phenomenon under investigation does not occur.' Mill suggests that we should compare instances where X is present with other things or instances differing from our positive instance as widely as possible. According to this injunction, a 'negative instance' in an enquiry into typhoid fever at Birmingham might be anyone or anything at Birmingham or Timbuctoo so long as he or it was not suffering from typhoid fever. What Mill really intended, as his choice of illustration perfectly shows, is that we should compare a positive instance with something having as many points of *agreement* with it as possible, but in which the phenomenon is absent. It would, for example, be important in investigating the causes of typhoid fever in Birmingham to consider people who were in Birmingham at the time of the outbreak, drinking the town's water, bathing in the pools, but not suffering from typhoid. Such negative instances will differ from any set of positive cases in a variety of ways; but what makes them interesting is the points of relevant agreement, and it is on their account that we use the phrase 'negative instances'. For example:

(3) ABC is followed by X.
(4) ADE is followed by X.
(5) BD is followed by not-X.
(6) CE is followed by not-X.
(Neither BD nor CE is sufficient for X.)

And, of course, if we could find two cases, one positive and one negative, which seemed to agree in all relevant circumstances except one (besides the typhoid) we should be inclined to say that this was the cause of the fever. And indeed if we could *know* that our positive instance differed from our negative instances only by the addition of a single factor A, we should be entitled to infer that A was a sufficient condition (or included in a sufficient condition) of X, i.e., the fever. We could not, of course, know that nothing else would cause the fever. Even at its ideal best the Method of Difference (or Second Canon) would not enable us to infer a necessary cause. But it would enable us to infer a sufficient cause.

(3) ABC is followed by X.
(7) BC is followed by not-X.
(A is sufficient for X.)

However, the difficulty is to make sure that of two instances, one positive and one negative, the only relevant differences between them have been identified. Can we ever *know* that we have identified and analysed all the features of a given instance? Or even all the possibly relevant features? It seems not. What we do in practice is to apply Mill's Joint Method (Third Canon): this enables us to eliminate as not sufficient, factors in which positive and negative cases agree, and to eliminate as not necessary those factors which occur in some of the positive cases, but not in all. But once again, besides the conclusive negative inferences, there is an inconclusive positive inference based on enumeration. As we gather differing instances, we feel growing assurance that we have found a factor sufficient for X. This assurance arises only as we

161

come to regard a positive instance and a negative instance as alike in all relevant respects except for the presence of the phenomenon and one other factor (or complex of factors).

The Method of Concomitant Variations (Fifth Canon) suggests that, instead of omitting the factors one by one, we vary their intensity one by one; where a variation in an antecedent factor is always followed by a variation in the degree of the effect, this suggests a causal connexion. Where, on the other hand, it makes no difference to the effect however much we vary a given antecedent factor, then this can be eliminated as not necessary to the effect. The Method therefore works as a method of elimination of sufficient causes only in the investigation of *effects:* and it suffers from precisely the same practical difficulties as the other methods. Can we be sure that we are varying one factor only and not upsetting the others? Unless we can be sure of this, our inference is not decisive.

(c) *Are they Methods of Discovery?*

Do the methods provide a 'key to unravelling the web' of causal connexions? I think the answer is that they are Methods of Discovery, but for use at a later stage of the process than Mill sometimes seems to suggest.

Before the methods can be applied, we must be in the position to enumerate a manageable selection of independently variable antecedent factors, every one of which is relevant to the effect. Unless we can do this we are faced with an impossible question: Which of all the factors in the immediate past may have been the cause? There will *always* be an indefinite number of such factors. We must know before we begin to apply the Methods that the cause might be, or might include, A or B or C, etc. Clearly we cannot *know* all there is to be known about a given phenomenon: but we can have, in some cases, *a reasonable assurance* that we have considered all the relevant features. Unless we have this, we should find ourselves with an indefinite number of hypotheses: time would fail us to examine them; and unless the number really is finite, elimination cannot lead to a proof.

Where does a 'reasonable assurance' come from? How do we recognize the alternative possible hypotheses? Whewell raises this difficulty in his book *The Philosophy of Discovery;*

> Upon these methods the obvious thing to remark is, that they take for granted the very thing which is most difficult to discover, the reduction of the phenomena to formulae such as are here presented to us ... where are we to look for our A, B, C? ... Nature does not present to us the cases in this form; and how are we to reduce them to this form?[10]

Nature does not present us with the relevant factors, but *experience* may do so. In his discussion of the methods as applied in the social sciences (Book VI), Mill fully acknowledges this; and the experience upon which we depend is not deliberate experiment nor prepared observation, but experience unrecorded and unanalysed. And it is not by common experience only that possible causes leap to the mind. There are many cases of discovery where the possible causes leapt only to very uncommon minds, minds of great intuitive and generalizing powers, minds which have (in Aristotle's words) 'an eye for resemblances'. But whether we consider the genius or the empiric, we have to look for Methods of Discovery in powers of memory and imagination. Given these, Mill's methods may indeed be fruitful in spite of the fact that the only *decisive, conclusive* steps they allow us to take are negative.

(d) Are they Methods of Proof?

In his reply to Whewell, Mill says that even if his methods were not methods of discovery 'it would not be the less true that they are the sole methods of Proof.' He remarks that Whewell does not seem to understand that a scientific hypothesis stands in need of proof: he writes as though any hypothesis which is uncontradicted by existing knowledge and accumulating evidence was a *tenable* hypothesis. This, according to Mill, is a 'radical misconception of the nature

10. From a long extract quoted by Mill with characteristic candour, *Logic*, III, ix (6).

of the evidence of physical truths.' In his view, physical truths are hypotheses *which have been proved*.

We have already seen that the connexion between the evidence for a generalization, and the generalization itself, cannot be that of logical entailment. The truth of the evidence does not in itself *necessitate* the truth of the conclusion. Yet evidently Mill held that in favourable cases general empirical propositions can be *proved* with the help of evidence collected in accordance with his methods. But the proof always also depends upon something else: upon a principle which Mill calls the Law of Universal Causation and which he refers to as an 'assumption':

> The validity of all the Inductive Methods depends on the assumption that every event, or the beginning of every phenomenon, must have some cause, some antecedent, on the existence of which it is invariably and unconditionally consequent.[11]

4. THE UNIFORMITY OF NATURE

In his chapter on the Evidence of the Law of Universal Causation, Mill distinguishes two kinds of induction: (i) Natural ('inartificial') inductions by simple enumeration; (ii) Scientific Inductions which have undergone certain tests. But neither of these would result in a *proof*, had we not an assurance that all aspects of nature are uniform; in their succession, subject to laws of causation; and in their co-existences to the laws of mathematics. How then do we know that nature is uniform in these ways? To this Mill replies that we know it by simple enumeration:

> The most universal class of truths, the law of causation for instance, and the principles of number and of geometry, are duly and satisfactorily proved by that method alone, nor are they susceptible of any other proof.[12]

Evidently the principle of the Uniformity of Nature is meant to be wider than the Law of Universal Causality. We

11. *Logic*, III, xxi (1).   12. *Logic*, III, xxi (3).

know by observation that various kinds of uniformity exist in nature: the property of being a triangle, for example, is *always* accompanied by (or co-exists with) the property of having three interior angles equal to two right-angles; the property of being red is always accompanied by the property of reflecting light waves of a certain length and frequency; the property of being a hen's egg duly incubated is always followed by the property of being a hen's chicken. Observing then many uniformities, we may make the inference that 'all phenomena take place according to general laws'. This principle is known by induction *per enumerationem simplicem*.[13]

But it is not this wide principle which really enables us to apply the Methods of Induction. In order to apply methods of elimination, we must be able to say: 'The occurrence of this property has some other *kind* of occurrence always associated with it: and that other occurrence is to be looked for within a limited range.' We can say this in the case of laws of causation: for here the range is limited *in time*, to the immediate antecedents or consequents of the phenomenon under investigation. And, according to Mill, we know that there is some law of antecedent sufficient causation applying to every event whatsoever: but *no other* general principle which applies to every event whatsoever. For example, in respect of many phenomena we can say: 'No doubt this has a material cause', i.e. 'Research would no doubt show that the structure we have now identified is correlated with a more minute structure in the same thing or state.' But can we say this of all phenomena whatsoever? To do so would involve us in an infinite regress: but is there no more guarded form in which it might be asserted? Mill does not consider this principle: he would probably have rejected it as not universal or as not certainly known. He therefore ostensibly confines his methods to arguments about causes antecedent in time. In fact, however, eliminative induction can be employed wherever we have assurance that X has a correlate and that the correlate is to be found in some determinate relationship to it. To admit non-

13. *Logic*, III, iii (1).

temporal relationships here is to admit as *determining* relationships many relations which are loosely spoken of as causal, though they involve no temporal sequence. (e.g. The moon's path *depends on* the gravitational attraction of the earth.) In expanding Mill's principle we have to ask: But do we know which phenomena have material causes? Do we know which variations must be correlated with other variations? If we do know, then *how* do we know? But of course we have to ask the same question about Mill's own law of antecedent causality. How does Mill suppose that we know that every event whatsoever has an efficient cause?

Mill says that this is known by observation of particular causal uniformities: by observation and induction. Our scientific knowledge of causal laws has therefore the following genesis:

(i) By passive observation and induction *per enumerationem*, we reach an unscientific knowledge of many causal uniformities;

(ii) We note that there are everywhere examples of causal uniformity and no well-authenticated examples of events which have no antecedent causes.

(iii) We come to the conclusion (once again, by crude induction) that every event has an antecedent cause even if we have not yet identified it.

(iv) This principle enables us to discover causes by the methods of elimination.

Of course Mill does not say that our scientific knowledge of causal laws is dependent upon methods which themselves presuppose knowledge *of a causal law*. For the Law of Universal Causation is not itself a causal law – it does not state that events of a certain kind have a certain kind of antecedent. It is more like the principles of logic and mathematics which, according to Mill's view, are also known by simple induction.

The crux of the argument is in the second step: Have we never found an event without a cause? Mill says that in all cases 'sufficiently open to our observation', we find causal uniformity. Of course there are all sorts of phenomena whose causes have never been investigated: and all sorts of phenomena whose causes have never been *identified*. Again, where it has been established that B has A as its cause we seem to find 'exceptions' – an A, not followed by a B. But, as Mill justly remarks, in none of these cases should we say that we had established an exception to the principle of causation. Where no cause can be identified, this may be because the phenomena are not 'sufficiently open to our investigation': where A seems to fail to produce B, this may be because a part of A is absent, or because some third factor not yet identified is present and prevents B or masks it.

This leads us to ask: In what circumstances should we be able to say that an uncaused event occurred? As we have seen, there is a fatal objection to the view that the principles of arithmetic and geometry are known by observation and induction. The objection is that there is no procedure for identifying an exception to these principles in experience. And precisely the same objection holds against the view that the Law of Universal Causation is known by induction. By what procedure should we be justified in asserting an uncaused event? Clearly there is no such procedure.

But even if we could claim to know by some other means that 'Nature is Uniform', or that there must be in nature uniformities of certain types, the finding of an unbroken connexion of A's and B's in experience would not be any sort of *proof* that this particular connexion is a universal one. *It might not be.* Nor does Mill ever clearly state at what point the accumulating evidence in favour of a generalization becomes a *proof* – or rather becomes a proof when taken in conjunction with the Law of Universal Causation. The methods do not bring about a crisis of proof: though they may, of course, bring about a crisis of disproof. What we find is a gradual increase in confidence, as a given generalization is tested in accordance with the methods. But a gradual increase of confidence is not what Mill has in mind when he speaks of 'methods of proof'. Indeed this 'gradualism' is precisely what he condemns in Whewell: in Mill's view it is the hall-mark of a genuinely scientific hypothesis that it is not destined always to remain a mere hypothesis. It will be disproved or proved.[14]

Mill completely fails to show how a knowledge of a general law of causation could be derived by induction from experience; and how, if we had that knowledge, it could constitute a major premise by means of which particular generalizations could be demonstrated. The 'assumption' which he formulates turns out not to be a matter-of-fact proposition at all. The other necessary condition which he does not explicitly formulate – that we can know all about our 'phenomena' – is clearly not realizable. It is a fact, of course, that we can be confident that we know the field well enough to formulate the possible alternatives. What is finally achieved from this starting-point, however, could not be regarded as *demonstrated*.

5. INDUCTION AND PROBABILITY

Mill's methods enable us to test causal generalizations and to feel a superior confidence in those which pass the tests. This confidence may amount to practical certainty (we act on them without hesitation); or theoretical certainty (reflection rejects all doubts). But even in such cases if pressed we should admit that it might perhaps be necessary some day to revise our belief in them. And in the case of many general beliefs we should disclaim *knowledge* and say that we merely believe them to be true, that they are only probably true. The philosopher

14. But in his discussion of ultimate and derivative laws of nature Mill admits that we can never be absolutely certain that any of the laws we know are unconditional. Even the law of gravitation, for example, might be conditioned by causal forces operating throughout that part of the universe with which we are acquainted. That is to say, there might be some different and general law which holds *throughout nature*, and which (in conjunction with the local circumstances of our part of the universe) produces a derivative law which is the law of gravitation as we know it. In regard to the most general laws we know, the only doubt Mill would admit would be whether forces outside our 'Cosmic Epoch' might some day disturb them.

in his generalizing manner has long ago extended the use of the word 'probable' to all beliefs that fall short of knowledge; and it is customary for philosophers to say that all empirical general beliefs are only probable. The evidence for a general proposition has been viewed as though it were a fraction between o and 1, rather like the odds in favour of a given horse – a fraction which can be increased by further evidence. If we adopt this language we shall say that the inconclusive evidence which gradually accumulates for a general proposition gives it a certain probability; that by collecting positive instances and comparing them with negative instances, in the way recommended by Mill, we are able to increase the probability of a given general proposition or to disprove it.

Mill himself naturally recognizes that we have better grounds for believing some general propositions than for believing others. He recognizes 'probability' in Locke's sense – as a belief which falls short of knowledge: but (unlike Locke) he believes that knowledge is *possible* in the physical sciences. Mill has little enough to say on the notion of probability. At all events, he sees no special connexion between inductive beliefs and 'matters of probability' or matters of *chance*, as this phrase is used in connexion with games of chance.

Mill's own chapter on the calculation of chances is concerned with statistical generalizations only. He accepts Laplace's 'Principle of Uncertainty' – though with manifest uneasiness. Mill tries to confine the use of the calculus of chances as narrowly as possible:

Except ... in such cases as games of chance, where the very purpose in view requires ignorance instead of knowledge, I can conceive no case in which we ought to be satisfied with such an estimate of chances as this.[15]

However, if we are decided that induction cannot be shown to be a form of demonstrative argument, we ought to consider the attempts that have been made by some of Mill's successors to justify induction as a form of problematical argument. We

15. *Logic*, III, xviii (3).

have to ask then whether Mill's methods really enable us *to increase the probability* of a general proposition.

The attempted justification begins where Mill began, by regarding the generalization as a kind of conclusion, and the evidence as constituting premises of a kind. To say that a generalization has a certain probability is always to make reference (whether explicit or not) to the evidence upon which it rests. A proposition has a certain probability *upon certain evidence;* on different evidence its probability might be higher or lower. Normally our reference is to the sum total of evidence available to us at the time. If we are able to add to this evidence by fresh observation, this may incline us to say that in relation to the new premises (i.e. to the evidence *now* available) the conclusion has a higher (or lower) degree of probability. For although the notion of degree of probability may be vague enough, we certainly do *compare* the degree of probability of the same general proposition in relation to different sets of premises (e.g. the evidence as it was yesterday and the evidence as it is to-day). Sometimes, where evidence does not point all one way, we can say that upon a given body of evidence one general conclusion (e.g. that the fine weather will hold to-day) has a higher probability than another (that it will hold until to-morrow evening).

Such a solution has appealed to a number of philosophers since Mill's day. It allows us to regard inductive inference as inconclusive and gradualistic. We can say (as a rough general rule) that the greater the number and variety of instances of a connexion A – B that have been found the greater the probability of the universal *All A is B*; but that there is no point at which we should be justified in excluding the very possibility of an exception. At the same time, this view seems to make intelligible the connexion between the evidence and the universal which is inferred from it. The connexion requires an independently known principle of limitation of variety in the world of our experience. Granted this principle as an additional premise, we can say that our 'premises' as a whole are connected with our 'conclusion' in a *logical* manner: but the

logic of the connexion is not syllogistical – it is the logic of
the calculus of chances. Inductive arguments are seen to be
analogous with arguments about extracting balls from a bag,
tickets from a hat, cards from a pack. In all such cases, given
a number of instantial propositions such as:

> 1st draw, red ball;
> 2nd draw, white ball;
> 3rd draw, red ball. ...

we make an inference about the probability of a certain constitution of the whole set of balls. But such an inference is
grounded not only on these particular pieces of evidence, but
also upon some independently acquired knowledge about the
set – e.g. that over half the balls are of the same colour. In
the case of inductive arguments, the general principle is some
form of the Uniformity of Nature – there is not unlimited
variety in the universe; not *all* combinations of characteristics
are possible.

This amended view of induction, then, also has to answer
the question which Mill's theory unsuccessfully tried to
answer: How do we know that there are uniformities in
Nature? Is Nature a set of objects put together in accordance
with some rational plan – like a pack of cards? Is there,
strictly speaking, a *set of objects* which is called 'Nature' or
'the Universe'? It is all very well to show that inductive arguments would be like arguments about balls in a bag, *if Nature
were a very large bag*. But it seems very obvious that we could
never know whether it is a very large bag or not: so that our
confidence in inductive arguments cannot derive from a
knowledge about the bag. Nor, I think, from a belief about
the bag either: since (as I hold) we all know that we do not
know anything at all about the constitution of the alleged bag.

I suspect that all such arguments are built upon a *false
analogy*. The connexion between the evidence and the universal
cannot be such that the evidence, together with a principle of
uniformity, entails a problematic universal conclusion. The
connexion is not syllogistic (as Mill thought); nor is it prob-

lematic (in the sense appropriate to questions of chances). Inductive arguments are not any kind of deductive argument at all.

Undoubtedly, in an inductive argument, we do offer *reasons* for our conclusion. And the most important of these reasons turn on the very considerations which Mill brings forward. For if we tried to say what general considerations lend positive weight to a generalization, independently of other generalizations, we should have to rely on the enumerations of instances and on their variety. On what grounds do we hold that A causes X? We should, I think, include the following considerations amongst our *reasons:*

(i) Our antecedent experience of the operation of A and X, B and C, D and E, and analogous factors.

(ii) The variety of circumstances in which our positive instances have been chosen. The connexion of A and X has been found to hold, not merely where the relevant factors B and C are present, but where they are absent and other relevant factors, D and E, are present. A – X holds in the presence and absence of important factors which might well affect the connexion. This leads us to suppose that A – X will hold in all other circumstances in which they may occur.

(iii) The number of instances of A – X observed – including all those we know to have been observed but not recorded.

(iv) Where, by control and experiment, we feel confident that A, B, C, were the only relevant factors present when X occurred; and we feel sure that A is the only relevant factor omitted where X fails; in such a case we feel confident that A and X are connected.

Now, on these lines, good reasons, sometimes overwhelming reasons, may be offered for the generalization. But what if an objector were to say: 'But still you haven't *proved* that A is the cause of X'? We might answer (1): 'What possible further proof could you need? Would it be reasonable to overlook or ignore all my reasons?' Or we might answer (2): 'Of course this is not a proof at all in the sense in which we prove a theorem in a calculus of geometry, nor in the sense in which we solve a problem about cards in a pack or balls in a bag. But to yearn for a mathematical proof of matters of fact and experience is to yearn for the impossible and the ridiculous. It is (in the blunt language of scripture) to go 'whoring after strange gods'.

This answer implies that the problem of Induction was misconceived by Mill. For the 'problem' as he presents it, and as most of his successors have presented it, consists in trying to show that the reasons we give for accepting factual general propositions can really be stated in the form of a deductive argument. What emerges from Mill's discussion is that induction by enumeration is indispensable to every genuine form of inference. Clearly, Mill ought to hold that the accumulation of positive instances in a variety of circumstances is the only procedure which gives independent positive strength to a generalization. For what, after all, does his account of the methods of induction accomplish? It shows that 'scientific' arguments about causes involve deduction. But (according to Mill) all valid deduction is tautological: deductive logic is a logic of mere consistency: we can never, by any pattern of deduction, arrive at any conclusion not already contained in our premises. In Mill's view, the vital premise in causal arguments is the Law of Universal Causation, which is known by 'the loose and uncertain mode of induction *per enumerationem simplicem*'. It would seem, therefore, he proceeds, that this mode

is not necessarily an illicit logical process, but is in reality the only kind of induction possible. [16]

It is not my business here to insist upon any revision of the problem of induction. It is rather my business to show that Mill's Law of Universal Causation does not provide a solution to his problem; and that the attempted reconstruction of Mill, while it recognizes the problematic character of induction, is still open to one of the main objections to Mill: that we are supposed to know something about the universe which it seems clear we don't know.

16. *Logic*, III, xxi (2).

Mill was therefore mistaken in supposing that his methods
ed to the *proof* of inductive generalization in any sense of
'proof' which he seems to have had in mind. He was quite
right in thinking that evidence collected by these methods
does provide grounds on which a reasonable man may rest
his belief. It also seems to me that he was negatively right in
not trying to interpret inductive arguments by analogy with
deductions in the calculus of chances, i.e. in not connecting
probability in Locke's sense with probability in the sense of
numerical odds.

6. SCIENTIFIC METHOD: INVESTIGATION AND EXPLANATION

(a) Types of Explanation

Mill's preoccupation with antecedent efficient causes reflects
his concern with practical affairs; his interest in 'improvement', or 'the application of science to human welfare'. It
dominates his views of explanation also. To explain an observed regularity is to show that it follows from causal laws
together with statements of the actual arrangement of causes
in operation. Mill holds that we may know general propositions without being able to see how they follow from causal
laws. But what we know is that there is *some* causal law, connecting the terms of the general propositions. To seek for an
explanation is to try to discover these laws. Science already
includes 'truths irrevocably acquired and universally assented
to'. And Mill supposes that it is by induction alone that we
come to know both the empirical connexions and the explanatory laws. The methods of science are refinements and elabora-
tions of induction: that is to say, of the one and only method
of genuine inference.

General propositions serve equally for prediction and for
explanation. We can say:

> All men are animals: therefore all will die.
> All men will die, because all are animals.

Where we see a general connexion between animals' nature and mortality, we may take this as an explanation of the fact that all men die.

The more we can explain the more we can predict. But an experimental science is a body of knowledge and aims at the systematic inter-relation of the general propositions known to be true in its field of enquiry. This, in the simplest cases, is to show that certain of them can be inferred from certain others. The scientist tries to explain things which we all know to happen: his discovery of things which we did not know to happen is very often a mere stage on the way to understand matters of common knowledge or common observation. Mill gives examples of two very simple types of scientific explanation:

(i) We explain an empirical uniformity by showing that it can be deduced from a causal law or laws together with facts about the agents operating. Here the laws used in the explanation are more general than the empirical one.

(ii) We explain the empirical law that C always follows A, by showing that there is a third term B, and that A causes B, and B causes C. Here also the $A - B$, $B - C$ laws are of a wider generality than the empirical law. For the $A - C$ connexion holds only where B supervenes – it is really an $AB - C$ connexion.[17]

(b) *The Geometrical Method*

Mill correctly perceives that the type of explanation found in geometry cannot be achieved in the experimental sciences. For geometry is not a science of causation and does not require or admit any 'summing-up' of the effects of different cause-factors. In geometry we explain particular features of a figure by showing that they are an instance of a general law which is itself either an axiom or a theorem of the system. Thus in an equilateral triangle we find the interior angles equal. We do not have to consider at the same time any other feature of the triangle: the relation of sides to angles does not

17. *Logic*, III, xii.

vary with size or position, nor do the principles of area measurement in any way conflict with the laws of sides and angles.

What is proved true from one geometrical theorem, what would be true if no other geometrical principles existed, cannot be altered and made no longer true by reason of some other geometrical principle.[18]

What in fact makes this type of explanation impossible in all the natural sciences is the concurrence of causes and the resulting inter-mixture of effects.

(c) The Concurrence of Causes

Mill first studied the concurrence of causes in the mechanical theory of the composition of forces. Here we are permitted to calculate an effect by a mode of addition of the separate forces in operation. This procedure is legitimate in dynamics and in applied mathematics, but apparently not so in chemistry. At this point in his reflexions, Mill recalled that this was one of the distinctions between chemical and mechanical phenomena in the introduction to Thomson's *System of Chemistry*, which had been his favourite reading in boyhood.

I now saw that a science is either deductive or experimental, according as, in the province it deals with, the effects of causes when conjoined, are or are not the sums of the effects which the same causes produce when separate.[19]

In mechanics, the joint effect of forces A and B is a simple function of the effects each would produce in isolation. In chemical changes, on the other hand, this is not so: the joint effect of hydrogen and oxygen is a phenomenon altogether new; the laws of the original agents 'cease entirely, and a phenomenon makes its appearance, which, with reference to those laws, is quite heterogeneous.' The connexion of cause and effect can be found only by special experiments. We can

18. *Logic*, VI, viii.
19. See *Autobiography*, pp. 17 and 160; *Logic*, III, x, and VI, ix.

discover what (if anything) results from the combination of two substances, provided we can be sure that no other relevant causes are operating. If the resulting compound is one already familiar to us in nature, then our experiment has enabled us to *explain* that compound as an effect of the two substances. Moreover, it often happens that the chemical process is reversible in certain special circumstances: we can, for example, form water from the explosion of a mixture of hydrogen and oxygen, and we can dissociate the two gases in steam by electrolysis.

7. THE EXPERIMENTAL SCIENCES

This mode of explanation, however, is extremely limited.

(i) There was in the early days of chemistry no general law which would enable a scientist to *predict* the effect of oxygen upon iron or upon hydrogen. The only general law of the nature of oxygen was a mere compendium of special laws each established by a specific experiment. It was therefore difficult to say whether the law of the combination of two elements was an empirical law, itself capable of further explanation, or an ultimate law of nature.

(ii) Moreover, observers were apt to find exceptions to their laws. For no accountable reason substances might fail to combine, or might yield variations in their effects. As everyone understood, the isolation even of prepared chemicals is not absolute. Factors hitherto unconsidered (temperature, pressure, the nature of the vessels used), when present in certain degrees, vary or nullify the result. The very notion of isolation could be interpreted as an equilibrium of forces which, if present in isolation, or if accidentally strengthened or weakened, might affect the experiment. The inaction of other forces might, in fact, be a complex and delicate interaction. All physical properties are, as Locke said, 'but retainers upon other properties'. Mill did not hesitate to prefer the Newton-Locke view of what a science might become to the Baconian view as to what a science was.

Mill's dissatisfaction with 'the Chemical or Experimental Method' is not a dissatisfaction with chemistry or with experimental methods. Mill actually held that chemistry was becoming, and had indeed become, a Deductive Science. The Chemical Method is simply the Experimental Method, not the method of chemistry. Nor does Mill wish to deny that an Experimental Science is a science; but the epithet 'experimental' is here used to indicate its theoretical poverty and perhaps also a mistaken notion of what a genuine causal law is really like.

A causal law must not be thought of as a guarantee of a certain result in certain specified circumstances. It must be thought of as the statement of a *tendency*. In other words, all genuine scientific principles are to be expressed in terms analogous with those of Newton's laws of motion.[20]

8. THE DEDUCTIVE METHOD

In mechanics, and to a less extent in physics generally, Mill saw his ideal of scientific law and of scientific explanation. Here it is assumed as a general rule that a change takes place as the result of a number of separate forces; that the laws of the different forces 'apparently frustrate or modify one another's operation, yet in reality all are fulfilled, the collective effect being the exact sum of the effects of the causes taken separately.' For example, a body kept in equilibrium by two equal and opposite forces:

One of the forces if acting alone would carry the body in a given time a certain distance to the west, the other if acting alone would carry it exactly as far towards the east; and the result is the same as if it had first been carried to the west as far as the one force would carry it, and then back towards the east as far as the other would carry it, that is, precisely the same distance; being ultimately left where it was found at first.[21]

The laws of these forces have no exceptions, just because they are abstract – or tell us only what a given force *would do*

20. *Logic*, III, x (5).   21. *Logic*, III, x (5).

if acting alone. But the general assumption is that the forces described do not act alone, but in combination. Hence, where the expected result of certain forces is not exactly achieved, this is always because some other force, not allowed for, has impinged upon the original forces.

In a Deductive Science it is possible to employ the Deductive (or Physical) Method. This serves both for investigation and for explanation. For once the laws of the separate forces are known we may (i) by calculation predict what will be the result of a certain measured collocation of such forces; and (ii) by calculation determine what definite collocation of forces could have produced a given phenomenon. It is obvious that, as a method of explanation, the Deductive Method alone cannot lead to any definite conclusion. For it will normally be the case that different sets of forces, present in different strengths, could have produced the same determinate result. But taken together with some independent information about the causes, it may lead to a more or less determinate conclusion.

The task is to explain why A is always and everywhere followed by B. The connexion of A and B may be a well-established empirical law, or it may be a connexion observed only in a limited field. The explanation has three stages. (i) We must show by analysis that A consists of a certain function of a set of ultimate forces (or forces taken as ultimate for the purposes of the enquiry). Suppose A is analysed into f' (a b c d). (ii) We must also show that by the operation of these forces, through any necessary intermediate stages or crises, there would result another function f" (a b c d), and that this function is itself an analysis of B. (iii) Wherever possible, an experimental verification should be carried on; f' (a b c d) should be constructed to operate, as far as possible, without the interference of any other forces: and the ultimate result must be compared with B.

The verification is primarily a test of the explanation, and not of the empirical law. What we want to show is that there is no force omitted in our analysis of A, that all the forces have their appropriate strengths, and that the calculations have been correctly carried out. A positive result, where f'' (a b c d), corresponds to B, confirms the explanation, and, as Mill remarks, may serve also to confirm the laws of the separate forces. (For if these had been wrongly formulated, the result could correspond with B only by chance.) Where, again, the connexion of A and B had not been thoroughly established this also may be confirmed. (We now see *why* A should always be followed by B.) A negative result, where f'' (a b c d) does not correspond with B, will lead, not to a *rejection* of the explanatory hypothesis, but to its revision. Forces overlooked in the analysis of A may have to be included, the co-efficients modified, the calculations revised.

9. CAUSES AND FORCES

We must now examine the grounds of Mill's preference for the Deductive Method over the Experimental Method. Mill's arguments show that he entertained the belief that the laws of motion are ultimate natural laws, but that he felt great doubt about experimental laws of the type which he illustrated from chemistry. What are the grounds of this discrimination?

(i) One objection to an Experimental Science was that its laws depend too much upon 'specific experiments': they are *too concrete*. But, of course, Mill is not going to hold that what distinguishes the laws of motion is that they are known independently of experiment and observation. The objection to the experimental type of laws was that they were insufficiently general, not linked by wider laws. The progress of the sciences suggested that these experimental laws *could* somehow be linked.

(ii) Mill was satisfied that the laws of motion, as laws of tendency, had been established by observation and experiment along the lines indicated in his Methods of Induction. These methods worked satisfactorily because it was always assumed that the same effect might result from a variety of alternate causes – a variety arising from the different forces which might be co-operating to produce the effect. But how was it possible to discover the laws of these fundamental forces themselves? Mill held that this had been done in mechanics, but not (for example) in physiology. The reason he gives is that in mechanics we are able to study each tendency

in cases in which that tendency operates alone, or in combination with no agencies but those of which the effect can, from previous knowledge, be calculated and allowed for.[22]

In mechanical phenomena the causes suffer themselves to be separated and observed apart. Not of course completely separated: we cannot observe a body moving on a frictionless plane; but we can observe what happens as the friction is progressively increased or diminished. From these results we can calculate what would happen if the tendency of a body to move on a plane were to operate without any friction.

(iii) How can we be sure that all the purely mechanical laws are known? Mill would claim that our certainty derives from the all-pervading character of the observations themselves. The laws of mechanics rest upon our common practical knowledge of handling moving bodies and of moving our own bodies. They are part of the skill of the 'rude Mechanicals' of all ages. Weight, force, size, speed, angle, distance, density of packing, roughness of surface – all these, and also the manner of their association, belong to common knowledge. On this basis the founders of modern science could work in analysing the laws of these forces.

10. ULTIMATE AND DERIVATIVE LAWS

Mill takes it to be the aim of scientists to explain empirical laws by means of more general laws; and to reach laws which are ultimate, i.e. unconditional.

We are not sure that any of the uniformities with which we are yet acquainted are ultimate laws; but we know that there must be ultimate laws, and that every resolution of a derivative law into more general laws brings us nearer to them.[23]

22. *Logic*, III, xi (1).   23. *Logic*, III, xiv (1), and xvi (1).

A *derivative law* is one which is not unconditional: it is an ultimate law operating under certain conditions or collocations of natural agents. An *empirical law* is one which is believed to depend upon the operation of a more general law in some particular collocation, but these have not been identified.

Besides ultimate laws, there must then be ultimate particular *facts:*

There is ... no uniformity, no *norma*, principle, or rule, perceivable in the distribution of the primeval natural agents through the universe.[24]

Since any derivative law holds only so long as its conditions persist, we cannot be absolutely certain of even the most general derivative laws. Mill's final conclusion ought to be that, since any of the laws we know may be falsified where some special conditions are not fulfilled, they are none of them known, or proved, in the strict sense. This conclusion is reached in Chapter xiv, but not generally applied.[25]

Mill is inclined to regard the fundamental causes at work in the universe as *forces* of a kind. He speaks in one place of apparent exceptions to causal principles as being always due to 'some other and distinct principle cutting into the former; some other force which impinges against the first force and deflects it from its direction.' The word 'principle' is here intended quite generally, and Mill explains in a footnote that his use of the word 'impinge' must not be held to imply 'any theory respecting the nature of force'. It is, however, one of many hints of his preference for a mechanical view of forces. This arises in part from his insistence upon 'speaking Newtonically' in opposition to the Baconian language of Macaulay and the empiricists. But it also reflects a deep-rooted prefer-

24. *Logic*, III, xvi (3). Mill believed, on the other hand, that there are ultimate laws of the co-existence of properties in natural kinds: not all laws governing the association of properties are laws of co-existence. In normal observable cases the connexion is causal: both properties depend upon the same antecedent. But some laws of co-existence of properties are (Mill held) ultimate laws of nature. See xxii (3).

25. See above, footnote 14.

ence for mechanical modes of explanation. The preference was still dominant in mid-nineteenth century physics, but it is by no means confined to scientists and philosophers. The laws of mechanics provide us with a satisfactory model of explanation: if we can 'see' how a change could have come about mechanically, we feel that a good explanation has been offered. What philosophers have done is to make us believe that it is the *only* satisfactory model. This apparently was Mill's view: and he seems to be unaware that he has made a choice, or indeed that there was anything else that might have been chosen.

This view of explanation brings out a point of capital interest in Mill's theory of scientific method. He talks of explaining an empirical law by reference to a more general law: and the ultimate laws are entirely general, unconditional, and abstract. But they are still altogether *empirical* in the wider sense that they express the laws of the behaviour of genuine characteristics of events. Let us suppose, as Mill in effect does, that the Laws of Motion are ultimate. That a particle is tending to persist in motion in a straight line is a perfectly genuine property of a perfectly observable entity. It is true that the same entity has an indefinite number of other properties and that some of those are inevitably relevant to its tendency to move in a straight line. Such a tendency nowhere exists without the co-presence of counter-tendencies. It is for this reason that we say of such a property that it is 'abstract', that there is no such thing as a body which perfectly exhibits the property.

Mill's notion of the explanatory laws of nature is the subtlest refinement upon crude empiricism. But it presupposes that scientific explanation is always carried out by means of laws which are descriptive of *verae causae*.[26]

He failed to see that there are features of scientific theory

26. This is most strongly insisted upon in the chapter on Hypotheses [III, xiv (4)]. In this same chapter, Mill quotes with approval from Bain's *Logic:* 'Scientific explanation and inductive generalization being the same thing, the limits of Explanation are the limits of Induction.'

whose justification is less directly empirical, less avidly experimental. For concepts may be introduced which describe no new observable entities, nor help us to ferret out any new facts; or which, if they do these things, also do something more. In some cases the chief point of the new concept is to summarize or simplify the theory (i.e. the deductive system) of the enquiry; or to emphasize certain structures or aspects of facts already known. Such features are introduced chiefly from mathematics, and alternatives to them are always possible. Different branches of mathematics have (from time to time) been found appropriate; and not all of these concepts have been interpretable by mechanical analogies.

It must be remembered that Mill's *Logic* was completed in 1841, at a very early stage in the scientific revolution of the nineteenth century. Moreover, his own interest in scientific methods lay in their possible application to morals and politics, and a life of devotion to philosophy and political activities prevented Mill from maintaining a lively contact with the scientists themselves. Mill's account of the basic laws of science reflects the tendency of his day: the attempt to derive chemical laws from physical laws; to offer a mechanical explanation of heat, light and electricity; the attempt to introduce the same mechanical notions into physiology. Mill was a mechanist: and it is difficult to see how he could have been anything else without an altogether more fundamental view of language. His theory of language presupposes that all words (except the purely logical signs) are descriptive of properties or relations which we can observe – and all descriptive in the same straightforward sense. Thus 'three' and 'four' describe visible and tangible properties of collections: the structural, conventional elements in the use of numerals are overlooked. For Mill, the characteristic structure of the arithmetical calculus derives from the structure of things. He usually overlooks the fact that principles of explanation in science have structural properties which, while they cannot conflict with what is observed, cannot be said to be based upon observation in the straightforward sense appropriate to the definition of 'man' or 'water'; nor to have as their purpose the ferreting out of any new observable facts. In other words, Mill's attitude to the explanatory laws of nature remained 'realistic' in the unphilosophical sense of that word.

The theory of language is the Achilles' heel of Mill's philosophy. To it can be traced the glaring defects of his theory of mathematics and subtler defects in his theory of ethics and science.

CHAPTER SIX

Appearance and Reality

On Man, on Nature, and on Human Life,
Musing in solitude.   WORDSWORTH

*

I. INTRODUCTION

W E have now tried to trace Mill's views of science, including
the science of society and of individual character. It has been
seen that these imply definite views of the objects known to
science; a doctrine of Nature and of Human Nature. There
are objective laws of sequence and of co-existence; there is a
Natural Order, a structure in things. And Man himself is a
part of this natural order, a part of Nature 'in the true scientific
sense of the word'. In considering Mill's ethical views, we
have taken account of some of the difficulties of this position.
How, for instance, can Man be free to make genuine moral
choices if his character is determined (in the end) by external
forces? And, still more difficult, how can he be free to discriminate correctly between the right and the wrong, if his
morality is imposed upon him by tradition and early education? Moreover, there is a parallel question about purely
theoretical knowledge: How can Man be free to describe the
world correctly, if his perceptions, and his responses to his
perceptions, are determined by external stimulation and internal habits and associations? Mill never really faces these
questions: but it has been suggested that it is necessary
to separate altogether questions of antecedent causes from
questions of validity. When this is done, it may now be added,
the remaining questions of validity will not be of the form:
'How is it possible to make the correct judgement?', but
rather 'Has he in fact made the correct judgement here?'[1]

1. See above, ch. ii (§§ 6 and 7).

Into these questions it is not possible to enter further. We must now attempt to see as a whole Mill's broader views of Nature, Man, and God, and of the attitude which may suitably be taken up towards 'a probable God' or a possible God. But in doing so, we must take into account the profound influence upon Mill of those studies which he sometimes calls psychology and sometimes metaphysics. These studies derive from Locke's *Essay on the Human Understanding*, as that work was sifted and sorted, abbreviated and expanded, by Berkeley, Hume, Reid, and Hartley. They concern the relations between mind and body, and especially the relation of the mind to the object which it claims to know; and in Mill's estimation, the most developed and comprehensive work on the subject was his father's *Analysis of the Human Mind* – in which Berkeley's views were made more consistent and less plausible than ever before.

These studies exercised a profoundly disturbing effect upon Mill's account of human knowledge. It is difficult to combine the commonsensical, practical doctrines of the *Logic* with the 'received opinions of modern metaphysicians' as these are given in his chapter on 'Things Denoted by Names', and in the *Examination of Hamilton's Philosophy*. An attempt to see the connexions will be made in this chapter. We shall consider the following topics:

The objectivity of our knowledge of the physical world (§ 2); Phenomenalism (§§ 3–5); What is known in general concerning man's place in the world; the hypothesis of the existence of a God (§ 6); Mill's views on Religion (§§ 7 and 8).

2. THE OBJECTIVITY OF JUDGEMENTS

The word 'fact' which so dominates the *Logic* is used by Mill to mean something that is the case whatever one thinks about it and whether or not one happens to be perceiving it. It is the view of the Experience Philosophy that we become aware of facts in experience. This is very much taken for granted in the

Logic; perhaps on the grounds that Mill has as his subject-matter, not knowledge in general, but only that part of our knowledge which consists of inferences from truths previously known. In his later metaphysical work, *The Examination of Sir William Hamilton's Philosophy,* Mill enters more fully into the question of the nature of that basic knowledge which (as Locke says) we have 'without pains, labour, or deduction'. Mill's doctrine of judgement contains two fundamental propositions:

(1) Properties are universals, with a nature invariable from time to time and from place to place;

(2) There are unconditional connexions of universals: these hold without reference to place and time.

The Experience Philosophy arranges judgements in an 'epistemic order': there are singular judgements which are based upon particular perceptions or other experiences; and there are universal judgements which are based upon singular judgements. In singular judgements of perception, we ascribe a property to an actual thing. 'This is a table' is an example. In order to make this judgement, to be sure, we have to have a notion of a table: that is to say, we have to have an understanding of the use of this general term. But we cannot make any singular judgement as to what is a table, merely by analysing our notion. What the verbal proposition lacks, and the judgement of perception has, is a reference to 'actual things' (not words), to 'facts'.

The very meaning of a judgement, or a proposition, is something which is capable of being believed or disbelieved; which can be true or false; to which it is possible to say yes or no. And though it cannot be believed until it has been conceived, or (in plain terms) understood, the real object of belief is not the concept, or any relation of the concept, but the fact conceived.[2]

It is by asserting a property *of a thing* that a judgement exposes itself to the hazard of falsehood.

This doctrine of judgement requires a Realistic view of

2. *Examination,* p. 348.

universals, or properties. In describing an object as 'a table', I am certainly not merely adding it to a group of objects which I have formed – the group whose members I call 'table'; nor merely to the group which *we all* call 'table'. Any such view of prediction would reduce the judgement to a merely verbal one. Accordingly, in ch. xviii of the *Examination*, we find Mill insisting that judgements are *intensional* in their ultimate signification: he holds that

all concepts and general names which enter into Propositions, require to be construed in Comprehension, and that their Comprehension is the whole of their meaning.[3]

This Realistic view of attributes or properties can be traced in Mill's later discussions of causal judgements. The only way to connect one fact with another not contained in the first is to show that one *property* or *kind* is connected with another. If we say that all we can do is to show that one aggregate (or class) is connected with another, then this is either nonsense, or the word 'class' is used to mean an 'open', infinite, class, and not an enumerable group. 'That all men are bipeds' (Mill says) cannot mean

that we have examined the aggregate whole 'all men', and the still greater aggregate whole 'all bipeds', and that all the former were found among the latter.[4]

This would require infinite power. This judgement also must be understood intensionally: i.e. as a connexion of universals which holds without reference to the mere spatio-temporal positions of the instances. It is, or is supposed to be, *unconditional*.

3. PHENOMENALISM

Since the mind, in all its thoughts and reasonings, hath no other immediate object but its own ideas, which it alone does or can contemplate, it is evident that our knowledge is only conversant about them.[5]

3. *Examination*, p. 362.
4. *Loc. cit.*
5. Locke, *Essay*, Book IV, opening words.

We have to try to see how these famous words of Locke's affect Mill's doctrine of the objectivity of our judgements about nature.

Consider, as an example, the following remarks which occur in the discussion on immortality in his last published work.

Feeling and thought are much more real than anything else; they are the only things which we directly know to be real. ...

All matter apart from the feelings of sentient beings has but an hypothetical and unsubstantial existence: it is a mere assumption to account for our sensations. ...

Mind ... is in a philosophical point of view the only reality of which we have any evidence: and no analogy can be recognized or comparison made between it and other realities because there are no other known realities to compare it with.

... the brain ... is, like matter itself, merely a set of human sensations either actual or inferred as possible, namely those which the anatomist has when he opens the skull, and the impressions which we suppose we should receive of molecular or some other movements when the cerebral action was going on, if there were no bony envelope and our senses or our instruments were sufficiently delicate.[6]

We must remember (in justice as well as in charity) that the essay from which these crude and incoherent statements are taken 'had not undergone the many revisions which it was' (we are told) 'the Author's habit to make peculiarly searching and thorough'.[7] As they stand, they are sufficient to convey the grand metaphysical objection, warning, complaint, that while I *know* that thoughts and feelings exist, I can never really be absolutely certain that material objects exist.

Descartes remarks that we say that we *see* people passing before the window, when in fact all that we can see is hats and cloaks, which might be moved by machinery. So that, while

6. *Three Essays on Religion*, p. 198, etc.
7. *Op. cit.* Introductory Notice by Helen Taylor.

we might be inclined to claim that we *know* that there are people in the street, it appears on reflection to be more correct to say that we know that there are hats and coats and infer from this that there must be people inside them. Such inferences may be mistaken: and there is a Test of Experience which will show us when they are mistaken and when not. To such a test one may properly appeal against any opinion, however long accepted.

But, of course, the Cartesian doubt did not stop at hats and coats. I also say that I *see* a piece of wax, or an orange, or a table, or a room heated by a stove: but is it notorious that seeing (in the sense here used) is not always *knowing*. What I see may turn out to be a mirror image or an image in my own mind. Moreover, even where no such illusion is discoverable, doubts may begin to arise. For it is usually the case that when two people are apparently perceiving the same object, we find that they can be persuaded to disagree in their descriptions of what they are perceiving. One can be induced to say that the penny looks elliptical, the other that it looks round; one, that it looks white and shining; the other, that it looks brown. And so on. But the penny cannot be round and elliptical, white and brown: both observers cannot really *know* although both are really *seeing*. But if perception does not *always* give us knowledge of the real properties of physical objects, how can we distinguish those cases in which it does? Is it not prudent to introduce here the distinction which we made in the case of the hats and coats? To say that we see *something* which has definite sensible properties, and *infer* that there must exist some sort of external object which is the cause of such perceptions in different people?[8]

But this inference is mysterious. It is not inductive. By inductive inference I decide that hats and coats probably conceal passers-by: for here is a connexion which I have learned from experience of hats and coats and of passers-by. And the inference *to passers-by* can, of course, be checked by further experience. The inference from what we perceive *to material*

8. Compare the opening of the seventh paragraph of *Logic*, I, iii.

things is not of this kind. For, it is held, we have no experience of material things *except* our experiences in perception. 'Of the outward world,' says Mill, 'we know and can know absolutely nothing, except the sensations which we experience from it.'

To adopt Mill's (and Locke's) language, experience may teach us to expect regular sequences and co-existences in our sensations; it cannot teach us to expect the co-existence of a set of sens..ions *with a material object*. Nor, therefore, can experience provide us with any check upon our belief (if we have such a belief) that, on a given occasion, certain sensations are caused in us by an external material substance. The sense, therefore, in which we may speak of a material substance as 'the cause' of sensations in us is not the sense of 'cause' which is discussed in Book III of the *Logic*.

From Locke to James Mill, there continued a complicated debate about the way in which we know physical objects; Reid and Hamilton providing an intelligent opposition to the sensationist school. Two important questions should be distinguished:

(1) Can our conceptions of *the properties* of physical objects be shown to derive from ideas of sensation? Do we, for example, form the notion of extension in three dimensions, from our ideas of sight and touch? Berkeley's *New Theory of Vision* is one of the answers offered by the sensationists. Mill certainly held that all our concepts of physical properties are derived from ideas of sensation.

(2) Does our belief *that a particular physical object exists* involve anything more than a belief in the co-presence of various sorts of sensible properties? Reid held that it is an original part of our natures to believe that our ideas of sensation are caused in us by an external and non-sensible object; and Locke himself had held that when we see the sun by day we have a non-sensuous intuition of the actual entry of our ideas of sensation from an external body.

On this second question, Mill holds that the notion of an independent, persisting cause of our sensation is one which we form by reflection and 'negative abstraction'; that there is no reason to believe that any such thing exists; and that our ordinary unreflective belief in the existence of a physical object makes no reference to anything but what we observe through the senses.

He argues on the following lines:

Sensations (Berkeley had said) occur in regular sequences and patterns. By association, therefore, one sensation comes to suggest the *possibility* (if only one waits, or moves over to another position, or puts out one's hand) of the other sensation following. Such possibilities have definite conditions which relate in every case to some movement (or state of rest) on the part of the observer's body: 'If I put out my hand until I see it on top of the colour I am now looking at, then I shall feel something hard.'[9]

Such 'possibilities' hold (as conditional statements) whether we proceed to carry out the condition or not; they hold whether we wish it or not. And they are permanent.

Though the sensations cease, the possibilities remain in existence; they are independent of our will, our presence, and everything which belongs to us.[10]

The *kind* of connexion which Mill has in mind here is that which would lead us to say that a *succession* of sensations of colour and shape were perceptions of the same continuing object from different points of view. Any one of these sensa-

---

9. Contrast the statement: 'If this kettle were heated, it would emit steam.' This is a valid conditional sentence, but it does not lead us to say that the steam *is really here now*. For the antecedent, the conditioning clause, does not refer simply to the bringing into play of my sense organs. See A. J. Ayer, *Foundations of Empirical Knowledge*, p. 256, and the whole of his final chapter.

Mill distinguishes more clearly than Berkeley had done between uniform connexions between physical objects and those connexions amongst our sensations which lead us to talk of physical objects. Berkeley was of course mistaken (as Hume well understood) in saying that the sensations themselves occur in uniform sequences. The point is discussed fully in H. H. Price's *Hume's Theory of the External World*, Oxford, 1940.

10. *Examination*, p. 196.

tions suggests to me that I could now have one of the others *merely by moving my own sense organs*. (The appearance of the front of an object immediately suggests the possibility that I could now see the back if I changed my position: the back is there awaiting me.) I therefore ascribe the colour or shape I now see to a three-dimensional object: 'The book is faded on this side.' This kind of connexion needs to be distinguished from a universal or causal connexion. I say 'This snow is white', not implying that snow might not be dirty or stained; but rather that there is here a 'fixed group' (as Mill calls it) in which whiteness can be experienced along with dampness, coldness, softness, etc., in any order – or, rather, in an order dictated solely by the way in which I make use of my senses. The predicational form of sentence indicates this connexion: whereas 'There is snow and noise' does not – it is not asserted that the snow is noisy.

These connexions concern, not my own sensations only, but those of any normal observer. While no two people share the same sensation (Mill assures us), they seem to base their expectations and their conversation and their conduct upon the same patterns or groups of possibilities. Mill therefore argues that it is to these permanent patterns, governing everybody's sensations, that we give the name 'material object.' This is all that the ordinary man means by matter unless he is drawn into a philosophical discussion. So far, Mill agrees with Berkeley's caption: 'The philosophic, not the vulgar, substance taken away.' But Berkeley claims that there is no other notion of substance: that even in philosophical discussion the word must mean either this or – nothing at all. Mill, on the contrary, admits another sense to the word, and tries to show how it was formed:

(1) Whenever we clearly form the notion of *a kind*, we also form the notion of *whatever is not of this kind*. This he calls negative abstraction. (We form the notion of 'the remainder class'.)

(2) When we realize that we never find anything in the outer world except ideas of sensation, we proceed to form

the notion of something external, but *not* sensation (or possibility of sensation).

(3) If we are brought to wonder what is the cause of our sensations, our only notion is something external but not either a sensation or a possibility of sensation. To this, if pressed, we give the old name of 'material substance'.

The use which Mill makes of the notion of 'possibility of sensation' is certainly a crude one. We may, however, rephrase his doctrine in more modern terms. He is arguing that all that we ever try to say in categorical statements about the existence of physical objects in the 'outer world' can be re-expressed, without any loss or change of meaning, in statements about what sensations we and other people actually have, together with hypothetical statements. In these hypothetical statements, the antecedent clause always refers to a re-orientation of our own, or any other normal observer's, sense organs; and the consequent refers to sensations which I (or the other normal observer) would then have. Even in this form many refinements need to be introduced, but they can be disregarded for the purposes of this discussion. The doctrine which we now ascribe to Mill is known as Phenomenalism.

4. UNPERCEIVED OBJECTS: OTHER MINDS

To this phenomenalism there are well-known objections. There is, for example, the question of unperceived objects, especially objects in the remote past, before there were any minds to perceive anything. And there is the question of the existence of other people.

(1) What happens to the cow in the field when there is nobody there to perceive her? To say that she is there is most certainly to imply that if any normal observer were to go into the field, he would see her colour and shape, and hear her characteristic noises. But do such implications convey, and exhaust, the meaning of the statement that she is there now? The proposed elucidation of our statement changes a cate-

gorical statement into a series of hypothetical ones. And the Phenomenalist has to argue that, if only the hypotheticals are supplied generously enough to cover what might be called 'indirect evidence of there being, or having been, a cow in the field', then the elucidation is really a complete analysis. But is it? 'The cow is there now' certainly seems to assert that she is there for the field and the grass and for the other cows *now;* and, above all, that she is there for herself; as well as implying that she would be there for me if I went to look.[11]

(2) But even if we are satisfied that phenomenalism is able to give a good account of cows, are we able to accept its account of the existence of other human beings? Consider Mill's remarks on the existence of Calcutta, a city which he had never seen:

> I believe that Calcutta exists, though I do not perceive it, and that it would still exist if every percipient inhabitant were suddenly to leave the place, or be struck dead. But when I analyse the belief, all I find in it is, that were these events to take place, the Permanent Possibility of Sensation which I call Calcutta would still remain. ...[12]

Mill here seems to suppose that the question of the existence of Calcutta becomes acute only when it ceases to be perceived by its normal inhabitants. And throughout his exposition of the meaning of material-object statements, he assumes that the objects are 'fixed groups' of possible sensations, for *any normal observer*, although in describing objects I am in fact describing *my own* sensations. But what does he mean by talking of the existence of sensations in observers other than himself? Does he, in asserting the existence of 'other successions of feeling besides those of which I am conscious', accept a hypothetical interpretation of his words or not? Certainly he does not. Whether I see you, hear your words, or have the remotest knowledge of what you are feeling or thinking, you are really there – there for yourself. This is Mill's view. And

11. See the great debate between Ansell and Tilliard in the opening scene of E. M. Forster's *The Longest Journey*.

12. *Examination*, p. 199.

not only are your present feelings there for you: you are some-how aware also of your past and your future states. So that *what* you are is indeed 'inexplicable'; as Mill himself admits in the twelfth chapter of the *Hamilton*. But whatever you are, you are not merely a 'conditioned possibility' for me.

In discussing the question, 'How do we know that other minds exist?' Mill offers only the usual arguments from analogy. When, therefore, he says (in the statement quoted at the opening of this paragraph) that *mind* 'is in a philosophical point of view the only reality of which we have any evidence', he must intend to speak of 'minds', not of his own mind. And in fact Mill never once supposes that a statement about the existence of another mind is to be interpreted in purely hypo-thetical terms. But if these statements cannot be interpreted in phenomenalist language, we must feel considerable doubt as to whether statements about the existence of physical objects are really exhausted by a phenomenalist analysis. Moreover, the second kind of statement seems to involve the first: physical objects are there to be perceived by any normal ob-server; they are in fact often perceived by many observers at the same time. At least by implication, therefore, they seem to involve a statement about other minds.

In the following sections I shall try to show that the pheno-menalist analysis gains its plausibility from the doctrine of sensationism, and that this provides no adequate account of our knowledge of the physical world.

5. APPEARANCE AND REALITY

We have first to ask: Does the Phenomenalist analysis pre-serve the objective character of judgements about physical objective? In saying 'The snow is white', I am saying that an object has a certain quality which I now perceive, and which any suitably-placed observer may perceive – must perceive whether he likes it or not.

Locke made a distinction between *quality* and *idea of sensa-tion*. The quality, according to him, is a specific power in the object which can cause us to have a physical sensation, of which we normally become conscious – of which we normally have an idea. The idea of whiteness is thus something quite distinct from the quality: for the former is private to the observer, the latter is not.

Mill admits a nominal distinction between physical quality and sensation; he will go no further. He holds that the same identical *quale* is called a sensation when it is considered in one context, and a quality of an object when it is considered in another context. When viewed as occurring along with my own feelings and desires, and the whole stream of my consciousness, it is called 'sensation'; when viewed as something occurring in a 'rigid complex', it is called 'quality'. Hence

the distinction which we verbally make between the properties of things and the sensations we receive from them, must originate in the convenience of discourse rather than in the nature of what is signified by the terms.[13]

According to Mill, to say 'The snow is white' is to assert the existence of a plurality of sensations (coldness, glitter, etc.) along with a sensation of whiteness: and to imply the present possibility (conditioned only upon my body making certain movements) of other sensations of taste, smell, etc. The object is *actual*, because whiteness, coldness, glitter, are now actually present. And because these sensations have in the past regularly occurred together with a certain taste, smell, etc., I take them as a sign of the remainder and give to the present possibility of sensation the name 'snow'.

Can we accept this view of judgement of perception? The judgement we are considering is undoubtedly intended to give an account of a quality of a real thing: and Mill's doctrine is intended as a contribution to the Philosophy of Experience; to say what exactly the Test of Experience means when it is applied to very simple judgements about physical objects. Is he correct?

13. *Logic*, I, iii (9). But should we not say that the distinction between 'man' and 'son' is a distinction in nature, even though the terms have the same extension?

A judgement of perception is to be distinguished from judgements about the way things look or appear or seem to me. Let us consider two different examples: (1) If I were looking down from a high window, I might say: 'The policeman's helmet appears as if it were between his boots'. And it would be understood that I was not asserting that the policeman was doubled up with his head between his feet, nor performing any other trick. But in making this remark I should suppose that, if anybody else were to come to the window, he would agree with me that the helmet appears to be between the boots; and equally agree with me that the helmet is really on the policeman's head. (2) On the other hand, if I suffered from a defect of vision, or were ill or very tired, I might say: 'The words on the page seem to be jumping about'; and in this case, of course, I should not expect other people to say that the words seem to them to be jumping about. And everyone would understand that I was not really saying that the words were actually moving about or that they would seem to be doing so to anyone who looked over my shoulder. If I were to judge that the words *were* jumping about, I should be making a mistaken judgement of perception. If I came to realize this mistake I might say: 'The words *seemed* to be jumping about but of course they were not really doing so.' This again is a straightforward statement about the way things really were. It is when (as might happen in such a case) I say 'And of course they still *seem* to me to be jumping about' that I am making a judgement about the way things *seem* to me in contrast to the way they really are.

There is clearly a big difference between these two cases. In the first case, while I am not saying that the policeman's head is between his boots, I am saying that from this position *anyone* would think the policeman's head was between his boots if he were to overlook, ignore, abstract from, those features which 'give away' the actual state of affairs. In the second case, my judgement about the letters is a judgement about me; about the effect of the print on my eyes. In the first case the judgement is not *about me* at all. We may call the second an example of a judgement of sensation: the first (in my opinion) is an example of a *special kind* of judgement of perception.

Now in a special restricted sense, Mill wants us to believe *that any judgement of perception is about the way in which things appear to the speaker.* 'The snow is white' means that I have a *sensation* of whiteness along with various other sensations and possibilities of sensation. Of course the snow is also perceived (or perceptible) by other people: but when I describe the snow, *what I am doing is to describe the quality of my own sensations,* not theirs. 'The snow appears white to me now, it appears to have other qualities and would appear to have still other qualities if I were to change my position, etc.' But it is important to notice that a sensation is not *any* kind of appearance: it is an appearance supposed to arise through the stimulation of one or other of the sense-organs. And Mill himself assures us that, in the presence of the same physical object, people do not have *exactly* the same sensations, for the sense-organs will be slightly different from person to person. What, then, am I trying to do when I offer a description of the snow – when I name its colours, for example? Am I really trying to describe the particular way it appears to me now? No. Nor is it the case (as Mill goes on to suppose) that I am trying to guess how it will appear to anybody else. What I am trying to do is to apply the word 'white' as I have learned to do from other people at home and at school. And the test of the *correct* application of such a word is certainly *not* to be found simply by comparing the appearance of the snow with the appearance of other things that have been described to me as 'white'. What reassures me that I have given a correct description of the object is that nobody disputes it; that there is general agreement between normal observers that this is the correct word to use on this occasion. And, of course, this agreement is limited to those who have learned the use of the word; that is, to those who speak English.

Now no doubt I am incited to use the word 'white' partly by the way the snow appears to me now – by the sensation I am at the moment enjoying. The sensation helps me to identify the colour of the object. But it is not the only factor: and I might judge the snow to be white, although it appeared yellow to me. For what I am trying to do is to apply to the snow the colour-adjective which everyone agrees to apply. Of course there are cases where it is not possible for us to reach agreement: it may be that the snow looks yellow to me, and I cannot but suppose that it really is so. Various ways of settling this question will at once suggest themselves. And I may in the end back down, ascribing my mistake to jaundice or sun-spectacles or to absence of mind. But the test clearly lies in general agreement. This is the Test of Experience, as applied to judgements of perception: not the test of my own private experience, but of many people in communication.

Mill's account seems to combine two incompatible theories of perception, both of which are mistaken.

(1) He wants to regard a judgement about a physical object as *an inference* from the way things appear to me. I have certain sensations; I infer that (on making certain bodily movements) I should have other sensations; and I infer that, if others were present and suitably placed, they would have sensations pretty much like my own. But these inferences must, of course, be capable of being tested *by experience*. And this can only mean, by the way in which things appear to me – or, rather, by the way they appear to me through one or other of my senses. This way of regarding judgements of perception derives from Locke's *Essay* (Book II, Chapter ix). In effect, it reduces them to a different type of judgement altogether – to judgements of sensation, such as 'This seems white to me'. All the ultimate premises from which a judgement of perception is inferred are supposed to be of this type. And it is by further judgements of sensation that all the inferences involved in judgements of perception are to be tested. Such judgements of sensation are supposed to be certain and beyond all possibility of revision: we cannot be mistaken about them.[14]

14. Of course there are judgements of sensation. But it is important to notice that when I use 'white' or 'yellow' to describe the appearance, I am using words whose meaning is derived from their use in judgements of

(2) Mill also wants, on the other hand, to regard a judgement of perception as a response – no doubt an 'appropriate
response' – to a stimulus from the physical environment of
my body. There is a continuous process supposed, from the
external object through the sense-organs to the brain. In the
brain, all kinds of 'traces' and connexions are touched off –
traces and connexions which have been established by the
peculiar experiences of the body, and which would not be the
same in all bodies. Then out comes the judgement – or the
expression of the judgement, whether in English or in Welsh
or in Chinese. All this is regarded as determined: and error
arises where the sense-organs are in an unusual condition,
where there is interruption of, or interference with, the
normal working of the brain, etc. Otherwise, the closeness or
directness of the causal connexion between stimulus and
response is a guarantee of the 'appropriateness' of the
response; i.e., of the truth of the judgement.

The second view greatly influenced Mill's statement of the
first view. Mill is anxious to secure as basic premises, judgements that are highly certain and reliable. The physiological
evidence suggested that the more-or-less immediate response
to an external stimulation would give the greatest possible
certainty. Hence the notion of 'sensation': that which appears
to me when light strikes my eyes from a plain surface, when
my hand moves over it, etc. In describing what I *seem to see*,
what I *seem to feel*, I can hardly go wrong. Moreover, physiology also suggested that all my genuine knowledge of the
physical world *must* come to me through the gateways of the
senses. Hence the doctrine of Experience is reduced to a
doctrine of direct awareness through the sense-organs,
supplemented by inferences based on the 'association' of ideas
and of feelings in the brain.

Now this certainly is a narrowing. If I look at a distant
snow-peak from a warm room, and am asked to describe what
I seem to see, I may very well say that the mountain shape

perception. This at once suggests that we could make mistakes in our use
of such words, even when we are describing sensations or images.

seems cold as well as white, and that it seems far in the background, as well as triangular. But the sensationist will reply that the shape cannot *seem* to be distant in the same sense as it seems to be triangular. It seems to have a certain shape and to have a certain position in my visual field, and these *suggest* the idea of distance – distance is inferred from the sensations of shape and position. Similarly, it will be objected that the shape cannot *seem* to be cold in the same sense as it seems to be white: it is the sensation of whiteness that leads us to *infer* coldness. The distance and the coldness are not immediate responses: they are associated with immediate responses by our past experiences. The distance and the coldness are therefore not acceptable as ultimate premises for a judgement of perception: analysis must derive the distance and the cold from those appearances which (according to the physiological theory) the thing immediately presents to me.

And it seems to me that both the inference-theory and the causal theory are mistaken.

(1) Do judgements about the way things seem to me always precede or accompany judgements of perception? Surely not. When we are trying to describe things as they really are, we do not bother to describe them as they *appear*: why should we? If I am asked to make a judgement *of sensation*, I do so by *contrasting* what appears with what is perceived. I ask myself, for example, what shape does the *circular* penny seem to present from this angle. I say 'It looks elliptical', and I mean that if I ignored altogether those features which assure me that it is lying face down at some little distance away from me and below me, then I should think that it really *was* elliptical. And 'it' in this context means the penny all the time – not a bogus entity called 'the appearance of the penny'. And in fact I do not think that the penny is elliptical; and it is only by considering it as cut out of its context that I can bring myself to admit that the answer to the highly abstract question is – 'elliptical'. This might be established more readily if only someone would make an elliptical penny.

It follows that when I judge 'The snow is white', I am not

asserting that whiteness is somehow compounded with other sensible properties in a rigid complex. It has, however, been admitted that it is normally when a thing looks white to me, or something like white, that I say that it is white. Sensations, then (not judgements of sensation) play an important role in the procedure of describing the world and of verifying descriptions. But not only sensations: other appearances, not acknowledged by the sensationists, play a precisely similar role. I say that the snow is crystalline, when it *looks* crystalline; that it is distant, when it *looks* distant; and the testimony of others is a further incitement to apply the description.

(2) The second theory is also mistaken.

The causal theory of perception begins with certain necessary conditions of perception. It is and always has been a part of common knowledge that I cannot see the shape of an object unless my body is in a suitable position and I have my eyes open. And we now certainly know a great deal about the physiological conditions which must be fulfilled if I am to see the shape. So that it is by what Locke called 'little excursions into natural philosophy' that we try to explain how it is that a given person is able to judge the colour of the flag, the size of the mountain, the shape of the penny. In all this discussion we are referring (i) to the percipient; (ii) to the object he is perceiving; (iii) to the effects of the object upon the outside and the inside of the percipient's body – but for which the perception would not have taken place. The mistake which gives rise to the characteristic difficulties of the causal theory of perception is to suppose that the perception of the object must really be the perception of some effect which the object has *inside the body of the percipient*. It is a further mistake to identify this (supposedly perceived) internal effect with an entity called 'the appearance of the object' – the something that *is* elliptical, where the object *looks* elliptical. Once these mistakes have been made, it becomes a question how one ever came to introduce the perceived object into the discussion at all.

No doubt there are occasions when I have a sensation and

do not know what it is of. I might, for instance, have such an 'unassigned' sensation of warmth, and wonder where it came from. In such cases I may really argue back from the effect on my body to an external and public cause – which may then become the *object* of a perception, whether by sight or touch or even through the very sensation of warmth. But we cannot suppose that all our sensations do or could occur in this way: it is only because we are able to make non-inferential judgements about external objects (by the help of the sense of sight and the sense of touch) that there is ever any question of making inferences to external objects. It is in any case not a cause of sensations that we ought to be in search of, but an object of perception, independent of my perceiving it, and perceptible by all. Such an object – and a world of such objects – is not far to seek. It is the world of objects which we refer to by names and demonstratives, and which we describe by the general terms of common speech.

We may conclude, then, that Mill's theory of knowledge makes great attempts to preserve the objectivity of statements about physical objects; that the attempt involves him in inconsistencies and confusions; and that an Experience Philosophy can remain plausible only if it retains a wide sense of the word 'experience'.

Setting aside, therefore, Mill's account of the relation between sensations and things, we must now enquire what general knowledge we have (in his view) of the order and arrangement of the world.

6. THE ORDER OF NATURE

Mill holds that facts have a wholly objective structure: there are kinds, and there are causal connexions, existing independently of anyone's knowing them. What precisely these are, is to be discovered piecemeal. Mill does not attempt to argue that all nature *must* obey regular laws. It is, in his view, a fact of experience that there is in nature such regularity as we are able to observe there. It is possible for us to conceive a world in which (could we by some miracle observe it) our experiences would be so chaotic that we should not attempt to formulate laws of sequence at all, or laws of co-existence. Universal judgements, in such a world, would have no use. And Mill says that such a chaos may even now exist 'in distant parts of the stellar regions'; and might, at the end of the present age, succeed the cosmos in which we now live. But in the whole of that part of the universe which is accessible to us by experience, we have good reason to suppose that every change has its regular antecedent, and that the laws of perspective and of geometry and arithmetic are everywhere observed.[15]

But even in the cosmos, some reference to chance is unavoidable. There are, at any given moment, certain fundamental causal forces operating in the world, and these are arranged in a certain pattern. By tracing individual causal sequences, we can in part explain how the pattern of to-day arises out of the pattern of yesterday. And so we can trace backwards from one configuration to another: but at each stage the antecedent configuration has to be accepted as a fact of chance. And if we suppose a beginning to the order of things in which we live, we must suppose there to have been a primaeval configuration of causes, for which we have no law. The kind of law we should need (presumably) would be a law of co-existence. And laws of co-existence are known to us: the laws of mathematics and of the basic natural kinds. But clearly the distribution of *forces* (or of matter) cannot be inferred from any purely geometrical laws. Nor will laws of the co-existence of properties in natural kinds be of any use. For they determine the character of the ultimate agents themselves: they are laws of such repeatable structures as are not known to be derived by causation from antecedent structures. They do not determine the total distribution of such agents. The primaeval configuration must therefore remain a matter of chance.[16]

It is because the total configuration at *any* given moment is

15. *Logic*, III, xxi (4), etc.   16. *Logic*, III, v (8).

in fact unknown to us that we cannot say of any of the formulae which we are inclined to regard as laws of causality, that they are *known* to be unconditional. For they may, in fact, hold only in the presence of certain causal agents in a certain configuration; just as unsupported bodies tend towards the centre of the earth only in its immediate neighbourhood.

In his later writings, Mill conceived the ultimate causal agents in the physical world to be material particles possessing force. He believed that minds have at least one power which is not possessed by matter: the power of *remembering*. Minds also have the power to change the distribution of physical forces: but Mill was not convinced that this was done otherwise than in accordance with physical laws. However, he was willing to examine this hypothesis, and also to give serious consideration to the view that the transformation of forces and (presumably) the operation of minds, might be partly under the control of a Divine Intelligence and Will.

In discussing the hypothesis of God's existence, Mill is at the greatest pains to set aside all purely religious considerations. By this I mean considerations that arise from the desire to worship God, to serve God, or to obtain the consolations of religion. 'We are looking at the subject,' he remarks in the early part of the *Essay on Theism*, 'not from the point of view of reverence, but from that of science.'[17]

By 'God', Mill means a Being having intelligence and will and capable of doing right and wrong. In some sense, God would be a person – indeed, he would be (in Mill's view) as much a separate person from any of his creatures as one man is separate from another. Could such a Being be *infinite* in his intelligence, power, and moral goodness? Mill holds that the notion of each of these infinites is clear, and the notion of their union in one Being is also clear. But he holds that a mere glance at the world of our experience shows that no such Being in fact exists. For our world contains every species of evil, along with all kinds of good. If we think of God as truly infinite, this world must derive from his power and survive

17. *Three Essays on Religion*, 3rd ed., p. 136.

by his acquiescence. We know, therefore, that God cannot be infinite in all his attributes.

But Mill is prepared to discuss the possibility of the existence of a Being who is limited in power, and perhaps also in intelligence, and whose goodness is to be judged from his creation. There is, he thinks, no value whatsoever in any of the *a priori* proofs of God's existence, but there is some value in the Argument from Design. This he regards as something more than a mere argument from analogy: it rests upon a direct induction from experience. For there are marks in the world of deliberate contrivance to secure definite ends: and in all our experience *within the world* such marks are always the work of an intelligent mind. Mill thus permits a transition from argument about things in the world, to arguments about the world as a whole. Many philosophers refuse to admit that this is ever a legitimate procedure: the transition is one which Mill does not seem to notice.

There are certain features of the world, then, which suggest that they are the result of the operation of a mind on a scale which all but exceeds our imagining. But only certain features of the world show this planning: others seem to be inconsistent with any notion of contrivance or foresight. The Theos is no more than a Demiourgos. He is certainly limited in power: in all probability, matter and force are coeval with him. He may also be limited in wisdom and skill: for some of those parts of the world which show marks of planning also show marks of clumsiness and stupidity. Is he morally good? Are his aims right aims? Mill is very cautious on this point. There is evidence that the creator or architect of the world desired the pleasure of his sentient creatures: why else should he have arranged that pleasure should accompany the normal working of organisms, and pain only the abnormal? But, even so, it cannot be said that pleasure has prevailed over pain in the world: geological ages of misery have passed by: and even the normal process of replenishing the higher species mingles brief pleasure with prolonged pain. Indeed, Mill says that those few who have lived happy lives seem to have done so chiefly by their own exertions – that is, very often, by struggling *against* the normal processes of nature. The credit for this belongs to them and not to the Author of Nature.

If there be a God, then, the pleasure of his creatures is only one of his purposes; and one which he often subordinates to other purposes of which we know absolutely nothing. The Demiourgos is a remote being: and it seems that we are not his favourite children. Any 'idea of God more captivating than this comes only from human wishes, or from the teaching of either real or imaginary Revelation'.[18]

If, as Mill believed, there is some genuine evidence for the existence of a God, it is not possible to pass over in complete silence the claims that have been made in favour of special revelations. If there is a God, then it may be that certain events are due to his direct intervention, and they may be intended by him as a means of communicating with his creatures. But Mill decides that a so-called revelation must be judged by external marks, and not by the internal character of the truth revealed. For no truth, however profound, is altogether beyond the unaided powers of humankind. He therefore confines his discussion of revelation to the external evidence; that is, to the supposed supernatural events which accompanied it. He rehearses many of Hume's arguments against the acceptance of events as being miraculous, and comes to the conclusion that there is never sufficient evidence to prove that an event is an exception to a genuine law of nature. (This, of course, he must hold: for he has admitted that there is never sufficient evidence for a final decision as to whether a given formula is an unconditional law.) He therefore rejects all so-called revealed knowledge of God. 'The whole domain of the supernatural is thus removed from the region of Belief into that of simple Hope.' And there it is likely to remain.

For, while Mill holds that the evidence of design is genuine enough, he regards it as insufficient for proof, and as 'amounting only to one of the lower degrees of probability'.[19] And he expresses the conviction that a final decision on rational

18. *Three Essays on Religion*, pp. 167 and 195. 19. *Op. cit.*, pp. 242–4.

grounds will not be reached in any foreseeable time. He also adds that if Darwin's view on the 'survival of the fittest' were shown to be valid, this would provide a quite different account of the appearances of design in Nature, and would greatly attenuate the evidence for the existence of a divine intelligence.[20]

This, then, is Mill's view of the physical world: it consists of matter acted upon by forces: perhaps these forces are (in some way which he does not specify) under the control of finite minds: and perhaps all are to some degree under the control of God.

Man's body is a part of this physical world; and his will is frequently thwarted by the other forces acting in nature. He therefore must suffer Necessity in the full meaning of the word. He struggles against poverty, and sickness, and against his fellow-men, and he is often overcome by them. The fate of the whole human society very largely depends upon the struggle for food: Malthusianism illustrates the dependence of the race on the parsimony of the rest of Nature. Nevertheless, man also enjoys Freedom. For his will may prevail over other forces, and he then has that triumph which, within a deterministic system, is the opposite counterpart of the feeling of being necessitated. This freedom must be taken into account in any science of human nature: mankind cannot be understood even in their social aspects, except by reference to the individual, who enjoys a measure of freedom to achieve, not only the objects he desires to have, but also the character he desires to be.

Necessity and Freedom are alike subject to laws of determinism. The changes that take place in the body are supposed by Mill to obey some kind of physical laws. They are chiefly (if not wholly) known to us as empirical laws: we know that a given stimulus leads to a certain response; but we are fairly sure that this is due to a configuration of minute forces in the body – a configuration as yet unanalysed.

The changes that take place in the mind also have causes.

20. *Op. cit.*, p. 174.

The causes may be antecedent states of mind or states of body or both. Mill holds that sensations have for their immediate antecedents, states of body; and that the laws governing sensations manifestly belong to the province of physiology. But whether our thoughts, emotions, and volitions are similarly dependent on physical conditions is an unsettled question.[21] Mill is inclined to hold that there is, so far as our observations go, a widespread concomitance of mental and bodily states. 'All theories of mind which have any pretension to comprehensiveness' must be engaged in trying to discover such connexions. But he is confident that psychology cannot be studied as a branch of physiology. For we are able, by introspective methods, to discover laws of mind which cannot be derived from any physiological laws known to us. The laws of association are examples. Such purely mental laws may not be ultimate, but the proper method is to study them first as empirical laws, and to explain them by whatever method of analysis proves most fruitful. Mill therefore adopts a methodological principle of psycho-physical parallelism.[22]

That mental states exist without accompanying bodily states is not known to be the case: but Mill insists that it is logically possible. Hence (he argues) the existence of a mind without a body is also logically possible. If minds were to exist without bodies, there could not, in the nature of the case, be any available evidence of this. Hence the complete lack of evidence in favour of the religious belief in immortality does not raise a strong presumption against the hypothesis. It is, Mill holds, one of those rare questions on which there is no evidence either way.[23]

If it is logically possible that thoughts and feelings and memories should exist without any connexion with a brain and body, then it follows *a fortiori* that thoughts and feelings

21. *Logic*, VI, iv (2).
22. *Logic*, *loc. cit.*, and *Three Essays on Religion*, p. 198, etc.
23. *Three Essays on Religion*, p. 203. Mill was not prepared to give serious consideration to the alleged evidence of communication with disembodied spirits. See *Letters*, I, p. 259.

and memories cannot actually be states of body described in a special (unscientific) language. Mill does not expressly discuss this view: but the arguments which he brings against those who hold that mental and bodily states are *necessarily* connected are in fact directed against it. We know that it *cannot* be shown that all facts are facts about bodies, because the received opinions of Associative Psychology teach us the direct converse of this doctrine. What we call bodies and brains are *certain of our sensations* described in a special language.

7. MILL'S VIEWS ON RELIGION

In his *Autobiography* Mill describes himself as 'one of the very few examples in this country, of one who has, not thrown off religious belief, but never had it'. In his childhood he had looked on the religious beliefs of his own day, exactly as he did on those of ancient times, as something which in no way concerned him.[24] But there came a time when these beliefs did concern him: and certainly his father was always concerned with them. James Mill had once been a candidate for Holy Orders: he had abandoned his beliefs after a struggle, and he knew that they must be taken seriously. His objections to Christianity were moral as well as logical. He found it morally repugnant to believe that this world is the work of a perfectly good and powerful deity: still less could he accept the Christian belief in 'the Omnipotent Author of Hell'. Such a doctrine he believed to be immoral in a plain honest sense of the word.

John Mill also never loses an opportunity, in his published writings and in his private correspondence, of insisting upon the same point. We can condemn the orthodox belief in omnipotence on the grounds that it is incompatible with a belief in perfect goodness. This implies that the acceptance of the canons of right and wrong are in no way dependent upon a belief in a god: and so, of course, all the Utilitarians believed. We can recognize right and wrong, good and bad, and can

24. P. 43.

imagine the highest perfection, without having to accept the existence of any order higher than the human. This doctrine of the autonomy of morals was carried a stage further in the arguments of 'Philip Beauchamp'. Beauchamp discussed the view that society in general (apart from a few intellectuals) cannot be maintained in a healthy moral state unless there is a widespread belief in the existence of a supernatural order which rewards goodness and badness hereafter; or which, by some means, at least contrives to make goodness prevail in the long run. As we have seen, John Mill was given the book to read at the age of sixteen, and accepted the author's refutation of this argument. And at a later time, after his marriage, he re-read it, and his *Essay on the Utility of Religion* shows that he was still in substantial agreement with it. The second of the *Three Essays*, that on *Nature*, written at about the same time, is an attempt to show that it is possible and desirable to take a religious view of Man himself. This is an adaptation of Comte's 'Religion of Humanity': and Mill argues that it contains in it all that is true and ennobling in the best of the historical faiths. But he was never altogether satisfied with this view.[25]

The last of the *Three Essays*, that on *Theism*, was written much later – between 1868 and 1870. In it, Mill makes a sustained attempt to consider again the rational grounds for belief or disbelief in the existence of a personal God, and in the immortality of the soul. We have already seen that his conclusions are almost entirely negative: and in this state of theoretical scepticism Mill died, as he had lived. But at various periods, and especially late in his life, he tried to assess *the moral value* of a belief in God – to find out, as Bain says, 'what there was in religion to commend it to the best minds among its adherents'. And this led him to enquire also whether something of this moral virtue might not be available in 'the region of simple Hope'. His reflections on this subject are given in the last sections of the *Essay on Theism*.

It is not now a question of the subjection of ordinary

25. cf. Mill's letter to Capt. de Chément, 1854, Vol. I, p. 183.

sensual man to the threats and bribes of a world-to-come. It is a question of the response *of the best minds* to the contemplation of the idea of God. And, inevitably, his enquiry centres upon Christianity and on the revelation of God to be found in the first three gospels.

In 1833, Mill mentioned in a letter to Carlyle that he has been reading the New Testament: 'properly I can never be said to have *read* it before'. But in a subsequent letter he explains that this reading has only served to strengthen his previous convictions about the life of Jesus; unbounded reverence for Christ was not a new thing in his life, but it was now becoming a living principle in his character. Mill's idea of Christ derived from the Synoptic Gospels: the Fourth Gospel was a misrepresentation and the source of much bad theology. His Jesus is a man, a moral teacher and leader; not a miracle-worker, not a sacrificed god, and (one might almost add) not the Head of the Christian Church.[26] But Mill recognized clearly enough that much in the purely moral teaching of Jesus would be meaningless apart from his belief in God. And in many letters, throughout many years, he discusses the question of the influence of the idea of God upon the imagination and the will.

In 1859, in a letter to Dr W. G. Ward, Mill remarks that, just as the believer would recoil from the idea of not being in unison with God, so even the unbeliever might have a similar feeling towards an *ideal* God; 'as there may be towards an ideally perfect man, or towards our friends who are no more, even if we do not feel assured of their immortality'. To another correspondent (an unbeliever), he wrote in 1868 of the value of prayer even to those who doubt whether prayer can alter the course of nature. There is, he held, a kind of prayer in which a man endeavours 'to commune and to become in harmony with the highest spiritual ideal that he is capable in elevated moments of conceiving. This effect may be very powerful in clearing the moral perceptions and intensifying the moral earnestness'.[27]

26. *Letters*, I, pp. 68 and 93.   27. *Letters*, I, p. 231; II, p. 115.

In the *Essay on Theism* Mill discusses the extremely difficult question of the relation between hopes and beliefs. Hopes are the work of the Imagination, the idealizing and transforming faculty; and Poetry, the Poetry of Insight, is the religion of the unbelieving. What principles ought to govern the Imagination, in order, on the one hand, to prevent it from disturbing the rectitude of the intellect and the right direction of the actions and the will; and, on the other hand, to permit it as much freedom as possible to perform its great task of increasing human happiness and goodness? Mill answers in a passage which at once recalls his account of the great lessons he learned in the years following 1826:

> To me it seems that human life, small and confined as it is, and as, considered merely in the present, it is likely to remain even when the progress of material and moral improvement may have freed it from the greater part of its present calamities, stands greatly in need of any wider range and greater height of aspiration for itself and its destination, which the exercise of imagination can yield to it without running counter to the evidence of fact; and that it is a part of wisdom to make the most of any, even small, probabilities on this subject, which furnish imagination with any footing to support itself upon.[28]

In a letter to Edwin Arnold, of the same period, Mill states that he does not expect that our uncertainty on these questions is ever likely to give way to knowledge. It is necessary to consider what ought to be the state of mind of thinking men of this and of all ages. 'I am convinced,' he writes, 'that the cultivation of an imaginative hope is quite compatible with a reserve as to positive belief, and that whatever helps to keep before the mind the ideal of a perfect Being is of unspeakable value to human nature.'[29]

These words are highly characteristic of Mill and of many of the best minds of the nineteenth century. All too earnest, all too moralistic, yet determined not to leave out imagination altogether; inordinately hopeful of the quick results of intelligent 'improvement', yet secretly disillusioned of its inward

28. *Three Essays*, p. 245.   29. *Letters*, II, p. 339.

value; making their bows, sadly but politely, to the clouded throne.

For Mill, then, the religion of Jesus has dwindled to 'the Theism of the imagination and feelings'. But the man Jesus lost nothing of his power. Mill could hope (but not believe) that Jesus received his message and his power from God. Mill found reasons for discarding all that was mysterious, miraculous, or eschatological from that message; he believed that Jesus had never himself claimed to be more than a prophet sent from God; 'greater than John the Baptist' but still a prophet. The teachings of Jesus, in so far as they concerned this world, seemed to him to express the highest conception of morality that has ever been offered to men. And besides, the life of Jesus is the ideal guide for humanity; so that even an unbeliever like himself could not find a better translation of the rule of virtue from the abstract to the concrete, than to try to live in the way which he could imagine Christ would approve. And if there was any one thing which Mill believed to be the great gift of religion, it was this translation of morality into a concrete example.

This is the verdict of Mill's later years. It is easy to object that to pick and choose amongst the sayings of Jesus, as Mill did, is to run the risk of missing essentials; that perhaps Mill did no more than rebuild his own creed from the scattered fragments. It is also possible that Mill's real moral creed was in some respects at variance with the gospel maxims which he accepts. But the philosopher was now in his latest years and the time for argument was drawing to a close.

8. MILL AND WORDSWORTH

It will be seen that Mill's attitude towards religion involves, in the last analysis, not belief but the 'cultivation of the feelings'. Wordsworth – the poet of *The Prelude*, not the poet of the *Ecclesiastical Sonnets* – remains a powerful influence. But Wordsworth takes up an attitude towards his own deepest feelings, which is very different from Mill's attitude towards his feelings. This is in part concealed by the fact that they were both ardent psychologists of the same school. Wordsworth was himself fascinated by attempts to trace the building up of moods and sentiments from associations formed in moments of excitement. In many of his poems he describes a moment of illumination, in which some natural scene or object, or some human situation, is invested with a new quality, a new light. And in many cases the poem also tries to show how this illumination was made possible by some previous experience (perhaps never regarded as of any special importance until now) in which a new association had been formed. Yet for all his psychology, Wordsworth constantly writes as if what is experienced in the moment of illumination gives us knowledge about the world as a whole, and not merely knowledge about our own minds and bodies. And he also writes as if these encounters with nature were not altogether accidental: as if something in nature had a concern to make itself known, and made use of psychological mechanisms to this end – as well as of other processes of nature.

I do not mean to suggest that Wordsworth ever seriously held that the feelings he experienced on a given occasion were simply and straightforwardly *properties* of the objects presented on that occasion. This would be to make nonsense of the whole doctrine of association and of preparation: and Wordsworth actually introduces these doctrines into the poems themselves. The power which he felt was certainly something far more deeply interfused. Still less do I suggest that Wordsworth regarded the encounters as wholly the result of pre-arrangement. On the contrary, he emphasizes strongly an element of chance – of sheer good luck. But it does seem that he believed that the one 'Wisdom and Spirit of the Universe' was *especially* present to him on certain occasions; and that there was something not altogether chance in the series of occasions which he experienced throughout a long and happy childhood, and afterwards. One might say that Wordsworth set the same store by these occasions as our Puritan ancestors set by 'providences'. 'Let us look into

Providences,' wrote Oliver Cromwell, 'surely they mean somewhat. They hang so together; they have been so constant, so clear, unclouded.'

If we ask what sort of power Wordsworth thought was revealed to him in these moments of illumination, his answer is: A power which operates in the same sort of way as the mind of man; especially, as the imaginative mind of the poet. We might compare this with the answer sometimes made by philosophers: God is a logician, a mathematician. This kind of answer need not be disconcerting. All the gods have always been Human Nature Gods. But it is a reminder that Wordsworth's power is not a truly universal power: for, after all, Wordsworth's Nature is his own abstraction, and excludes nearly all the cruelty and recklessness which Mill describes in his own *Essay on Nature*. It is a typically eighteenth-century abstraction. But does not very much the same sort of abstraction (and even fiction) always go into the imaginative conception of the god men worship? Although Wordsworth was so fully conscious of these imaginative processes, yet (he tells us) it was in a spirit of religious awe that he walked with nature.

Mill's approach was more narrowly human and moralistic. He denounces nature as immoral: 'In sober truth, nearly all the things which men are hanged or imprisoned for doing to one another, are nature's every day performances.'[30] But, as we have seen, he was able to frame in his imagination the conception of a being in whom all the highest of moral and human qualities were united. This being was to him an object of imaginative contemplation, not of religious awe. Wordsworth had Faith and Mill had not. And Mill always assumed that Faith must rest upon *an inference* – upon an inference from experience to the existence of a remote and separate being. He was unable to see any logical justification for such an inference. But does Faith always rest upon an inference, whether logical or illogical? Was it essential to Wordsworth's religion to believe something *about* his experiences? It would surely be more accurate to say simply that he *believed in* them.

30. 'Essay on Nature', *Three Essays on Religion*, p. 28.

Bibliography

I. WORKS BY J. S. MILL

The *Collected Works* are now being published jointly by Toronto University Press and Routledge. The General Editors are F. E. L. Priestly and J. M. Robson. A *Selection* of Mill's works, edited by J. M. Robson, is published as a paperback by the Macmillan Company of Canada. The original editions of the more important philosophical works are listed below, together with some of the many reprints.

Dissertations and Discussions, London, 1859–75 (4 vols).
   Including the essays on 'Sedgwick' (1835), on 'Civilisation' ('36), on 'Bentham' ('38), on 'Coleridge' ('40), on 'Tocqueville' ('40), on 'The Claims of Labour' ('45).
   The essays on 'Bentham' and on 'Coleridge' have been published with an introductory essay by F. R. Leavis.
Letters, edited by Hugh Elliot, London, 1910 (2 vols).
J. S. Mill and Harriet Taylor, letters edited by F. A. Hayek, London, 1951.
The Spirit of the Age, 1831, edited by Professor Hayek, Chicago, 1942.
A System of Logic, London, 1843 (2 vols).
   The 8th edition is still in print.
On Liberty, London, 1859.
   Reprinted in Everyman's Library (with *Utilitarianism* and *Representative Government*), World's Classics (with *Subjection of Women*), and Blackwell's Political Texts (with *Representative Government*), and in the Thinker's Library and in many paperback editions.
Representative Government, London, 1861 (see above).
Utilitarianism, London, 1863 (see above).
   The text is reprinted in *The English Utilitarians*, by J. Plamenatz, Blackwell, 1949.
Examination of Sir William Hamilton's Philosophy, London, 1865.
Autobiography, London, 1873.
   Reprinted in World's Classics with other papers and an introduction by Harold Laski.
Three Essays on Religion, London, 1874.

2. CRITICAL WORKS

This list makes no pretence to be complete; it includes works which have been found useful in the writing of this monograph. Other references will be found in scattered footnotes throughout the book.

(a) General

Leslie Stephen, *The English Utilitarians*, London, 1900 (3 vols).

A. V. Dicey, *Law and Opinion in England*, London, 1905 (2nd ed. 1914).

Élie Halévy, *The Growth of Philosophic Radicalism*, translated by Mary Morris, London, 1928 (reprinted 1950).

James Bonar, *The Tables Turned*, London, 1931.

J. Plamenatz, *The English Utilitarians*, Oxford, 1949.

Basil Willey, *Nineteenth-Century Studies*, London, 1949.

(b) On Mill

James M'Cosh, *Examination of Mr J. S. Mill's Philosophy*, London, 1866.

Alex. Bain, *James Mill, a Biography*, London, 1882.

Alex. Bain, *J. S. Mill, a Criticism*, London, 1884.

W. L. Courtney, *Life and Writings of J. S. Mill*, London, 1888.

Chas. Douglas, *J. S. Mill, A Study of his Philosophy*, Edinburgh, 1895.

Chas. Douglas, *The Ethics of J. S. Mill*, Edinburgh, 1897.

Thos. Whittaker, *Comte and Mill*, London, 1908.

Emery Neff, *Carlyle and Mill*, New York, 1926 (2nd ed.).

Reginald Jackson, *Examination of the Deductive Logic of J. S. Mill*, Oxford, 1941.

R. P. Anschutz, *The Philosophy of J. S. Mill*, Oxford, 1953.

M. St. J. Packe, *The Life of John Stuart Mill*, London, 1954.

K. W. Britton, *Concise Encyclopaedia of Western Philosophy and Philosophers*, 1960: articles on J. S. Mill, James Mill, Bentham and Utilitarianism.

K. W. Britton, 'Utilitarianism: The Appeal to a First Principle,' *Proceedings of the Aristotelian Society*, 1959–60.

INDEX OF SUBJECTS

INDEX OF PROPER NAMES

A CATALOGUE OF SELECTED DOVER BOOKS
IN ALL FIELDS OF INTEREST

A CATALOGUE OF SELECTED DOVER BOOKS
IN ALL FIELDS OF INTEREST

WHAT IS SCIENCE?, *N. Campbell*
The role of experiment and measurement, the function of mathematics, the nature of scientific laws, the difference between laws and theories, the limitations of science, and many similarly provocative topics are treated clearly and without technicalities by an eminent scientist. "Still an excellent introduction to scientific philosophy," H. Margenau in *Physics Today*. "A first-rate primer . . . deserves a wide audience," *Scientific American*. 192pp. 5⅜ x 8.
60043-2 Paperbound $1.25

THE NATURE OF LIGHT AND COLOUR IN THE OPEN AIR, *M. Minnaert*
Why are shadows sometimes blue, sometimes green, or other colors depending on the light and surroundings? What causes mirages? Why do multiple suns and moons appear in the sky? Professor Minnaert explains these unusual phenomena and hundreds of others in simple, easy-to-understand terms based on optical laws and the properties of light and color. No mathematics is required but artists, scientists, students, and everyone fascinated by these "tricks" of nature will find thousands of useful and amazing pieces of information. Hundreds of observational experiments are suggested which require no special equipment. 200 illustrations; 42 photos. xvi + 362pp. 5⅜ x 8.
20196-1 Paperbound $2.00

THE STRANGE STORY OF THE QUANTUM, AN ACCOUNT FOR THE GENERAL READER OF THE GROWTH OF IDEAS UNDERLYING OUR PRESENT ATOMIC KNOWLEDGE, *B. Hoffmann*
Presents lucidly and expertly, with barest amount of mathematics, the problems and theories which led to modern quantum physics. Dr. Hoffmann begins with the closing years of the 19th century, when certain trifling discrepancies were noticed, and with illuminating analogies and examples takes you through the brilliant concepts of Planck, Einstein, Pauli, Broglie, Bohr, Schroedinger, Heisenberg, Dirac, Sommerfeld, Feynman, etc. This edition includes a new, long postscript carrying the story through 1958. "Of the books attempting an account of the history and contents of our modern atomic physics which have come to my attention, this is the best," H. Margenau, Yale University, in *American Journal of Physics*. 32 tables and line illustrations. Index. 275pp. 5⅜ x 8.
20518-5 Paperbound $2.00

GREAT IDEAS OF MODERN MATHEMATICS: THEIR NATURE AND USE, *Jagjit Singh*
Reader with only high school math will understand main mathematical ideas of modern physics, astronomy, genetics, psychology, evolution, etc. better than many who use them as tools, but comprehend little of their basic structure. Author uses his wide knowledge of non-mathematical fields in brilliant exposition of differential equations, matrices, group theory, logic, statistics, problems of mathematical foundations, imaginary numbers, vectors, etc. Original publication. 2 appendixes. 2 indexes. 65 ills. 322pp. 5⅜ x 8.
20587-8 Paperbound $2.25

THE MUSIC OF THE SPHERES: THE MATERIAL UNIVERSE — FROM ATOM TO QUASAR, SIMPLY EXPLAINED, *Guy Murchie*
Vast compendium of fact, modern concept and theory, observed and calculated data, historical background guides intelligent layman through the material universe. Brilliant exposition of earth's construction, explanations for moon's craters, atmospheric components of Venus and Mars (with data from recent fly-by's), sun spots, sequences of star birth and death, neighboring galaxies, contributions of Galileo, Tycho Brahe, Kepler, etc.; and (Vol. 2) construction of the atom (describing newly discovered sigma and xi subatomic particles), theories of sound, color and light, space and time, including relativity theory, quantum theory, wave theory, probability theory, work of Newton, Maxwell, Faraday, Einstein, de Broglie, etc. "Best presentation yet offered to the intelligent general reader," *Saturday Review*. Revised (1967). Index. 319 illustrations by the author. Total of xx + 644pp. 5⅜ x 8½.
21809-0, 21810-4 Two volume set, paperbound $5.00

FOUR LECTURES ON RELATIVITY AND SPACE, *Charles Proteus Steinmetz*
Lecture series, given by great mathematician and electrical engineer, generally considered one of the best popular-level expositions of special and general relativity theories and related questions. Steinmetz translates complex mathematical reasoning into language accessible to laymen through analogy, example and comparison. Among topics covered are relativity of motion, location, time; of mass; acceleration; 4-dimensional time-space; geometry of the gravitational field; curvature and bending of space; non-Euclidean geometry. Index. 40 illustrations. x + 142pp. 5⅜ x 8½.   61771-8 Paperbound $1.35

HOW TO KNOW THE WILD FLOWERS, *Mrs. William Starr Dana*
Classic nature book that has introduced thousands to wonders of American wild flowers. Color-season principle of organization is easy to use, even by those with no botanical training, and the genial, refreshing discussions of history, folklore, uses of over 1,000 native and escape flowers, foliage plants are informative as well as fun to read. Over 170 full-page plates, collected from several editions, may be colored in to make permanent records of finds. Revised to conform with 1950 edition of Gray's Manual of Botany. xlii + 438pp. 5⅜ x 8½.   20332-8 Paperbound $2.50

MANUAL OF THE TREES OF NORTH AMERICA, *Charles Sprague Sargent*
Still unsurpassed as most comprehensive, reliable study of North American tree characteristics, precise locations and distribution. By dean of American dendrologists. Every tree native to U.S., Canada, Alaska; 185 genera, 717 species, described in detail—leaves, flowers, fruit, winterbuds, bark, wood, growth habits, etc. plus discussion of varieties and local variants, immaturity variations. Over 100 keys, including unusual 11-page analytical key to genera, aid in identification. 783 clear illustrations of flowers, fruit, leaves. An unmatched permanent reference work for all nature lovers. Second enlarged (1926) edition. Synopsis of families. Analytical key to genera. Glossary of technical terms. Index. 783 illustrations, 1 map. Total of 982pp. 5⅜ x 8.
20277-1, 20278-X Two volume set, paperbound $6.00

It's Fun to Make Things From Scrap Materials,
Evelyn Glantz Hershoff
What use are empty spools, tin cans, bottle tops? What can be made from
rubber bands, clothes pins, paper clips, and buttons? This book provides
simply worded instructions and large diagrams showing you how to make
cookie cutters, toy trucks, paper turkeys, Halloween masks, telephone sets,
aprons, linoleum block- and spatter prints — in all 399 projects! Many are easy
enough for young children to figure out for themselves; some challenging
enough to entertain adults; all are remarkably ingenious ways to make things
from materials that cost pennies or less! Formerly "Scrap Fun for Everyone."
Index. 214 illustrations. 373pp. 5⅜ x 8½.   21251-3 Paperbound $1.75

Symbolic Logic and The Game of Logic, *Lewis Carroll*
"Symbolic Logic" is not concerned with modern symbolic logic, but is instead
a collection of over 380 problems posed with charm and imagination, using
the syllogism and a fascinating diagrammatic method of drawing conclusions.
In "The Game of Logic" Carroll's whimsical imagination devises a logical game
played with 2 diagrams and counters (included) to manipulate hundreds of
tricky syllogisms. The final section, "Hit or Miss" is a lagniappe of 101 additional puzzles in the delightful Carroll manner. Until this reprint edition,
both of these books were rarities costing up to $15 each. Symbolic Logic:
Index. xxxi + 199pp. The Game of Logic: 96pp. 2 vols. bound as one. 5⅜ x 8.
                                                      20492-8 Paperbound $2.50

Mathematical Puzzles of Sam Loyd, Part i
selected and edited by M. Gardner
Choice puzzles by the greatest American puzzle creator and innovator. Selected
from his famous collection, "Cyclopedia of Puzzles," they retain the unique
style and historical flavor of the originals. There are posers based on arithmetic,
algebra, probability, game theory, route tracing, topology, counter and sliding
block, operations research, geometrical dissection. Includes the famous "14-15"
puzzle which was a national craze, and his "Horse of a Different Color" which
sold millions of copies. 117 of his most ingenious puzzles in all. 120 line
drawings and diagrams. Solutions. Selected references. xx + 167pp. 5⅜ x 8.
                                                      20498-7 Paperbound $1.35

String Figures and How to Make Them, *Caroline Furness Jayne*
107 string figures plus variations selected from the best primitive and modern
examples developed by Navajo, Apache, pygmies of Africa, Eskimo, in Europe,
Australia, China, etc. The most readily understandable, easy-to-follow book in
English on perennially popular recreation. Crystal-clear exposition; step-by-
step diagrams. Everyone from kindergarten children to adults looking for
unusual diversion will be endlessly amused. Index. Bibliography. Introduction
by A. C. Haddon. 17 full-page plates, 960 illustrations. xxiii + 401pp. 5⅜ x 8½.
                                                      20152-X Paperbound $2.25

Paper Folding for Beginners, *W. D. Murray and F. J. Rigney*
A delightful introduction to the varied and entertaining Japanese art of
origami (paper folding), with a full, crystal-clear text that anticipates every
difficulty; over 275 clearly labeled diagrams of all important stages in creation.
You get results at each stage, since complex figures are logically developed
from simpler ones. 43 different pieces are explained: sailboats, frogs, roosters,
etc. 6 photographic plates. 279 diagrams. 95pp. 5⅝ x 8⅜.
                                                      20713-7 Paperbound $1.00

PRINCIPLES OF ART HISTORY,
H. Wölfflin

Analyzing such terms as "baroque," "classic," "neoclassic," "primitive," "picturesque," and 164 different works by artists like Botticelli, van Cleve, Dürer, Hobbema, Holbein, Hals, Rembrandt, Titian, Brueghel, Vermeer, and many others, the author establishes the classifications of art history and style on a firm, concrete basis. This classic of art criticism shows what really occurred between the 14th-century primitives and the sophistication of the 18th century in terms of basic attitudes and philosophies. "A remarkable lesson in the art of seeing," *Sat. Rev. of Literature.* Translated from the 7th German edition. 150 illustrations. 254pp. 6⅛ x 9¼. 20276-3 Paperbound $2.25

PRIMITIVE ART,
Franz Boas

This authoritative and exhaustive work by a great American anthropologist covers the entire gamut of primitive art. Pottery, leatherwork, metal work, stone work, wood, basketry, are treated in detail. Theories of primitive art, historical depth in art history, technical virtuosity, unconscious levels of patterning, symbolism, styles, literature, music, dance, etc. A must book for the interested layman, the anthropologist, artist, handicrafter (hundreds of unusual motifs), and the historian. Over 900 illustrations (50 ceramic vessels, 12 totem poles, etc.). 376pp. 5⅜ x 8. 20025-6 Paperbound $2.50

THE GENTLEMAN AND CABINET MAKER'S DIRECTOR,
Thomas Chippendale

A reprint of the 1762 catalogue of furniture designs that went on to influence generations of English and Colonial and Early Republic American furniture makers. The 200 plates, most of them full-page sized, show Chippendale's designs for French (Louis XV), Gothic, and Chinese-manner chairs, sofas, canopy and dome beds, cornices, chamber organs, cabinets, shaving tables, commodes, picture frames, frets, candle stands, chimney pieces, decorations, etc. The drawings are all elegant and highly detailed; many include construction diagrams and elevations. A supplement of 24 photographs shows surviving pieces of original and Chippendale-style pieces of furniture. Brief biography of Chippendale by N. I. Bienenstock, editor of *Furniture World.* Reproduced from the 1762 edition. 200 plates, plus 19 photographic plates. vi + 249pp. 9⅛ x 12¼. 21601-2 Paperbound $3.50

AMERICAN ANTIQUE FURNITURE: A BOOK FOR AMATEURS,
Edgar G. Miller, Jr.

Standard introduction and practical guide to identification of valuable American antique furniture. 2115 illustrations, mostly photographs taken by the author in 148 private homes, are arranged in chronological order in extensive chapters on chairs, sofas, chests, desks, bedsteads, mirrors, tables, clocks, and other articles. Focus is on furniture accessible to the collector, including simpler pieces and a larger than usual coverage of Empire style. Introductory chapters identify structural elements, characteristics of various styles, how to avoid fakes, etc. "We are frequently asked to name some book on American furniture that will meet the requirements of the novice collector, the beginning dealer, and . . . the general public. . . . We believe Mr. Miller's two volumes more completely satisfy this specification than any other work," *Antiques.* Appendix. Index. Total of vi + 1106pp. 7⅞ x 10¾. 21599-7, 21600-4 Two volume set, paperbound $7.50

THE BAD CHILD'S BOOK OF BEASTS, MORE BEASTS FOR WORSE CHILDREN, and A MORAL ALPHABET, *H. Belloc*
Hardly and anthology of humorous verse has appeared in the last 50 years without at least a couple of these famous nonsense verses. But one must see the entire volumes — with all the delightful original illustrations by Sir Basil Blackwood — to appreciate fully Belloc's charming and witty verses that play so subacidly on the platitudes of life and morals that beset his day — and ours. A great humor classic. Three books in one. Total of 157pp. 5⅜ x 8.
20749-8 Paperbound $1.00

THE DEVIL'S DICTIONARY, *Ambrose Bierce*
Sardonic and irreverent barbs puncturing the pomposities and absurdities of American politics, business, religion, literature, and arts, by the country's greatest satirist in the classic tradition. Epigrammatic as Shaw, piercing as Swift, American as Mark Twain, Will Rogers, and Fred Allen, Bierce will always remain the favorite of a small coterie of enthusiasts, and of writers and speakers whom he supplies with "some of the most gorgeous witticisms of the English language" (H. L. Mencken). Over 1000 entries in alphabetical order. 144pp. 5⅜ x 8.
20487-1 Paperbound $1.00

THE COMPLETE NONSENSE OF EDWARD LEAR.
This is the only complete edition of this master of gentle madness available at a popular price. *A Book of Nonsense, Nonsense Songs, More Nonsense Songs and Stories* in their entirety with all the old favorites that have delighted children and adults for years. The Dong With A Luminous Nose, The Jumblies, The Owl and the Pussycat, and hundreds of other bits of wonderful nonsense. 214 limericks, 3 sets of Nonsense Botany, 5 Nonsense Alphabets, 546 drawings by Lear himself, and much more. 320pp. 5⅜ x 8. 20167-8 Paperbound $1.75

THE WIT AND HUMOR OF OSCAR WILDE, *ed. by Alvin Redman*
Wilde at his most brilliant, in 1000 epigrams exposing weaknesses and hypocrisies of "civilized" society. Divided into 49 categories—sin, wealth, women, America, etc.—to aid writers, speakers. Includes excerpts from his trials, books, plays, criticism. Formerly "The Epigrams of Oscar Wilde." Introduction by Vyvyan Holland, Wilde's only living son. Introductory essay by editor. 260pp. 5⅜ x 8.
20602-5 Paperbound $1.50

A CHILD'S PRIMER OF NATURAL HISTORY, *Oliver Herford*
Scarcely an anthology of whimsy and humor has appeared in the last 50 years without a contribution from Oliver Herford. Yet the works from which these examples are drawn have been almost impossible to obtain! Here at last are Herford's improbable definitions of a menagerie of familiar and weird animals, each verse illustrated by the author's own drawings. 24 drawings in 2 colors; 24 additional drawings. vii + 95pp. 6½ x 6. 21647-0 Paperbound $1.00

THE BROWNIES: THEIR BOOK, *Palmer Cox*
The book that made the Brownies a household word. Generations of readers have enjoyed the antics, predicaments and adventures of these jovial sprites, who emerge from the forest at night to play or to come to the aid of a deserving human. Delightful illustrations by the author decorate nearly every page. 24 short verse tales with 266 illustrations. 155pp. 6⅝ x 9¼.
21265-3 Paperbound $1.50

THE PRINCIPLES OF PSYCHOLOGY,
William James
The full long-course, unabridged, of one of the great classics of Western literature and science. Wonderfully lucid descriptions of human mental activity, the stream of thought, consciousness, time perception, memory, imagination, emotions, reason, abnormal phenomena, and similar topics. Original contributions are integrated with the work of such men as Berkeley, Binet, Mills, Darwin, Hume, Kant, Royce, Schopenhauer, Spinoza, Locke, Descartes, Galton, Wundt, Lotze, Herbart, Fechner, and scores of others. All contrasting interpretations of mental phenomena are examined in detail—introspective analysis, philosophical interpretation, and experimental research. "A classic," *Journal of Consulting Psychology*. "The main lines are as valid as ever," *Psychoanalytical Quarterly*. "Standard reading . . . a classic of interpretation," *Psychiatric Quarterly*. 94 illustrations. 1408pp. 5⅜ x 8.
20381-6, 20382-4 Two volume set, paperbound $6.00

VISUAL ILLUSIONS: THEIR CAUSES, CHARACTERISTICS AND APPLICATIONS,
M. Luckiesh
"Seeing is deceiving," asserts the author of this introduction to virtually every type of optical illusion known. The text both describes and explains the principles involved in color illusions, figure-ground, distance illusions, etc. 100 photographs, drawings and diagrams prove how easy it is to fool the sense: circles that aren't round, parallel lines that seem to bend, stationary figures that seem to move as you stare at them — illustration after illustration strains our credulity at what we see. Fascinating book from many points of view, from applications for artists, in camouflage, etc. to the psychology of vision. New introduction by William Ittleson, Dept. of Psychology, Queens College. Index. Bibliography. xxi + 252pp. 5⅜ x 8½.
21530-X Paperbound $1.50

FADS AND FALLACIES IN THE NAME OF SCIENCE,
Martin Gardner
This is the standard account of various cults, quack systems, and delusions which have masqueraded as science: hollow earth fanatics, Reich and orgone sex energy, dianetics, Atlantis, multiple moons, Forteanism, flying saucers, medical fallacies like iridiagnosis, zone therapy, etc. A new chapter has been added on Bridey Murphy, psionics, and other recent manifestations in this field. This is a fair, reasoned appraisal of eccentric theory which provides excellent inoculation against cleverly masked nonsense. "Should be read by everyone, scientist and non-scientist alike," R. T. Birge, Prof. Emeritus of Physics, Univ. of California; Former President, American Physical Society. Index. x + 365pp. 5⅜ x 8.
20394-8 Paperbound $2.00

ILLUSIONS AND DELUSIONS OF THE SUPERNATURAL AND THE OCCULT,
D. H. Rawcliffe
Holds up to rational examination hundreds of persistent delusions including crystal gazing, automatic writing, table turning, mediumistic trances, mental healing, stigmata, lycanthropy, live burial, the Indian Rope Trick, spiritualism, dowsing, telepathy, clairvoyance, ghosts, ESP, etc. The author explains and exposes the mental and physical deceptions involved, making this not only an exposé of supernatural phenomena, but a valuable exposition of characteristic types of abnormal psychology. Originally titled "The Psychology of the Occult." 14 illustrations. Index. 551pp. 5⅜ x 8. 20503-7 Paperbound $3.50

FAIRY TALE COLLECTIONS, *edited by Andrew Lang*
Andrew Lang's fairy tale collections make up the richest shelf-full of traditional children's stories anywhere available. Lang supervised the translation of stories from all over the world—familiar European tales collected by Grimm, animal stories from Negro Africa, myths of primitive Australia, stories from Russia, Hungary, Iceland, Japan, and many other countries. Lang's selection of translations are unusually high; many authorities consider that the most familiar tales find their best versions in these volumes. All collections are richly decorated and illustrated by H. J. Ford and other artists.

THE BLUE FAIRY BOOK. 37 stories. 138 illustrations. ix + 390pp. 5⅜ x 8½.
21437-0 Paperbound $1.95

THE GREEN FAIRY BOOK. 42 stories. 100 illustrations. xiii + 366pp. 5⅜ x 8½.
21439-7 Paperbound $1.75

THE BROWN FAIRY BOOK. 32 stories. 50 illustrations, 8 in color. xii + 350pp. 5⅜ x 8½.
21438-9 Paperbound $1.95

THE BEST TALES OF HOFFMANN, *edited by E. F. Bleiler*
10 stories by E. T. A. Hoffmann, one of the greatest of all writers of fantasy. The tales include "The Golden Flower Pot," "Automata," "A New Year's Eve Adventure," "Nutcracker and the King of Mice," "Sand-Man," and others. Vigorous characterizations of highly eccentric personalities, remarkably imaginative situations, and intensely fast pacing has made these tales popular all over the world for 150 years. Editor's introduction. 7 drawings by Hoffmann. xxxiii + 419pp. 5⅜ x 8½.
21793-0 Paperbound $2.25

GHOST AND HORROR STORIES OF AMBROSE BIERCE, *edited by E. F. Bleiler*
Morbid, eerie, horrifying tales of possessed poets, shabby aristocrats, revived corpses, and haunted malefactors. Widely acknowledged as the best of their kind between Poe and the moderns, reflecting their author's inner torment and bitter view of life. Includes "Damned Thing," "The Middle Toe of the Right Foot," "The Eyes of the Panther," "Visions of the Night," "Moxon's Master," and over a dozen others. Editor's introduction. xxii + 199pp. 5⅜ x 8½.
20767-6 Paperbound $1.50

THREE GOTHIC NOVELS, *edited by E. F. Bleiler*
Originators of the still popular Gothic novel form, influential in ushering in early 19th-century Romanticism. Horace Walpole's *Castle of Otranto*, William Beckford's *Vathek*, John Polidori's *The Vampyre*, and a *Fragment* by Lord Byron are enjoyable as exciting reading or as documents in the history of English literature. Editor's introduction. xi + 291pp. 5⅜ x 8½.
21232-7 Paperbound $2.00

BEST GHOST STORIES OF LEFANU, *edited by E. F. Bleiler*
Though admired by such critics as V. S. Pritchett, Charles Dickens and Henry James, ghost stories by the Irish novelist Joseph Sheridan LeFanu have never become as widely known as his detective fiction. About half of the 16 stories in this collection have never before been available in America. Collection includes "Carmilla" (perhaps the best vampire story ever written), "The Haunted Baronet," "The Fortunes of Sir Robert Ardagh," and the classic "Green Tea." Editor's introduction. 7 contemporary illustrations. Portrait of LeFanu. xii + 467pp. 5⅜ x 8.
20415-4 Paperbound $2.50

EASY-TO-DO ENTERTAINMENTS AND DIVERSIONS WITH COINS, CARDS, STRING, PAPER AND MATCHES, *R. M. Abraham*
Over 300 tricks, games and puzzles will provide young readers with absorbing fun. Sections on card games; paper-folding; tricks with coins, matches and pieces of string; games for the agile; toy-making from common household objects; mathematical recreations; and 50 miscellaneous pastimes. Anyone in charge of groups of youngsters, including hard-pressed parents, and in need of suggestions on how to keep children sensibly amused and quietly content will find this book indispensable. Clear, simple text, copious number of delightful line drawings and illustrative diagrams. Originally titled "Winter Nights' Entertainments." Introduction by Lord Baden Powell. 329 illustrations. v + 186pp. 5⅜ x 8½.   20921-0 Paperbound $1.00

AN INTRODUCTION TO CHESS MOVES AND TACTICS SIMPLY EXPLAINED, *Leonard Barden*
Beginner's introduction to the royal game. Names, possible moves of the pieces, definitions of essential terms, how games are won, etc. explained in 30-odd pages. With this background you'll be able to sit right down and play. Balance of book teaches strategy — openings, middle game, typical endgame play, and suggestions for improving your game. A sample game is fully analyzed. True middle-level introduction, teaching you all the essentials without oversimplifying or losing you in a maze of detail. 58 figures. 102pp. 5⅜ x 8½.   21210-6 Paperbound $1.25

LASKER'S MANUAL OF CHESS, *Dr. Emanuel Lasker*
Probably the greatest chess player of modern times, Dr. Emanuel Lasker held the world championship 28 years, independent of passing schools or fashions. This unmatched study of the game, chiefly for intermediate to skilled players, analyzes basic methods, combinations, position play, the aesthetics of chess, dozens of different openings, etc., with constant reference to great modern games. Contains a brilliant exposition of Steinitz's important theories. Introduction by Fred Reinfeld. Tables of Lasker's tournament record. 3 indices. 308 diagrams. 1 photograph. xxx + 349pp. 5⅜ x 8.20640-8 Paperbound $2.50

COMBINATIONS: THE HEART OF CHESS, *Irving Chernev*
Step-by-step from simple combinations to complex, this book, by a well-known chess writer, shows you the intricacies of pins, counter-pins, knight forks, and smothered mates. Other chapters show alternate lines of play to those taken in actual championship games; boomerang combinations; classic examples of brilliant combination play by Nimzovich, Rubinstein, Tarrasch, Botvinnik, Alekhine and Capablanca. Index. 356 diagrams. ix + 245pp. 5⅜ x 8½.   21744-2 Paperbound $2.00

HOW TO SOLVE CHESS PROBLEMS, *K. S. Howard*
Full of practical suggestions for the fan or the beginner — who knows only the moves of the chessmen. Contains preliminary section and 58 two-move, 46 three-move, and 8 four-move problems composed by 27 outstanding American problem creators in the last 30 years. Explanation of all terms and exhaustive index. "Just what is wanted for the student," Brian Harley. 112 problems, solutions. vi + 171pp. 5⅜ x 8.   20748-X Paperbound $1.50

SOCIAL THOUGHT FROM LORE TO SCIENCE,
H. E. Barnes and H. Becker
An immense survey of sociological thought and ways of viewing, studying, planning, and reforming society from earliest times to the present. Includes thought on society of preliterate peoples, ancient non-Western cultures, and every great movement in Europe, America, and modern Japan. Analyzes hundreds of great thinkers: Plato, Augustine, Bodin, Vico, Montesquieu, Herder, Comte, Marx, etc. Weighs the contributions of utopians, sophists, fascists and communists; economists, jurists, philosophers, ecclesiastics, and every 19th and 20th century school of scientific sociology, anthropology, and social psychology throughout the world. Combines topical, chronological, and regional approaches, treating the evolution of social thought as a process rather than as a series of mere topics. "Impressive accuracy, competence, and discrimination . . . easily the best single survey," *Nation.* Thoroughly revised, with new material up to 1960. 2 indexes. Over 2200 bibliographical notes. Three volume set. Total of 1586pp. 5⅜ x 8.
20901-6, 20902-4, 20903-2 Three volume set, paperbound $9.00

A HISTORY OF HISTORICAL WRITING, *Harry Elmer Barnes*
Virtually the only adequate survey of the whole course of historical writing in a single volume. Surveys developments from the beginnings of historiography in the ancient Near East and the Classical World, up through the Cold War. Covers major historians in detail, shows interrelationship with cultural background, makes clear individual contributions, evaluates and estimates importance; also enormously rich upon minor authors and thinkers who are usually passed over. Packed with scholarship and learning, clear, easily written. Indispensable to every student of history. Revised and enlarged up to 1961. Index and bibliography. xv + 442pp. 5⅜ x 8½.
20104-X Paperbound $2.75

JOHANN SEBASTIAN BACH, *Philipp Spitta*
The complete and unabridged text of the definitive study of Bach. Written some 70 years ago, it is still unsurpassed for its coverage of nearly all aspects of Bach's life and work. There could hardly be a finer non-technical introduction to Bach's music than the detailed, lucid analyses which Spitta provides for hundreds of individual pieces. 26 solid pages are devoted to the B minor mass, for example, and 30 pages to the glorious St. Matthew Passion. This monumental set also includes a major analysis of the music of the 18th century: Buxtehude, Pachelbel, etc. "Unchallenged as the last word on one of the supreme geniuses of music," John Barkham, *Saturday Review Syndicate.* Total of 1819pp. Heavy cloth binding. 5⅜ x 8.
22278-0, 22279-9 Two volume set, clothbound $15.00

BEETHOVEN AND HIS NINE SYMPHONIES, *George Grove*
In this modern middle-level classic of musicology Grove not only analyzes all nine of Beethoven's symphonies very thoroughly in terms of their musical structure, but also discusses the circumstances under which they were written, Beethoven's stylistic development, and much other background material. This is an extremely rich book, yet very easily followed; it is highly recommended to anyone seriously interested in music. Over 250 musical passages. Index. viii + 407pp. 5⅜ x 8.
20334-4 Paperbound $2.25

THREE SCIENCE FICTION NOVELS,
John Taine
Acknowledged by many as the best SF writer of the 1920's, Taine (under the name Eric Temple Bell) was also a Professor of Mathematics of considerable renown. Reprinted here are *The Time Stream*, generally considered Taine's best, *The Greatest Game*, a biological-fiction novel, and *The Purple Sapphire*, involving a supercivilization of the past. Taine's stories tie fantastic narratives to frameworks of original and logical scientific concepts. Speculation is often profound on such questions as the nature of time, concept of entropy, cyclical universes, etc. 4 contemporary illustrations. v + 532pp. 5⅜ x 8⅜.
21180-0 Paperbound $2.50

SEVEN SCIENCE FICTION NOVELS,
H. G. Wells
Full unabridged texts of 7 science-fiction novels of the master. Ranging from biology, physics, chemistry, astronomy, to sociology and other studies, Mr. Wells extrapolates whole worlds of strange and intriguing character. "One will have to go far to match this for entertainment, excitement, and sheer pleasure . . ."*New York Times.* Contents: The Time Machine, The Island of Dr. Moreau, The First Men in the Moon, The Invisible Man, The War of the Worlds, The Food of the Gods, In The Days of the Comet. 1015pp. 5⅜ x 8.
20264-X Clothbound $5.00

28 SCIENCE FICTION STORIES OF H. G. WELLS.
Two full, unabridged novels, *Men Like Gods* and *Star Begotten*, plus 26 short stories by the master science-fiction writer of all time! Stories of space, time, invention, exploration, futuristic adventure. Partial contents: *The Country of the Blind, In the Abyss, The Crystal Egg, The Man Who Could Work Miracles, A Story of Days to Come, The Empire of the Ants, The Magic Shop, The Valley of the Spiders, A Story of the Stone Age, Under the Knife, Sea Raiders,* etc. An indispensable collection for the library of anyone interested in science fiction adventure. 928pp. 5⅜ x 8.
20265-8 Clothbound $5.00

THREE MARTIAN NOVELS,
Edgar Rice Burroughs
Complete, unabridged reprinting, in one volume, of Thuvia, Maid of Mars; Chessmen of Mars; The Master Mind of Mars. Hours of science-fiction adventure by a modern master storyteller. Reset in large clear type for easy reading. 16 illustrations by J. Allen St. John. vi + 490pp. 5⅜ x 8½.
20039-6 Paperbound $2.50

AN INTELLECTUAL AND CULTURAL HISTORY OF THE WESTERN WORLD,
Harry Elmer Barnes
Monumental 3-volume survey of intellectual development of Europe from primitive cultures to the present day. Every significant product of human intellect traced through history: art, literature, mathematics, physical sciences, medicine, music, technology, social sciences, religions, jurisprudence, education, etc. Presentation is lucid and specific, analyzing in detail specific discoveries, theories, literary works, and so on. Revised (1965) by recognized scholars in specialized fields under the direction of Prof. Barnes. Revised bibliography. Indexes. 24 illustrations. Total of xxix + 1318pp.
21275-0, 21276-9, 21277-7 Three volume set, paperbound $8.25

HEAR ME TALKIN' TO YA, *edited by Nat Shapiro and Nat Hentoff*
In their own words, Louis Armstrong, King Oliver, Fletcher Henderson, Bunk Johnson, Bix Beiderbecke, Billy Holiday, Fats Waller, Jelly Roll Morton, Duke Ellington, and many others comment on the origins of jazz in New Orleans and its growth in Chicago's South Side, Kansas City's jam sessions, Depression Harlem, and the modernism of the West Coast schools. Taken from taped conversations, letters, magazine articles, other first-hand sources. Editors' introduction. xvi + 429pp. 5⅜ x 8½.   21726-4 Paperbound $2.00

THE JOURNAL OF HENRY D. THOREAU
A 25-year record by the great American observer and critic, as complete a record of a great man's inner life as is anywhere available. Thoreau's Journals served him as raw material for his formal pieces, as a place where he could develop his ideas, as an outlet for his interests in wild life and plants, in writing as an art, in classics of literature, Walt Whitman and other contemporaries, in politics, slavery, individual's relation to the State, etc. The Journals present a portrait of a remarkable man, and are an observant social history. Unabridged republication of 1906 edition, Bradford Torrey and Francis H. Allen, editors. Illustrations. Total of 1888pp. 8⅜ x 12¼.
20312-3, 20313-1 Two volume set, clothbound $30.00

A SHAKESPEARIAN GRAMMAR, *E. A. Abbott*
Basic reference to Shakespeare and his contemporaries, explaining through thousands of quotations from Shakespeare, Jonson, Beaumont and Fletcher, North's *Plutarch* and other sources the grammatical usage differing from the modern. First published in 1870 and written by a scholar who spent much of his life isolating principles of Elizabethan language, the book is unlikely ever to be superseded. Indexes. xxiv + 511pp. 5⅜ x 8½. 21582-2 Paperbound $3.00

FOLK-LORE OF SHAKESPEARE, *T. F. Thistelton Dyer*
Classic study, drawing from Shakespeare a large body of references to supernatural beliefs, terminology of falconry and hunting, games and sports, good luck charms, marriage customs, folk medicines, superstitions about plants, animals, birds, argot of the underworld, sexual slang of London, proverbs, drinking customs, weather lore, and much else. From full compilation comes a mirror of the 17th-century popular mind. Index. ix + 526pp. 5⅜ x 8½.
21614-4 Paperbound $2.75

THE NEW VARIORUM SHAKESPEARE, *edited by H. H. Furness*
By far the richest editions of the plays ever produced in any country or language. Each volume contains complete text (usually First Folio) of the play, all variants in Quarto and other Folio texts, editorial changes by every major editor to Furness's own time (1900), footnotes to obscure references or language, extensive quotes from literature of Shakespearian criticism, essays on plot sources (often reprinting sources in full), and much more.

HAMLET, *edited by H. H. Furness*
Total of xxvi + 905pp. 5⅜ x 8½.
21004-9, 21005-7 Two volume set, paperbound $5.25
TWELFTH NIGHT, *edited by H. H. Furness*
Index. xxii + 434pp. 5⅜ x 8½.   21189-4 Paperbound $2.75

LA BOHEME BY GIACOMO PUCCINI,
translated and introduced by Ellen H. Bleiler
Complete handbook for the operagoer, with everything needed for full enjoyment except the musical score itself. Complete Italian libretto, with new,
modern English line-by-line translation—the only libretto printing all repeats;
biography of Puccini; the librettists; background to the opera, Murger's La
Boheme, etc.; circumstances of composition and performances; plot summary;
and pictorial section of 73 illustrations showing Puccini, famous singers and
performances, etc. Large clear type for easy reading. 124pp. 5⅜ x 8½.
20404-9 Paperbound $1.25

ANTONIO STRADIVARI: HIS LIFE AND WORK (1644-1737),
W. Henry Hill, Arthur F. Hill, and Alfred E. Hill
Still the only book that really delves into life and art of the incomparable
Italian craftsman, maker of the finest musical instruments in the world today.
The authors, expert violin-makers themselves, discuss Stradivari's ancestry, his
construction and finishing techniques, distinguished characteristics of many
of his instruments and their locations. Included, too, is story of introduction
of his instruments into France, England, first revelation of their supreme
merit, and information on his labels, number of instruments made, prices,
mystery of ingredients of his varnish, tone of pre-1684 Stradivari violin and
changes between 1684 and 1690. An extremely interesting, informative account
for all music lovers, from craftsman to concert-goer. Republication of original
(1902) edition. New introduction by Sydney Beck, Head of Rare Book and
Manuscript Collections, Music Division, New York Public Library. Analytical
index by Rembert Wurlitzer. Appendixes. 68 illustrations. 30 full-page plates.
4 in color. xxvi + 315pp. 5⅜ x 8½. 20425-1 Paperbound $2.25

MUSICAL AUTOGRAPHS FROM MONTEVERDI TO HINDEMITH,
Emanuel Winternitz
For beauty, for intrinsic interest, for perspective on the composer's personality,
for subtleties of phrasing, shading, emphasis indicated in the autograph but
suppressed in the printed score, the mss. of musical composition are fascinating
documents which repay close study in many different ways. This 2-volume
work reprints facsimiles of mss. by virtually every major composer, and many
minor figures—196 examples in all. A full text points out what can be learned
from mss., analyzes each sample. Index. Bibliography. 18 figures. 196 plates.
Total of 170pp. of text. 7⅞ x 10¾.
21312-9, 21313-7 Two volume set, paperbound $5.00

J. S. BACH,
Albert Schweitzer
One of the few great full-length studies of Bach's life and work, and the
study upon which Schweitzer's renown as a musicologist rests. On first appearance (1911), revolutionized Bach performance. The only writer on Bach to
be musicologist, performing musician, and student of history, theology and
philosophy, Schweitzer contributes particularly full sections on history of German Protestant church music, theories on motivic pictorial representations
in vocal music, and practical suggestions for performance. Translated by
Ernest Newman. Indexes. 5 illustrations. 650 musical examples. Total of xix
+ 928pp. 5⅜ x 8½. 21631-4, 21632-2 Two volume set, paperbound $4.50

THE METHODS OF ETHICS, *Henry Sidgwick*
Propounding no organized system of its own, study subjects every major methodological approach to ethics to rigorous, objective analysis. Study discusses and relates ethical thought of Plato, Aristotle, Bentham, Clarke, Butler, Hobbes, Hume, Mill, Spencer, Kant, and dozens of others. Sidgwick retains conclusions from each system which follow from ethical premises, rejecting the faulty. Considered by many in the field to be among the most important treatises on ethical philosophy. Appendix. Index. xlvii + 528pp. 5⅜ x 8½.
21608-X Paperbound $2.50

TEUTONIC MYTHOLOGY, *Jakob Grimm*
A milestone in Western culture; the work which established on a modern basis the study of history of religions and comparative religions. 4-volume work assembles and interprets everything available on religious and folkloristic beliefs of Germanic people (including Scandinavians, Anglo-Saxons, etc.). Assembling material from such sources as Tacitus, surviving Old Norse and Icelandic texts, archeological remains, folktales, surviving superstitions, comparative traditions, linguistic analysis, etc. Grimm explores pagan deities, heroes, folklore of nature, religious practices, and every other area of pagan German belief. To this day, the unrivaled, definitive, exhaustive study. Translated by J. S. Stallybrass from 4th (1883) German edition. Indexes. Total of lxxvii + 1887pp. 5⅜ x 8½.
21602-0, 21603-9, 21604-7, 21605-5 Four volume set, paperbound $11.00

THE I CHING, *translated by James Legge*
Called "The Book of Changes" in English, this is one of the Five Classics edited by Confucius, basic and central to Chinese thought. Explains perhaps the most complex system of divination known, founded on the theory that all things happening at any one time have characteristic features which can be isolated and related. Significant in Oriental studies, in history of religions and philosophy, and also to Jungian psychoanalysis and other areas of modern European thought. Index. Appendixes. 6 plates. xxi + 448pp. 5⅜ x 8½.
21062-6 Paperbound $2.75

HISTORY OF ANCIENT PHILOSOPHY, *W. Windelband*
One of the clearest, most accurate comprehensive surveys of Greek and Roman philosophy. Discusses ancient philosophy in general, intellectual life in Greece in the 7th and 6th centuries B.C., Thales, Anaximander, Anaximenes, Heraclitus, the Eleatics, Empedocles, Anaxagoras, Leucippus, the Pythagoreans, the Sophists, Socrates, Democritus (20 pages), Plato (50 pages), Aristotle (70 pages), the Peripatetics, Stoics, Epicureans, Sceptics, Neo-platonists, Christian Apologists, etc. 2nd German edition translated by H. E. Cushman. xv + 393pp. 5⅜ x 8.
20357-3 Paperbound $2.25

THE PALACE OF PLEASURE, *William Painter*
Elizabethan versions of Italian and French novels from *The Decameron,* Cinthio, Straparola, Queen Margaret of Navarre, and other continental sources — the very work that provided Shakespeare and dozens of his contemporaries with many of their plots and sub-plots and, therefore, justly considered one of the most influential books in all English literature. It is also a book that any reader will still enjoy. Total of cviii + 1,224pp.
21691-8, 21692-6, 21693-4 Three volume set, paperbound $6.75